Lunch with Charlotte

LEON BERGER

grey gecko press

This book is a memoir/biography, as told to the author by the subject herself. To the best of the author and publisher's knowledge, the events in this book are true and factual. No offense is intended or should be inferred.

Published by Grey Gecko Press, Katy, Texas.

www. greygeckopress. com

Printed in the United States of America

Design by Grey Gecko Press

Library of Congress Cataloging-in-Publication Data

Berger, Leon
Lunch with Charlotte / Leon Berger
Library of Congress Control Number: 2012942898

ISBN   978-0-9854400-8-4
10 9 8 7 6 5 4 3 2 1

First Edition

Charlotte Urban

née Liselotte Goldberger

1919 — 2010

⚜ **Prologue** ⚜

"How's the coffee?"

"It's good, thanks."

"Is it strong enough? I don't know, what do you think?"

"No, it's excellent."

"You sure? I thought maybe it wasn't strong enough."

This was how it was whenever I went to visit my good friend Charlotte. Often, she'd go out of her way to purchase some special item, like Viennese-blend coffee, then fret that she hadn't prepared it to my taste. At ninety-one, she was still stubbornly independent, yet she was always searching for praise—and this was just one of her many contradictions.

Friday lunch was our usual time together, at least when I wasn't traveling. Although I lived just twenty minutes from Charlotte, my consulting business occasionally took me away from Montreal, either to nearby New York or distant Beijing, but whenever I was in town, I'd call to say I was on my way.

Each time I'd arrive, she'd already have covered half the dining room table with the kind of items I only seemed to consume with her. They were a reflection of her more traditional fare from the old world—hard-boiled eggs, pickled cucumbers, herring in brine, black bread and cream cheese.

We'd supplement this with ethnic staples that were more North American in origin, like the poppy-seed bagels and Pacific lox that I'd pick up en route, but these were for my own benefit. She wasn't so keen on them herself. Sometimes, to add variety, she would struggle out to buy chicken livers and a pound of onions and then spend her afternoon chopping it all by hand, the way it used to be done.

As if that wasn't enough, she'd follow up by laboring through the evening to bake a deep-dish apple cake for dessert. Such preparations would inevitably exhaust her, and I'd often protest at the inordinate amount of work, but she insisted on making the effort because, as she often said, I was the son she'd never had, and it was her duty to make a fuss.

Yet, with Charlotte, the food was always secondary to the talk—eclectic waves of chatter about everything and nothing, from geopolitics to trivia, from the profound to the just plain silly.

In between, she'd invariably sprinkle anecdotes of her extraordinary life experience, told with either twinkling humor or bitter sadness in her lilting Austrian syntax. Such episodes were never in chronological sequence but scattered through our myriad conversations over a period of twenty-five years.

She recounted events as she remembered them, and she'd return time and again to the same incident because of elements she'd forgotten or misplaced. Often, she'd be totally entwined in every detail, even reproducing chapter and verse of a conversation, but then, without any warning, she'd come to a sudden halt in her monologue due to some totally arbitrary reason.

It might have been an inquiry about the food or the coffee, but it could equally have been a telephone call she had to make, or an invoice she hadn't paid which couldn't be delayed a minute longer. It was difficult to absorb it all in such a haphazard fashion, and although I developed a certain expertise at decrypting these sessions, I sometimes became mystified as to who or what we were talking about at any given moment.

To assist my comprehension, she would often illustrate her recollections by hauling out her cherished photographs, which ranged from the sepia tones of her youth to the fading grays of her middle years. In the early snapshots, she appeared robust and willing, a source of girlish laughter and vibrant enthusiasm, but these impressions were far removed from the woman who sat facing me.

By the start of her tenth decade, she'd become philosophical—mentally capable but physically handicapped. As she said, "The engine's still good, but the bodywork's falling apart." Once an imposing figure, Charlotte had become shrunken by osteoporosis, and a surgical operation for her crumbling hip had left her with one leg a full inch shorter than the other.

She was mobile only by means of a specially built shoe and a steel walker, yet despite the effort it took just to get out of bed each morning, she coped majestically. She always presented herself to callers showered, dressed, and groomed, a mark of self-respect and old-world propriety.

In these later years, she came to epitomize the quintessential ethnic mother figure—the dignified survivor with the silver hair and the big heart. Everybody who met her loved her. She had a charismatic personality and a generous spirit which seemed to overflow to the world around her. Yet there was another, more tragic side to Charlotte that nobody knew—a paradox.

Deep within, she suffered from a profoundly wounded soul, and it was only when she was with me in private that she revealed her despair. Sometimes, during our Friday lunch, it would all just pour out of her: the grief, the doubt, and the guilt, along with the relentless flow of tears.

Finally, toward the end of her long life, she took me into her confidence and entrusted me with her most guarded secret, the shattering trauma she'd suffered, which affected every aspect of her existence and gave rise to the emotional volatility that only I ever witnessed.

Her friends, her neighbors, even her family, all came and went without ever discovering this innermost truth, but I came to realize that this was the essence of who she was. This was the real Charlotte, and it was at the very heart of her extraordinary story.

1

According to Charlotte, ever a believer in the power of destiny, the origins of her life-changing trauma could be traced back to a precise moment four years before she was born.

It happened in the early spring of 1915, nearly a year after the start of the Great War, when a stocky, prematurely balding serviceman arrived on leave in the Austro-Hungarian Empire's grandiose capital of Vienna.

His name was Jakob Georg Goldberger, and it was on that afternoon that he first glimpsed and fell instantly in love with a high school girl, Franzi Gutmann, thirteen years his junior. Was it sordid? Just another tiresome example of male foolishness? Or was it more romantic, a lonely soldier searching for innocence in a misery-soaked world?

Raised in the medieval city of Krakow in Galicia, Jakob had been drafted at the outbreak of hostilities, along with countless others, by the Imperial Army of the Royal House of Habsburg. However, he wasn't sent to the front, at least not directly. Thanks to an intuitive skill in languages—he was fluent in Polish, German, and Russian, competent in Czech, Hungarian, and Italian—he was trained in administrative duties and eventually transferred to a regional headquarters unit on the outskirts of Pressburg in Slovakia, close to the Austrian border.

So here he was, seizing the rare opportunity of a four-day pass to come see his sister, Berthe, who'd married a Viennese and was now a war widow, her husband having fallen on the Serbian front during that first summer of the conflict. Jakob hadn't seen her since she received the news, and felt he owed her a visit.

It hadn't been an easy night's journey. He'd been obliged to spend close to seven hours on a slow, crowded bus that smelled of human sweat and chicken excrement. With a grinding transmission and several noisy infants to keep him awake, Jakob was both ravenous and fatigued by the time the bus dropped him near the Stubentor, his eyes bleary and his limbs stiff. A bright sun was just beginning to creep over the ornate rooftops of the Altstadt, but he was in no condition to appreciate it.

He hauled his knapsack onto his back and then felt in his greatcoat pocket. There were just a few coins left from his monthly pay, and for a few moments he gazed at them lying in his grease-stained palm. Such a pitiful amount of change meant he had a decision to make.

He could purchase a roll and coffee from the bakery that he'd spotted on the other side of the street, or he could use that same money to take the Stadtbahn north to Bezirk 20 where his sister lived and save himself the trouble of having to walk the last few kilometers. Essentially, it came down to a uniformed man's age-old quarrel between his stomach and his feet, and as always, the stomach triumphed.

The rational excuse was that without nutrition nothing could be accomplished anyway, but the real reason was far more fundamental—the sensory pleasure of immediate gratification, based on the truism that a lowly private, at the end of the line for all things, never truly knew from one moment to the next whether he'd be alive or dead.

Each day, thousands were sacrificed, charging out of mud-filled trenches and blown to bloody pieces by constant shelling, and although he currently had the luckiest of duties as a paymaster's clerk, sitting all day at his desk, engaged in nothing more than stamping ration books and processing weekend passes, he was only too aware that such good fortune could change at any time.

On a superior's whim, he could be ordered directly to the front lines, where his lifespan would be measured not in weeks or days but more probably in a matter of hours.

The wafting aromas from the bakery were enticing, even from the street, and in the end, he couldn't help himself. As he entered, his senses were immediately overwhelmed by the pervasive atmosphere of fresh bread and pungent coffee while, all around him, staff and customers went about their affairs.

He found a small table by the window just as an elderly lady was leaving, but he had to wait for a well-scrubbed young waitress in a starched black uniform to wipe off the table. As she leaned over, he was very conscious of her full figure, ice-blue eyes, and white-blonde plaits pulled tightly back and curled into a neat bun.

It had been a while since he'd been this close to a woman, and suddenly, involuntarily, there were other things on his mind besides hunger. Obviously, he had no way to fulfill such fantasies, so he deliberately turned away from her to gaze out of the window at the passing parade of pedestrians and traffic.

The people, whether men or women, walking or riding, seemed to have a prosperous air about them, making him aware and then ashamed of his own appearance. He peeled off his shabby greatcoat, but underneath, his uniform was frayed and stained in several places. His third button was missing, too, which was all the more obvious because his tunic pulled open at the center.

As soon as the waitress had finished tidying, he sat down and gave his order, hoping nobody had noticed the sad state of his clothing, but he needn't have been concerned. The other patrons paid him no heed, as if he were a nobody, of zero consequence in the general scheme of things. Once she was gone, he slumped forward in his chair with his head in his hands, feeling very much alone and poverty-stricken, no more than a speck within the magnificence of this great metropolis.

By the time the waitress returned, Jakob's thoughts had wandered all over the continent. First, he thought about his elder sister, Berthe, and worried that she might be waiting for him. He hadn't told her what time he'd arrive, and he hoped she hadn't taken the day off work in anticipation. However, there was nothing he could do about that now. His roll and coffee were in front of him, and he was determined to enjoy them.

From Berthe, his thoughts went back to his home town, where his parents still took care of his younger brother, Adolfo, who'd been rejected as unfit for duty due to mental instability. The family derived their income from the patent royalties of a beer pump their father had invented in his youth, but such revenue was now scarce because the equipment was effectively obsolete.

At the start of the war, Jakob had tried to save enough from his wage pittance to send a little back every once in a while, but he had ceased on principle when he learned that his parents were giving it all to Adolfo, who had newly discovered the pleasant oblivion of alcohol.

These days, Jakob's letters contained nothing but greetings, which he tried to make as cheerful as possible to make up for the lack of money. Then, after Berthe and Adolfo, his thoughts traveled all the way to London and his older brother, Herschel—or Harry, as he was known over there—who had emigrated some years back.

At the time, it certainly seemed like a far-sighted move on Herschel's part, but such wisdom had since been tempered by the fact that he, too, had recently been conscripted. In Herschel's case, it was by the British Army, which meant they were now on opposite sides of the war.

Crazy world, thought Jakob, as he plastered his roll with free butter. He wondered what would happen if—by a one-in-a-million chance—they should ever come face-to-face on some God-forsaken battlefield. Would their respective platoon sergeants be yelling at them to fire at each other?

Suppose the brothers refused. Would they be executed for cowardice, or insubordination, or mutiny, or any of the other charges their respective armies could dream up? Officers had been known to shoot their own troops in the back for less.

Jakob shook himself. He often thought about his far-flung siblings, but he was essentially a pragmatist, and brought his mind back to the present. He saw his waitress once again sidling her way through the packed tables, and this time he felt her soft buttocks inadvertently caress his sleeve as she passed by. It was surreptitiously exciting, and he found himself shivering slightly at the sensation.

This is no good, he thought. *No good at all.* He finished up the last crumbs and drained the dregs of his coffee. He knew perfectly well that a man could get himself into a lot of trouble like that, and he strode out of the bakery hoping the cool air would clear his head of such thoughts.

For a moment, he just stood on the sidewalk, confused and disoriented in this unfamiliar city as the world passed by. He knew he had to find his way across the canal to the broad green space known as the Augarten, but he was unsure of the exact route through the complex grid of streets, so he was obliged to pause and ask further directions whenever he spotted a tradesman, or workman, or someone else of his status.

While they all recognized him as a foreigner, he appeared to be of their own class, so they helped him willingly enough, speaking their coarse slang and indicating directions with thick fingers. Yet, although he considered himself at the same economic level, he was self-educated and widely read, a habitual browser of newspapers and borrower of library books.

He'd learned all about the city prior to coming—about the culture of Schubert, Mahler, Klimt, and the Strauss family, and about the advanced psychoanalytic theories of Sigmund Freud. He'd have liked to take in some of the architectural sights, like the Schönbrunn Palace, the Leopold Museum, the State Opera, or especially the Spanish Riding School where they housed the famous Lipizzaner horses.

An animal lover, he really wanted to see the horses, but he'd have had to go far out of his way, and he possessed neither the energy nor the entrance fee. Maybe he'd manage to get there someday, but not today, so he locked away the promise in the back of his mind and kept walking.

Once over the waterway and beyond the band of commerce and industry which lined the banks, the city became more residential, with long rows of modest apartment buildings, mostly four stories, with all the attendant neighborhood facilities.

On the ground floor were grocery stores, repair shops, laundries, and pawnbrokers, while separate structures housed offices and small business showrooms. There were also synagogues and yeshivas, because this part of town was more ethnically mixed than elsewhere in Austria, which was almost uniformly Catholic. Here, Jakob felt a little more at ease.

Eventually he found the building he was seeking on Wallensteinstrasse, a busy thoroughfare that hadn't been cleaned in a while. There were still horse-droppings around, a rare sight in this city, and he was watching so closely where he placed his feet that he failed to see a pale girl approaching the same building from the other direction.

She was of high school age, dressed in a dark-blue uniform under a brown coat with a narrow fur collar: a young lady trying to look as fashionable as possible within the confines of correct attire. Her most distinguishing feature, however, was her hair, an auburn color so rich it seemed to glow.

Jakob almost bumped into her as they both arrived at the stone staircase at the same time. Instinctively, he stepped back with an apology on his lips. That's when it happened—the moment he looked at her for the first time. The difference between them was considerable.

While he was scruffy and world-weary, she was neat and clean, undoubtedly intelligent, and trying very hard to be mature but still retaining the shy naiveté of youth. Jakob stared at her for several long seconds, transfixed, until he remembered his manners and, with far too much gallantry under the circumstances, raised his cap to her.

She didn't smile and hardly even acknowledged his gesture, so he simply waited for her to mount the stairs, then followed at a discreet distance. He realized he'd behaved like an idiot but for some reason he couldn't take his eyes from her. Even after they'd entered the building he continued to watch from outside his sister's door on the ground floor as the girl continued up to whichever apartment she called home.

After she was gone, Jakob knocked loudly and heard movement from inside. The door creaked open and his sister yelled in delight, flinging her arms around him and clutching him tightly, her tears damp on his neck. Then she stood back to look at him, her expression creasing into a frown as she spoke to him in their native Galician Yiddish.

"About time you showed up. I've been waiting here all day."

He grinned at the ancient syntax, with all its implied sarcasm, and chose to reply in kind. "So? Who told you to wait?"

"If I hadn't, you'd have been sitting here on the doorstep."

"No, I'd have gone upstairs with that pretty girl I saw just now."

"A pretty girl? What pretty girl? Since when did you chase after pretty girls?"

"You'd be surprised."

She looked at him dubiously. She loved her brother, but he'd never been known to be much of a ladies' man. Even at school, he almost never had a girlfriend. "Talking of surprises, I've got one for you."

"What kind of surprise?"

"You'll see later. First things first."

They were still standing on the doorstep, so she told him to remove his coat and his boots before turning to lead him through the narrow passageway and into her cramped living room. From the kitchen came the powerful smell of hot stew simmering on the gas range—a traditional recipe from her mother—with potatoes, lentils, and butter beans, enhanced with as much fatty lamb as she could afford.

With pickles, black bread, and cheap local beer, it would make a filling repast, even for a half-starved soldier. It was typical of Berthe. She had once aspired to being a generous-hearted housewife, but that had all changed when she was told she wouldn't be able to have children. Then, when her husband was drafted, she'd decided she couldn't stay in the apartment alone all the time and went back to her old position at the municipal tax offices.

It had kept her occupied during the day but it was repetitive work and didn't pay well, so she'd had no qualms claiming she was sick so she could accommodate her brother's arrival.

For most of the day, she'd been cooking and cleaning but now that Jakob was here it was all worth it, just like old times: a big pot of food and a man who was hungry enough to eat it. She began taking out the dishes and setting the table but before she could serve, Jakob had slumped down into one of her sagging armchairs and closed his eyes, grateful at this chance to relinquish the world and all its chaos, even if only temporarily.

It was almost dark by the time he awoke and he had to rub his face with his hands before he could fully comprehend where he was. Then he saw his sister sitting patiently in the other armchair, half-dozing herself. She hadn't even lit the lamps, not wishing to disturb him.

"Good *Shabbos*," she said with a smirk.

The words formed the customary Sabbath greeting but she was only teasing. Few in the family had ever been very religious, even while growing up. They had regarded themselves as a little more enlightened than the people around them, a form of intellectual superiority that allowed them to maintain the traditions without being a slave to the rituals.

Their parents in Krakow typically spoke Yiddish at home because it came so natural, also Polish because it was the language spoken by the Gentiles all around them, but the literature they read was mostly High German, the language of Schiller and Goethe, and they had taught it to their children at a very early age.

From that point, the siblings' taste in languages varied. Berthe herself was fascinated by ancient Hebrew, not because of any spiritual influence but simply because she liked the Biblical stories of the great women—Esther, Miriam, Rachel, and so forth.

By contrast, Herschel, liked the western cowboy tales that found their way over from America, pulp shoot-'em-ups featuring Buffalo Bill Cody and Wyatt Earp and, in that way, he had learned his rudimentary English.

Jakob, for his part, had a friend at school who was half-Russian, and had told Jakob fine stories of the czars and their palaces. Once he had a grasp of Russian, Jakob moved on to Czech and other languages, allowing his mind to wander from one to the other whenever he took a momentary interest, like a butterfly constantly flitting across a bed of flowers.

Sadly though, Adolfo, the youngest, wasn't like the other three. He'd been born to their mother late in life, and this inherent handicap denied him their natural language abilities. So while his sister and two brothers equipped themselves industriously for the world around them, Adolfo was the one who remained at home, locally employed as a stable hand, while still living under the protection and guidance of his aging parents.

Perhaps it was not so strange that it was the two older ones who had ventured into marriage—Berthe with the Austrian, Hans, who was now in some anonymous muddy grave, and more recently, Herschel in England with Sarah, a native of Warsaw whom nobody in the family had ever met.

Next in line, according to familial lore, should have been Jakob, and it was Berthe who was most aware of it. That's why she'd insisted in her letters that he come visit her in Vienna as soon as he could. It was over their delayed meal that Friday evening that Berthe brought up the subject.

"You haven't asked me about the surprise I've got for you."

After Jakob had woken from his nap, he'd washed and changed into some of Hans' old clothes, and was now enjoying the warm glow of his adoring sister and the steaming food she'd served him.

He took a sip of his beer. "So tell me," he said simply.

Berthe smiled, anxious to impress him with her own cleverness but also a little embarrassed. In the end, she resorted to the old standby of Yiddish sarcasm.

"I arranged a *shidach*," she told him. In the old rural ghettoes, and sometimes even in the cities, a *shidach* was an arrangement of marriage, either organized by parents, or handed over to a third party, a matchmaker, usually an older woman who was supposedly wise in these matters.

Jakob glanced across the table, not surprised at all. Instead, he just shook his head with a sense of resignation. What else would anyone expect from an older sister? It wasn't the first time someone had tried to set him up. Back home it was his mother, then an aunt. Neither had been successful, yet here was Berthe, trying again.

"So who is she?" he asked, just for the sake of being polite. He really wasn't interested because he knew how it would work out.

Whoever it was would no doubt be plain and boring, unable to find a man to take any interest because she had no interest in anything herself.

Like most males, he believed a woman could either be beautiful and boring or plain and interesting. Both were acceptable. To find beautiful and interesting was an impossible dream, but plain and boring? That was a definite negative, and in his mind, he'd already dismissed Berthe's effort before she told him anything about it.

That's when she said, "It's a girl here in the building. I think you'll like her."

Jakob could hardly believe what he was hearing. "Here, in the building?"

"Are you deaf?"

He was about to ask if she was young with auburn hair, but he didn't dare. It would have been too embarrassing, too much of an admission. Instead, he just shrugged as if he were above it all and couldn't be bothered one way or the other. He wasn't sure if the pretense worked, but it didn't matter because his sister took his indecision as an approval of sorts.

"Don't you want to know what she's like?" she asked.

"If you want to tell me, so tell me."

"Well, where do I start? Let me think. Well, she's quite nice looking . . ."

"Only quite nice?" Jakob would have said the girl he met on the stairs was more than quite nice but he was prepared to acknowledge that males and females had different standards in such things.

"All right, *very* nice," said Berthe. "Also, very smart. A real head on her, that one."

"That's good."

"Sure, that's good. And she presents herself nicely—always well dressed, clean . . . What else?"

By this time, Jakob was definitely more interested, even though he was still feigning indifference. "What kind of things does she like?"

"Ah, that I'm not so sure. But I know she goes to the theater sometimes. And I've seen her reading. Good books, too, not just silly things."

Jakob shrugged again, this time with just a slight raise of the eyebrows to indicate that while he still had doubts, it was beginning to sound more reasonable.

"When do you want to meet her?" asked Berthe.

"I'm only here until Monday."

"Monday? That's all?"

"I was lucky to get that much."

"All right, all right. So how about Sunday afternoon?"

"If you like. What's her name, by the way?"

"Oh, that's right, her name, what am I thinking? Her name is Paula . . . Paula Gutmann."

"Paula," Jakob repeated, almost to himself. Although he was still taking great pains not to show it, he could hardly wait to be more formally introduced to his pretty Paula, and he continued thinking about it in silence as he ate. What he would say to her? How he should behave?

Certainly no more of that silly gallantry, he warned himself; in fact, no more games of any kind. He'd just try to be a little less shy, a little more confident than he normally was with the opposite sex, and hope that would be sufficient.

That weekend, Jakob wasn't able to see the wonders of Vienna as he'd promised himself. There just wasn't time and even if there had been, he didn't have the means. As it was, he'd have to borrow a little from Berthe just to get himself back to his unit. Yet he wasn't too disappointed because he now had something else to which he could look forward.

He was, therefore, content to spend the few hours he had available with his sister, talking and laughing the way they had once done. Such simple pleasure had been absent from both their lives for too long. Saturday morning, after breakfast, they did laundry together and Berthe sewed a button on his tunic. It didn't match the others but at least it closed the yawning gap.

Then they went out shopping, not to any Jewish stores, which were all closed for the Sabbath, but to the old Carmelite street market in nearby Leopoldstadt where they bought fresh vegetables and some salted fish for the evening meal.

Later, in the afternoon, they strolled in the Augarten where they paused to chat with a few of Berthe's friends. One had a dog, a small terrier of some sort, and Jakob spent a fun hour playing with it, running and jumping, chasing it around trees, throwing sticks, and even barking at each other until Berthe called a halt.

It was a happy interlude in Jakob's life, that Saturday afternoon. He was away from the war and all things military, he was here with his sister who'd always been his best friend, and on top of all that, he was about to see, once again, the girl he was certain he was going to marry.

In his own mind, Charlotte's future father had already ventured that far.

Sunday was the great day—the day Jakob was to be properly introduced to the petite, auburn-haired girl for whom he longed. It had only been forty-eight hours since he'd first seen her on the street outside his sister's building, yet the passion, whether real or imagined, had somehow taken over his life.

In preparation, he carefully ironed his shirt and his tunic, polished his boots to a high shine, and then heated up a large kettle of water so he could wash and shave, whistling as he did so. As a final touch, he applied several dabs of the cologne which Berthe had bought for her late husband on his last birthday before the war. The memories conjured by the scent brought moisture to her eyes but at least, she believed, it was now being put to good use.

At the front door, she gave Jakob a final head-to-toe inspection, as good as any barracks sergeant. Apart from readjusting his tie and smoothing down a couple of stray hairs, she decided he looked fine and gave him her blessing. His expression, however, revealed his nervousness. His face was paler than usual and she thought she could see signs of his lower lip quivering.

"You look scared," she told him. "Are you scared?"

"I'm fine."

"No, you're not, but that's all right. Scared is good the first time, makes you look sensitive. Girls like sensitive."

"They do?"

"What do you think? They like tough? Only boys like tough. Believe me, girls prefer sensitive."

"I didn't know that."

"No? So that explains a lot. All right, if you're ready, let's go."

She was about to lead the way upstairs but he held on to her arm, a way of delaying it.

"Wait, wait, what do I speak, German or Yiddish?"

"Yiddish? Are you crazy? These are educated people, very cultured. You speak only German . . . and High German, too, none of your army slang."

"German, good. Just so I know."

They had to climb two flights, but when they arrived at the door, he held her arm back yet again. "Do I look all right?"

"Very handsome. You want to do this, or not?"

"Yes, yes. Well, maybe no. I don't know. Maybe . . ."

He didn't get to finish his sentence as she rapped her knuckles loudly on the wooden door. The answer was prompt. A woman about Berthe's age but a little taller, a little slimmer, opened the door. She looked well-dressed and refined.

It was Berthe who spoke first. "Ah, good afternoon, Frau Gutmann, I hope we're not late. I'd like you meet my brother, Jakob."

They all shook hands self-consciously, then the woman looked at Jakob for what seemed like a long time, as if trying to sum him up all in one go. It was difficult for either Jakob or Berthe to read her thoughts because she offered no expression, none whatsoever.

She just stood back and said, "Please, come in. I'm sorry, my husband had an urgent appointment today. He was very much looking forward to meeting you."

The Gutmann apartment appeared to be larger than Berthe's, but it might just have been perception due to more tasteful furniture and decor. In the living room, on a chintz-style sofa, sat a young woman who stood to greet them as they entered, a gloved hand outstretched.

For Berthe, the glove seemed to be overdoing it a little, even for the Gutmanns, who were known to be a snobbish family.

She volunteered to make the introductions, as before.

"Fräulein Gutmann, please allow me to introduce my brother, Jakob Goldberger. Jakob, this is Paula."

"Pleased to meet you," said Paula, turning her attention to him. Although she and Jakob were about the same height, she appeared to be looking down at him, as if not entirely pleased with what she was seeing.

For his part, Jakob was equally unhappy. This Paula was not the auburn-haired girl on the stairs with whom he'd become so smitten. It was true, they looked a little alike, but Paula was older, she was definitely taller, and her hair was more a chestnut shade of brown.

For the moment, he seemed to have lost his voice. Worse, he'd turned pale, and Berthe had to nudge him slightly with her elbow to rouse him from his stupor.

"Hello," he said quickly in response. "Yes, pleased to meet you, very much so, very pleased." Without realizing it, he'd slipped back into Yiddish, and a very disjointed

Yiddish, at that. "Sorry," he said, switching back to his finest German. "Sorry, I meant to say . . ."

They all looked at him but he'd already sunk back into silence.

"Why don't we all sit down?"suggested Frau Gutmann, trying to ease the tension. "Paula, would you mind serving the tea?"

Paula was evidently not eager to play the servant's role, and probably not too used to it, but she was trying to be on her best behavior and nodded her acquiescence before leaving for the kitchen.

"So, Jakob," Frau Gutmann began. "Tell me a little about yourself."

Berthe had to nudge him again. "Jakob?" This time, her elbow seemed sharper.

""Yes, yes . . . Well, I'm in the army."

"Yes," said Mrs. Gutmann, "I can see that. Do you serve at the front?"

"Me? Oh, no, no . . . I'm in the paymaster general's office . . . Pressburg."

"Ah, good. That's something, at least. And what else can you tell me? What do you like to read? What do you like to do? What are your accomplishments?"

Jakob thought about it but his head just wouldn't seem to clear. "I like animals," he replied.

"You like animals, do you? I see." Frau Gutmann was finding the conversation a strain. "Any particular kind of animals?"

"No, not really. Horses, dogs . . . anything really. As long as . . ."

"As long as?"

"It's an animal."

Berthe, who was sitting right next to him, couldn't take much more of this. "He speaks many languages."

"Is that so?"asked Frau Gutmann, finally pleased to hear something intelligent.

"German, Polish, Russian, Czech and . . . what else, Jakob?"

"Yiddish, I speak Yiddish."

"Yes, we know. But wasn't there also Italian?"

"Yes, yes, a little. Well, a lot. It's a nice language."

"Yes," said Frau Gutmann, "I'm sure it's a very nice language. For the Italians."

It was at that point that she seemed to give up and seamlessly directed further dialogue at Berthe with such requests as "Tell me about the family," and "What does your father do?" and other generalities. While Berthe did her best to answer, Jakob just sat there in his own disappointment and misery.

After a few more minutes, Paula returned with a tray containing a small silver samovar with five glasses in ornate silver holders and a plate of shortbread.

Berthe wondered why there were five glasses until Paula delicately kicked at the beige, floor-length tablecloth. "For heaven's sake, Franzi, come out of there, will you? *Mutti*, tell her to come out. It's embarrassing."

"Francesca . . ." said Mrs. Gutmann, using the girl's full name like a rebuke. "Enough now, you can read later."

A slim hand appeared, then an auburn-crowned head, followed by a petite body with arms wrapped around a heavy old volume, a Tolstoy novel in its original Russian. When Jakob glanced at it, he recognized it as *Anna Karenina*, one of his favorites, but the book wasn't exactly the focus of his attention.

Franzi stood up and attempted to tidy a few stray wisps of glorious hair while smoothing out her blouse and skirt. She wasn't wearing her school uniform today and this ensemble, worn specially for company, made her seem less junior and more lady-like—but not by much. She still looked considerably younger than her sister, Paula.

"Hello, again," said Jakob, finding his voice.

There was some slight recognition from Franzi. "Hello," she replied more tentatively.

"You know each other?" asked Berthe.

Jakob wasn't sure how to respond, as if he'd been caught doing something amiss. "No . . . well, not really. We met on the street. Downstairs. Actually, *on* the stairs." He decided to stop right there before he did any more damage to himself.

"She likes to read under the table," explained Frau Gutmann. "God alone knows why."

"It's private," replied Franzi defensively. Then, without another word, she hurried from the room.

"Don't mind her," said Paula to the guests. "She's at that age."

"She reads Russian?" This was Jakob, still staring after Franzi, expecting her to reappear momentarily.

"She reads whatever she can get her hands on," said Frau Gutmann, but that really wasn't what she wanted to talk about, not this afternoon. "Paula, tell them what you like to do." When Paula didn't respond, Frau Gutmann added an edge to her tone which contained an undercurrent of warning. "Paula, please serve the tea, then sit down and tell our guests what you like to do."

It was easy to see that Paula was upset, by the disruption Franzi had caused and by her mother's tone, which implied some kind of comparison between the two daughters. Clearly, by her own standards, Paula was nothing like her sister, who was still just a baby in so many ways.

Berthe and Jakob accepted the tea she served, adding their own lemon and, in Jakob's case, an extra spoon of sugar. It was difficult to find sugar amongst army supplies. He also helped himself to the shortbread.

"I'm not sure what to tell you," Paula began, displaying the correct amount of modesty for a well-brought-up daughter. "I like many activities. I do well in mathematics and the sciences . . . and next year I'll be applying for a position to study biology. I would like to work in medicine."

"As a nurse?"asked Berthe.

Paula felt some disgust at the notion and revealed it in her expression. Undoubtedly, she wasn't eager to fetch bedpans and wipe up vomit for a living.

"Perhaps in a laboratory," she replied airily.

"Very good," said Berthe.

"In my spare time, I like to cycle . . . and to read, of course."

"Also Russian?"asked Jakob.

Paula looked at him dismissively. "No, I read German," she said, as if it was a ridiculous question.

At that, Jakob was cowed into submission and chose to hold back from all further comment. From that time onward, there was only so much that Berthe and Paula could talk about, so eventually the afternoon came to a very unsatisfactory close. Frau Gutmann, still the epitome of the good hostess, saw her guests to the door.

"Thank you for visiting. Please do call in again."

'Thank you for inviting us," answered Berthe, shaking her hand in the proper manner—just a simple clasp, not too firm. "Please give Herr Gutmann our regards. We're sorry to have missed him."

"Yes, I will. Well, thank you, again."

As soon as the door was shut, Berthe dug her brother in the ribs yet again, this time with her clenched fist, and tore into him in Yiddish.

"What was that about? I know shy, but that was. . . I don't even know what that was, can you tell me? *Nu*, what have you got to say for yourself?"

Jakob wasn't able to respond. How could he? How could he admit that even while he was being introduced to the elder Gutmann daughter, he'd fallen for the younger one? How would his own sister ever comprehend such a thing? He was lost, both to himself and to her.

"Jakob?" she asked.

They were now back at Berthe's front door but still he couldn't reply, couldn't say a word and, as soon as he was inside, he went directly to the tiny room where he was sleeping, the one with all the old boxes and other discarded items which might come in useful someday.

Ashamed of himself, he lay down on the cot and closed his eyes, wondering why he'd ever agreed to such old-world matchmaking and hoping it would now just go away.

Berthe, however, refused to leave him be and put her head around the door. "Jakob? What is it? All right, it didn't go so well, we both looked like fools, so what? No need to get upset. What's wrong with you? I've never seen you like this."

It was true, because he'd never been like this. Yet, even now, he couldn't admit to his emotions. The girl, who he now knew as Franzi, was just fifteen, thirteen years younger than he was.

He could see how indecent, how obscene that might be, and how presumptuous he was to imagine that there could be anything at all between them. Yet he couldn't help his feelings.

The moment Berthe closed the door, some moisture welled in his eyes, and although he was contemptuous of himself—he was, after all, a soldier in uniform—he just wasn't able to prevent it.

That evening, Jakob was a mess. After his disastrous visit to the Gutmann household when he thought he was going to see Franzi but met Paula instead, he remained in his tiny room and refused to emerge, either for supper or his sister Berthe's entreaties.

He thought himself a pedophile, a cradle-snatcher, and goodness knows what else. He also felt like a coward for not admitting everything to his sister, yet he couldn't bring himself to face her. She'd been good to him, his Berthe. She'd cooked and sewn for him, then introduced him to a fine family, and this was how he repaid her.

All in all, he loathed himself, and for one very brief moment in the early hours he actually considered the ridiculous idea of suicide. Back at camp, he had a gun, not a very good one since he was only an administrator, but it would surely be enough if that was what he really wanted.

All he'd have to do was insert the muzzle in his mouth and bang, it would all be over. Was that what he wanted, or was he too pathetic to do even that? He didn't know anymore. He simply didn't know who or what he was.

Meanwhile, he had another problem. The following day he was due back at the base by the start of curfew and if he didn't show up he'd be charged for being absent without leave, a serious wartime offense. He did some rapid math in his head. He estimated a seven-hour journey by bus, plus an hour long walk at each end.

He'd have to leave his sister's place by lunchtime at the latest just to have a chance of making it back in time. It meant he had just a few hours, either to do something, or let it alone and do nothing at all, but if he chose the former, what should he do? That night he slept little.

Early in the morning, he put in an appearance for breakfast and tried to apologize to Berthe for his behavior, but it came out awkwardly and he fell silent. She was concerned for him and tried to offer some reassurance that he was sure to find someone but to no avail. Eventually, she had to leave for work, so she hugged him goodbye and told him to leave the key hidden under the doormat.

Once she'd gone, he finished the dishes, hauled on his greatcoat and went for a walk in the Augarten. This time there was no happy chatter with his sister, no friends to meet and greet, not even a dog to chase.

It was Monday, so the park was empty and all he had was his own solitude, enhanced by the heavy gray clouds which seemed to have rolled in from nowhere just to add to his unhappiness. He sat down on a wooden bench, weary from his lack of sleep, and closed his eyes.

No sooner had he done so than he opened them again with a start. He'd had an idea. He was on his feet immediately and pacing his way back to the building. This time, Jakob didn't knock on his sister's door but went directly upstairs to the Gutmanns' apartment. It was Frau Gutmann who answered, obviously surprised to see him. There'd been no arrangement, no appointment. This was exceedingly unusual.

"Herr Goldberger . . ."

She wasn't as well-dressed today, back to the working housewife, with a large pinafore apron over a beige blouse and gray skirt. She was still wiping her hands on a dishcloth. Jakob raised his cap and moved swiftly into his most polished German.

"I apologize for disturbing you, Frau Gutmann, but I have little time and there's something I must speak to your husband about. Is he, by any chance, at home today? Please forgive me, but it really is extremely urgent."

"I see. Well, I'm sorry but my husband's at work. May I be of some assistance?"

"That's very kind, but it's really Herr Gutmann I need to see. May I ask if he works around here, I mean in Brigittenau?" Frau Gutmann seemed offended at the suggestion that her husband was so lowly as to work in some mere local office.

"No, Herr Goldberger, it's on Krugerstrasse, but my husband is very busy. Do you plan on going to see him?"

Jakob wasn't sure. He didn't know if he would have time, nor did he recognize the street name. For all he knew, Krugerstrasse could be on the other side of the city. Would he have time to call in on his way to the bus? He was still considering when Frau Gutmann interrupted his unfinished thoughts with a more pragmatic suggestion.

"He usually comes home for lunch at 12. 30. You can see him at that time."

Jakob's eyes brightened for an instant, then dimmed again when he realized it would give him precious little time to achieve anything.

Nevertheless, he thanked her profusely, shook her hand, and almost bowed like a Prussian in his gratitude, before scampering back down the stairs. He didn't have long to prepare what he was going to say.

This was the idea he'd come up with in the park—not to talk with Frau Gutmann but to have a dialogue, man-to-man, with her husband. *There would be no emotion involved*, he told himself. This would be a business proposition, cold and logical, nothing more.

At least, that was Jakob's intention. He wasn't at all certain he could handle it, but he was determined to make the effort. If he failed to do so, he knew he'd never be able to forgive himself.

Herr Gutmann worked for a German insurance company, headquartered in Frankfurt but with a large branch in the Austrian capital. He was in the actuarial department, which meant a high intellectual requirement but a low standard of pay. He was, however, a valued employee at a transnational enterprise and such a position afforded him a certain status within his home community.

As a consequence, he dressed conservatively and could often be seen strolling his own neighborhood, as if showing off his city attire.

Unlike his wife and his elder daughter, Paula, he wasn't especially tall, but he tried to make himself imposing with a bushy brown mustache and a black walking cane, which he swung like a wealthy boulevardier.

Under normal circumstances, Herr Gutmann's somewhat haughty demeanor might have deterred Jakob but not on this occasion. Instead of waiting for him to reach his apartment, Jakob decided to waylay him on the street, right on the stairs, in the very same spot where he first saw Franzi just three days earlier.

"Herr Gutmann, excuse me. Please forgive me."

The man glanced back at the soldier on the sidewalk. "I'm sorry, I have no change."

"No, please, you don't understand. I spoke to your wife and she very kindly said I might speak with you. I hope you don't mind. I just need a minute of your time. My name is Jakob Goldberger and yesterday . . ."

"Ah, yes, Herr Goldberger. You came to visit my daughter, I believe."

"That's right, that's what I wanted to talk to you about."

"I see. Well, to be frank with you, I'm not sure it will do any good. She has a mind of her own and I'm afraid you didn't make such a good impression. A pity, I'm sure, but thank you for your interest."

He turned to continue but Jakob was insistent.

"A minute, please, Herr Gutmann. Yes, I'm aware it didn't go so well, I know that, but you have two daughters."

There, it was done, spoken out loud, and Jakob couldn't take it back now, even if he wanted to. He waited for some reaction.

"Yes . . . that's perfectly true," said the man cautiously. "What of it?"

Jakob allowed himself to take a breath. "Well, it's just that . . ."

"Speak up, Herr Goldberger, I have very little time to stand around."

"Yes, of course, of course. I was about to say I'm actually quite fond . . . What I mean is . . ."

"You prefer Francesca to Paula, is that what you're trying to tell me? Well, is it?"

Herr Gutmann's direct attitude took Jakob completely by surprise and he wasn't sure how to respond. "Well, yes." It was all he could think to say.

"I see. All right, I suppose that's honest enough. But you realize, I hope, how young she is?"

"I do. Believe me, I do. But I'm in the army, there's a war. I was hoping that, maybe, when it's all over . . ."

"When do you return to your unit?"

"Today, right now."

"So that's the reason you assault me here, like a thief."

"I'm sorry, Herr Gutmann, I didn't mean . . ."

"I suppose your bravery does you credit. Very well, let me think about it. Good day to you, Herr Goldberger."

That was all Herr Gutmann said before hurrying into the building, already late for his midday meal. Nevertheless, it was sufficient to make Jakob a happy man and he reflected on his good fortune as he strode off to catch his bus with renewed vigor.

How frail the human condition must be, he thought, if it can pass from suicidal depression to joyous elation in under twelve hours.

The phone rang and our lunchtime conversation was interrupted yet again. Charlotte would always take the call, even though she had a fully functioning answering machine. She'd speak for a few minutes, then afterwards, once she'd replaced the receiver, she would invariably inform me what the call was about, which I believe was her way of apologizing for the interruption.

"That's Clara, her ceiling's damp," she might say. Or, "That's Mrs. Brizelli wants to come down, and bring me the check." Or: "That's Claude, thinks he found a new tenant, a Lebanese woman."

It was distracting but understandable that these calls took priority over everything else, because Charlotte was both owner and proprietor of the building in which she lived, a venerable, five-story walk-up of thirteen dwellings, older by a decade than Charlotte herself.

Located in the genteel borough of Outremont on the northern slopes of Mount Royal, it was conveniently close to stores, schools and subway, as well as one of the city's major universities, and although she received her regular government pension in addition to a modest annual amount in reparations from Austria, the cash flow generated by the building was her major source of income.

From the street, the brown-brick façade looked innocuous, like all the rest on that block, but passing through the front doors was like stepping back in time.

The hallways were lined with beige stucco, the floors were laid with the original checkerboard marble tiles and, everywhere, the authentic fittings still remained—handsculpted moldings, ornate sconces, plasterwork arches, wrought-iron banisters. The place was outmoded but it had become imbued with Charlotte's own aging personality—a dowager of an edifice, with a musty ambience and an evocative nostalgia.

As owner, she lived at number one on the ground-floor, a moderate-sized apartment crammed to capacity with unmatched furniture and countless mementos, plus all the minutiae of her daily life: newspapers, address books, coupons, and to-do lists.

Tucked out of sight in numerous drawers were tax files, mortgage contracts, and dozens of other folders, including her critical accounting ledgers in which both revenues and expenses were painstakingly entered by pencil in her precise script. This was an essential, if time-consuming function, because her preference was to control costs and keep rents low, which her tenants naturally appreciated.

Some of them seemed to have been there forever, making it not so much a residential building as a minuscule community, a true vertical village. Chitchat, fuss, demands, complaints...

At times, Charlotte's apartment on the ground floor could receive a call every few minutes, which she'd then relay through to the janitor, the thin and wiry Claude, a highly capable, if somewhat moody, handyman who also lived in the building.

"He can turn his hand to anything, that man. The painting, the plumbing, the electricity. He sands the floors, too, when I need it, patches the roof, does the bricks. Whatever *it is, he can do it. Sure, I pay him, maybe it's too much, I don't know. He gets it done, but he's not always so organized. Sometimes I have to remind him, do this, do that. He doesn't always remember."*

It was clear that Charlotte appreciated Claude, but unfortunately they had an unstable relationship—sometimes friendly, sometimes highly argumentative. Occasionally, despite being landlady and janitor, they wouldn't speak for days, which made for a strange atmosphere around the building. Somehow, though, the routine work continued and the countless range of things that fell apart in the old structure were miraculously fixed.

Given his personality, some were inclined to blame Claude for these eruptions but, as I can testify, it was often the fault of Charlotte's own involuntary temper, suddenly bubbling up like volcanic lava for almost no reason.

Afterwards, when she'd cooled a little, the regret would set in and I'd often arrive to find her head in her hands, her face lined with anguish and her cheeks cascading with tears. This was the paradox of Charlotte. Why she blew hot or cold had little to do with immediate reasons and everything to do with her own history, her memories, and her internal pain.

She knew what was happening but was powerless to prevent it, so it became my self-proclaimed task on these occasions to divert her despondency. Jokes, quips, wisecracks—I used whatever I could to make her laugh, and it usually worked. I'd make us a pot of coffee and we'd become involved in other topics.

It was as if nothing had happened. Yet I knew that after I left, she might just as easily slip back into the same despair.

2

Herr Gutmann was not entirely convinced about the idea of Jakob Goldberger as a future son-in-law, however it was his pragmatic compromise rather than his wife's high-minded ambitions which finally won the day.

Of course, he was in full agreement with her that this working-class *nebisch,* this nothing, was hardly the catch they'd originally had in mind, either in looks, prospects, or any other material way, but as a potential husband for their younger daughter, he might just suffice.

He came from a good family, and more importantly he was of sound character—honest, intelligent, dutiful—the kind of qualities which shouldn't be too quickly dismissed in such a *meshuga* world. A girl like Franzi, he felt, could certainly do a lot worse in life.

Jakob was with his unit when the unexpected letter arrived. It was noon-hour and he was in the mess at the time, sitting with a couple of his colleagues from admin, one from Budapest, and the other from Linz. In front of him, on a metal tray, were the picked-over remains of his meal: gristly sausage which contained very little meat, accompanied by a pungent sauerkraut which might, at some stage in history, have been fresh cabbage.

However, a spicy type of mustard was plentiful enough to camouflage the taste and render the food almost edible. Bread had once been in abundance, too, but as the war dragged on, it had become more of a rarity, appearing on the menu about once a week, mostly on Sundays.

At that moment, though, Jakob had the letter, so he wasn't too interested in food and he pushed the tray aside. Since he rarely received mail of any kind, its presence alone was cause for excitement, but when he saw that it bore a Vienna postmark, his fingers became shaky and he fumbled with the envelope.

Across from him, the Hungarian nudged his Austrian friend, having correctly guessed what the letter might contain: news of the redhead, about whom they'd been teasing Jakob mercilessly.

They didn't know the details, neither her age nor the initial mix-up with her older sister, but they did know he'd been mooning over her ever since he'd gotten back from Vienna. In fact, the entire regiment seemed to know. It had become that evident.

Appropriately enough, the first item that slid out from the folded notepaper was a small photograph of Franzi. It was a classic studio portrait in standard black-and-white, but a retouch artist had painted a pale rust-colored wash on the hair, plus the tiniest dab of gray-green for the eyes, crimson for the lips, a rosy white for the skin tones and a mid-turquoise blue for the dress.

The colors weren't exact but it was, nevertheless, skillfully executed and effective at offering a reasonable first impression. When Jakob turned it over, he saw her handwriting. There was no message, she'd simply signed it "Franzi" with the date, but that was enough.

The other two men peered across at the image, making all the usual whoops and catcalls on seeing such a young and attractive girl, but when they reached for it, Jakob pulled it away, refusing to let them touch it. For a few moments more, he gazed enthralled at the image, then tucked it safely inside his tunic, away from prying fingers and right next to his heart.

The letter itself was another matter. It wasn't written by her, as he'd hoped, but by her father in a formal copperplate script. The words, cautious in tone but flowery in phraseology, essentially informed him that it would be appropriate for him to see Franzi, should he wish to do so, whenever he next returned to Vienna on leave.

For Jakob, that was sufficient for a bout of elation. It called for a major celebration, and that evening he and his friends escaped from the base on a six-hour pass and kept ordering beer in a local workers' bar until the place closed.

They sang, they drank, they got up and danced, and in the morning when it was time to return to duty, they were sick to their stomachs, with Jakob in the worst condition of any of them. Nothing could take away from his joy, however, and he was more than happy to suffer the paralyzing headache because he still had both the letter and the photograph stuffed tightly into his pocket.

He wasn't sure when his next leave could be scheduled but being in the section that arranged for such permission, he had some personal influence.

Jakob continued to write to his parents in Krakow, full of guilt about not visiting, but that didn't change anything. Whenever he could, he chose the city of Vienna for his travels , where his widowed sister, Berthe, was always pleased to see him and looked forward to his arrival, enjoying the chance to take care of someone again.

Privately, she wasn't sure if she approved of the prospective liaison but she kept all such opinions to herself. He was, after all, her brother, and she was glad to see him so happy. It had been a long time since Jakob had been this joyful. Besides, the girl might be young right now but life was short and she'd age soon enough.

As for Franzi herself, no one seemed to know what she thought of the arrangement. She agreed to go for afternoon walks with Jakob, the normal courting ritual, sometimes allowing him to buy her a soda or an ice cream if he had the funds.

Yet, when the weekend was over and he returned to barracks, she just seemed to carry on with her life as if nothing had happened: reading her literature, studying her art, taking her cello lessons; all the cultural activities that Herr and Frau Gutmann considered essential for a modern, well-brought-up young woman.

She never spoke to them about Jakob, about what she thought of him, nor did she ever discuss it with her friends at school, as if it were the secret to some other life she was leading.

By the summer of 1916, Jakob had saved enough to be able to escort her on more distant outings. They frequently caught the Stadtbahn into central Vienna, so he could fulfill his longstanding desire to see the great sights, and she was content to oblige, chatting away about architecture and music, sometimes humming for him a cello piece she was rehearsing as they strolled the historic pavement.

Once, on a sudden whim and against all regulations, they even managed to sneak in behind a group of visitors to see the Lipizzaner stallions train in the magnificent Hofburg arena, an eighteenth century architectural masterpiece. It looked to all the world like some flamboyant opera house, except it had a base of sand for the horses' hooves.

Stealing in like they did was a daring act on their part but well worth the risk and they watched, fascinated, as the animals pranced their delicate maneuvers like a troupe of colossal ballerinas.

When it was over, and while they were still marveling at their own courage, he said he had a surprise for her. Intrigued, she began to spray him with questions, but all he would say was, "Later ... I'll tell you later."

Instead of continuing along the busy Herrengasse, they diverged onto the Michaelerplatz and entered the Grössenwahn, a fashionable coffee house. There, he ordered café-crème and strudel for two, a rare treat, as Franzi gazed around at the finely-clothed people smoking their cigarettes and reading their newspapers, at the bustling waiters in their black jackets, and at the tall windows, the vaulted ceiling and the potted plants.

It all seemed so sophisticated to a sixteen-year-old who'd hardly ever ventured out from her own ethnic neighborhood.

"Is this the surprise?" she asked softly, not wishing to raise her voice in such an august establishment.

"Do you like it?"

"It's ... wonderful."

He smiled, shaking his head. "Actually, no, this is not the surprise. Well, it's part of it, but only a small part." She looked back at him expectantly—such a pretty face with those petite features and gray-green eyes.

Her radiant hair shone like it was bathed in light and Jakob noticed that a few of the male customers couldn't help but sneak a glance over. It made him feel both proud and nervous at the same time. "Franzi, the army ... They're sending me to the front."

"Oh. Really? When?"

"Soon, very soon."

"But won't it be ..."

"Won't it be what?"

"I don't know? Dangerous? Won't they order you to fight?"

"To tell you the truth, I'll still be with admin, so I won't be in the direct line of fire . . . but I'll be close enough."

"Still dangerous, I'm sure. I hope you'll be careful."

"Franzi . . ." He took a look around him to see who might be listening, but while some of the clientele might have been attracted by her youth and appearance, they weren't at all interested in the couple's conversation. "I don't know how to say this."

She seemed to sympathize with his difficulty. "Jakob, do you want to break our friendship?"

"No, no . . . not at all. That's not what I mean." He was dismayed to hear her call it a friendship, nothing more, but he refused to let that dissuade him from what he wanted to say.

"No, on the contrary, I don't want to break anything. Actually, I was wondering . . . I was wondering how you'd feel if I were to ask your father . . . " Jakob's voice trailed off.

"Ask my father? Jakob? Ask him what?"

All of a sudden, he wanted to stop, to hold back, but he couldn't. He was too far along. He had no choice now but to come right out and declare it.

"Franzi, I would like us to get married." Before she could reply, he quickly added, "Not now, not immediately, but eventually. How would you feel about that? I'd give you a good life, I promise.

"You'd have your books, you could continue with your studies. I wouldn't be a demanding husband, I think you know that's not my way. We could be happy together, Franzi. I've got plans, I mean for after the war, to start my own business—import-export. I've already made some contacts.

"We could live here in Vienna, so you'd still be close to your family and . . . and . . ." Jakob forced himself to slow down, as if realizing all at once how he must sound.

Meanwhile, Franzi stared down at her half-finished coffee, thick with cream. She'd hardly touched the strudel. Then she looked up at him directly and asked a strange thing. "If we were engaged to be married, would it help you when you're at the front?"

It was such an unlikely response that, for a moment, he was confused. "Why? What I mean is, why would you ask that?"

"It's all right, I understand. I've read how, when a man's at the front and he has a sweetheart back home, it gives him comfort. Do you think it would give you comfort?" It was such an impossibly romantic notion that he was taken aback, until he realized it was exactly the kind of innocent comment that might be expected from a girl of her age.

All she knew of war was the patriotic propaganda the government posted, which was full of such imagery: men at the front with chiseled features, standing firm, rifles at the ready, while their loved ones displayed unbounded joy on receiving news of their brave exploits.

"Is that why you sent me the photograph?" he asked softly.

She didn't answer, a little embarrassed at this revelation of the truth, and a long silence enveloped them like a gentle cloud. It didn't feel like rejection, but Jakob was certainly tentative as he waited for an answer, not about the photograph but about his proposal of marriage.

It had taken so much effort just to work up the audacity to ask.

Eventually, the tension snapped and he just couldn't wait any longer. "So . . . what do you think?"

Finally, Franzi spoke: "I think it depends on my father."

"So you're saying yes? Is that what you're saying?"

"Jakob . . ."

"You must ask your father, I understand. But if he approves?"

"Then we'll see."

"Yes, of course. Good, good, no need to decide now. Plenty of time. I'll talk to your father first, how about that?"

She shrugged her narrow shoulders. "If you like."

Their journey back to Brigittenau was also made in silence, each of them lost in thought. The conversation about architecture and music had been forgotten, as had their escapade to view the horses, all replaced by the heavy presence of the proposal which hovered in the atmosphere above and around them. As for Jakob, he couldn't believe his own good fortune at reaching this stage without his nerve breaking, and already, even while still on the Stadtbahn, he was desperately trying to prepare himself for his meeting with her father. The man certainly wouldn't be too impressed if Jakob blurted it all out, the way he had just done with Franzi.

No, he told himself, he'd have to be more composed, more measured. It would have to be a thoughtful approach, some way to show his dedication, his total commitment to her happiness and welfare—which shouldn't be too difficult, he thought, because he profoundly meant it.

Gradually, Jakob began to believe that his life was changing, that he was now being carried along on a rising swell of good fortune. Not only had the Gutmanns given their cautious blessing to some potential future union between Jakob and Franzi, but the Imperial Army had also played a role.

Instead of being transferred to the bloody trenches in France—where the constant artillery shelling had turned the countryside into a wasteland, and where the rumors of poison gas being used as a weapon were turning out to be true—he was sent instead to the Italian front, to Carinthia near the Isonzo River, north-east of Trieste. Certainly, it would have been preferable to spend the entire war at his unit's base in Pressburg but if he did have to go to the front, he felt this particular posting was better than most.

He was still in an administration unit, for which he showed sound aptitude, being both nimble-minded and conscientious, but while his previous responsibilities were in the paymaster's office, he was now under the divisional quartermaster's authority. His principal work involved ordering up food, medical, and ammunition supplies, as well as checking the bulk shipments as they arrived.

Although his function was often dismissed by frontline troops as bureaucratic and, therefore, of little consequence, Jakob knew that if he made a mistake with his paperwork, it could end up costing lives. In addition, his station at a forward emplacement required him to assume his share of sentry duty like anyone else, even if he was just guarding a compound of crates and barrels against his own side's petty pilferers. As Franzi had predicted in her naiveté, the spiritual presence of a sweetheart helped Jakob considerably. Wherever he went, whatever he did, he carried that tiny portrait of her in his inside pocket, and when the danger had finally threatened, he was sure it was Franzi who had saved his life.

The incident occurred early one morning in the winter of 1917. Dawn had already broken over the Carnic Alps, and after an exhausting double shift of guard duty due to lack of manpower, Jakob had inadvertently fallen asleep while sitting with his back against a howitzer tractor. He was dreaming and heard a female voice as if she were right next to him. The tone was urgent, insistent. "Wake up Jakob, wake up!"

As instructed, he shook himself awake in time to hear the terrifying, high-pitched whistle of a falling bomb immediately overhead. Intuitively, he rolled under the tractor, just as the projectile erupted in a blast of light and heat and sound. Crates were splintered, drums exploded and massed coils of barbed wire were blown into fragments of flying metal.

Bad as it was, it could have been worse. Fortunately, the recent supplies of heavy ordnance had already been transported out to the lines, otherwise Jakob, too, would have been incinerated. As it turned out, the heavy vehicle managed to shield him from the brunt of it, and somehow he had emerged, wounded but alive, his lower limbs scratched and bruised but otherwise fully intact. Apparently, the bomb had been jettisoned by an aircraft, an Italian Caproni, whose port engine was on fire and trailing black smoke across the early skies. The fact that the explosive managed to strike the compound was, the authorities said, purely coincidental.

This was the closest Jakob ever came to death throughout those long years of war and he was never really sure why he was spared, or precisely whose voice was in his dream. Conceivably, it might have been his mother, or perhaps Berthe, but he was more inclined to think it was Franzi calling to him from right out of the photograph. It might have been wishful thinking on his part but the more he considered it, the more he became convinced that it must have been her, and when he was strong enough, he wrote to thank her profusely for saving his life. The letter was addressed "To my dearest auburn angel."

With frontline medical facilities at a premium, Jakob managed to get himself shipped home on extended disability. At his own request, he was sent not to Krakow, but to his sister Berthe in Vienna. It was she who had the fortitude and patience to nurse him back to health and strength.

Each night when she came back from work, she set about preparing him a hot supper, and each morning before she left, she made sure he had as much as he needed to survive the day on his own. Although food rations were limited, there was plenty of tea, also a change of bandages and some old books to read.

By this stage of the war, many essential items were in short supply, but just as Jakob had pulled strings to get back, so Berthe used whatever influence she had within her government office to obtain what she needed. The Goldbergers of Krakow were a resourceful family and it was this intrinsic ability which helped them get by.

On weekends, with Berthe as chaperone, Franzi was permitted to visit the apartment. Once Jakob felt capable, they began to take walks again along the neighborhood streets to the Augarten. However, it wasn't the same as before. This time he needed to tap along with a stout cane and that added an extra element of drama and emotion to their times together, especially for Franzi, who seemed very taken with her new role as convalescent nurse, walking arm-in-arm with her hero from the front.

She'd been deeply touched by the letter he'd sent and the concept of herself as an angel had become firmly locked inside her mind. In her vision, she was like some ethereal being with a golden halo, even though such a self-image was perhaps more a reflection of Christian art than Jewish scripture.

"Does it hurt?" she would ask him as they walked, her voice heavy with compassion. "Can I do anything for you?"

There was not a great deal she could have done since it was Berthe who did all the strenuous work, but Franzi's support was, nevertheless, very welcome to Jakob, and she was nothing if not consistent in her willingness to help. At one point, as he was resting with his hand on her shoulder, he leaned in and gave her a brief kiss on the cheek.

Despite all their outings, this was the first time he'd done such a thing and she wasn't sure what to make of it. She understood that it was meant simply as a show of gratitude, but it was in a public park and she flushed at the gesture, offering a shy smile only when she'd glanced around and reassured herself that nobody had noticed.

"Will you marry me?" he asked her quietly.

"Jakob, I've already . . ."

"What I mean is now, this summer, before I have to go back."

"This summer? I don't know. I'll have to . . ."

"You'll have to ask your father. I know, I know."

"Not just my father. My mother, too."

"But how do you feel about the idea yourself? If your parents approve, would you be willing?"

She didn't know if she'd be willing and had to think about it for the entire forty minutes it took to walk home.

"The situation," she said at last, "with the war and everything. It's not good, is it? My father is worried. He says he doesn't know what will happen."

They were on the sidewalk in front of the building. On either side, people hurried by and all seemed to have frowns on their faces, as if confirming what she'd just said. Everyone was concerned about the future, not just her father.

Meanwhile, out in the street, the driver of a large horse-drawn cart was delivering what little milk he could supply to the homes on his route: according to the rationing laws, no more than a half-cup a day for an entire family.

"No," said Jakob, replying to her question, "it's not good."

"You think it's the right time to get married?"

"We might not get another chance."

"Really?"

"I don't know."

She nodded, and that's when he knew the decision was set, based on little more than a feeling that it was possibly a final opportunity before . . . before what? That was the problem. Nobody could predict how it would all turn out. For a while, it had been inconceivable that the Central Powers' great Triple Alliance could actually lose the war, or what such a reality would mean, but the news headlines had become increasingly foreboding and the editorial opinions ever more critical.

Clearly, the situation here in the capital wasn't as physically grim as in the farther reaches of the empire, but since they were closer to the core, they felt the anxiety with more immediacy because they knew that the crushingly bad news was mostly true.

Before early summer, with Franzi still only eighteen years of age, they were married.

Was she already pregnant? That was Berthe's immediate suspicion, and she might not have been the only one to think that way. Although such impropriety was never as damnable for members of the Jewish community as it might have been for the Catholic population around them, it would still have represented a major social stigma, especially for a family like the Gutmanns with appearances to maintain.

Over the weeks, however, as Franzi failed to show any signs, these fears were allayed and a major wedding was planned, not to camouflage any shame that might be involved, but simply to satisfy the needs of Herr Gutmann's egocentric personality and match his self-perceived status within the community.

The ceremony was scheduled at the local synagogue, a tall structure with twin onion domes, which was located on Klukygasse, just off the main Wallensteinstrasse thoroughfare. Here, the Gutmanns' largesse could be on full display, almost the sole sign of hopeful optimism in the increasingly depressed atmosphere. Within their own modest neighborhood, the event had become the closest thing to a society wedding that anyone had seen in a long time.

To match the occasion, finely printed invitations in cream and silver were sent out to almost everyone who mattered, and by the time the service was due to start, the building was almost full to capacity.

In the pews were not only relatives and friends, but also members of the rabbinate, leaders of the district council, minor officials from Berthe's office, a local Jewish police officer, and several of Herr Gutmann's colleagues from the insurance company.

All were wearing their finest outfits to celebrate this most joyous occasion but, as with Berthe's original question, the murmurs still circulated and they couldn't seem to hide their curiosity as to why the more junior of the two Gutmann daughters was getting married first. Jakob could sense the mood and understood the whispered gossip, but with his liberalized attitude, he didn't care too much what people thought or said.

He believed them to be small-minded and in fact, when he was with Franzi, he sometimes liked to poke a little good-natured fun at the enclave of Brigittenau, referring to this tight little area between the canal and the river as "Matzo Island." It was a private joke between them and usually made her smile, but not on the day of their wedding.

"Looks like the whole island showed up," he said to her as they met, according to custom, in the bridal preparation room. This time, however, she didn't acknowledge the humor and her face remained immobile.

As far as Jakob was concerned, she was simply nervous, no more than that. *It's perfectly natural*, he thought, and he smiled at her as gently as he could. She was entering a new life and he well understood that, for someone so young, it was a frightening leap into the unknown.

He was just about to leave when she stood up and took him aside from her mother and sister who were still fussing with the dress. That's when she said something which both shocked and disturbed him.

"I want you to . . . to . . ." At first, she couldn't get the words out. She took a breath, trying to pull herself together, but was still so anxious not to be overheard that her voice was almost inaudible. "I want you to know something."

Jakob waited for several seconds but there was nothing further. She didn't even want to look at him.

"What?" he asked her. "What is it?" He lifted her chin so he could see her eyes but she just shook her head. He was very conscious now of her mother and sister waiting on the other side of the room, watching them, wondering what was going on. "Tell me, please. What is it? What is it you want me to know?"

She was about to refuse again but suddenly it burst out, all the more forcefully because she was still attempting to keep her voice as low as possible.

"What I want you know is that . . . is that you're marrying a woman who doesn't love you."

For a long moment, he just looked at her. He didn't know how to reply, whether to remain silent or to speak out loud. He raised his arms but then lowered them again in futility. He just didn't have the words to reply. With some effort, he told himself to relax a little, to think before saying anything at all.

From somewhere inside him, there came a momentary burst of logic when he realized that at least she wasn't calling it off. She wasn't walking out on him. She was still here and she was whispering, which meant she didn't want anyone to know. He replied with the only answer he could think to give her.

"You'll learn to love me," he told her softly.

Then he attempted another smile, but this one didn't work too well, so he just retreated from the room and closed the door gently behind him.

Half an hour later, they were together under the canopy, decorated with blossoms specially brought in from the country. Jakob was in a formal black suit, while Franzi looked like the angel of her own imagination in her long white dress and lace veil. Her lustrous auburn hair was tied up in curls. Seeing them so beautiful together, the congregation sighed collectively, with all thoughts of Franzi's suspected condition cast aside. So young, so pretty, they told each other. Jakob Goldberger was a truly lucky man.

The rabbi, middle-aged with a thick beard and intense eyes, spoke at length, offering his usual marriage sermon about love and respect, along with the wish for many healthy children. Yet Jakob couldn't hear him, couldn't focus on what was happening, because even as he went through the motions, her words continued to haunt him for the rest of the service, and when the time came to stamp his foot on the wine glass, the traditional gesture of good luck, he found this simple act difficult.

Not only did it confirm to him how much he loathed all this religious ritual, but it also suggested that this streak of fortune he'd enjoyed since he first met Franzi might not be as permanent as he'd thought.

Amongst the wedding guests were a number of black-garbed Hasidim and it was their celebratory zeal which was the most ardent. Sweeping objection aside, they transformed the synagogue's reception hall into their own function, herding women to one side and men to the other, with neither Jakob, nor anyone else, summoning up enough spiritual grit to prevent them. With the wine flowing and the hired *klezmer* musicians encouraged to play rousing melodies, they clapped their hands and stomped their feet and indulged in the precarious tradition of raising both bride and groom on chairs to shoulder height.

Following this spectacle was more rapturous drinking as some of the younger men showed off their dance skills, including their own versions of the *horah* as well as individual efforts in performing the Russian-inspired *hopak*, a challenge that involved ever longer periods of leg-kicking squats. This was all far too much for Jakob. Although Franzi was hesitant about leaving, he managed to persuade her to escape with him sooner rather than later. For another half-hour, they did the rounds, shaking hands and kissing cheeks while her purse and his pockets were stuffed with small envelopes of money.

Then, at last, they were away, sitting with their baggage in the back of a motor taxi which had been afforded, like everything else, by the generosity of the bride's father. Neither of them spoke as they drove off into the darkness of the sleeping city. The arrangements were for the taxi to take them to a modest hotel near the Nordbahnhof, from where they would take a train in the morning to a Tyrolean resort.

Both were fatigued from the day, both had drunk too much, but above all, both were acutely aware of those words she'd spoken just before the ceremony. "You're marrying a woman who doesn't love you." Now that they were alone together, its dire meaning hung between them like a barrier, preventing them from communicating, even from looking at each other.

Ultimately, the moment arrived when they were in their room with the door closed, but still, they couldn't say or do anything. They couldn't touch, they couldn't undress, so they just lay on the bed, apart and fully clothed. Jakob thought about moving closer but when he turned his head to look at her, she rolled over onto her side, facing away from him, eyes open, just staring into the blackness of the room.

The second night was a little better but not by much.

They were already at their destination, a village hostel on the slopes of Karlinberg, not expensive but rustic and quaint, with shutters on the windows and boxes bright with crimson geraniums. Perhaps it was the feeling of finally being away, or perhaps it was just the mountain air, but that night, after a quiet dinner, they went upstairs in a better frame of mind.

Unusual for that kind of establishment, their room at the front of the house had an attached bathroom and each of them used it in turn to change into their night clothes. Once under the covers, they moved tentatively towards each other. Franzi was breathing in a shallow manner, not in anticipation but in anxiety, while Jakob tried to keep his erection away from her in case she was overcome by her own nerves.

As gently as he could, he began by touching her hair, that beautiful auburn hair, and when she didn't pull away, he leaned in and kissed her very delicately on the cheek, just as he'd done that very first time in the park. Then he put his head back on the pillow and, without going any further, allowed her to fall asleep. It was a start.

During the days, they went for long walks through the lanes and pastures, then ate well when they returned, but all the while, Jakob was very conscious of his own reply to her and was trying to live up to it. "You'll learn to love me."

He was gentle and patient and tried to engage her in the kinds of conversations they used to have on their walks in Vienna about the arts she so adored.

Gradually, her attitude softened towards him, but even so, it took several nights for them to become intimate in any way. He was stocky, while she was petite, and far from the special moment she'd been told about by her mother, it seemed unnatural to have that throbbing flesh inside her and the first painful penetration actually brought her to tears.

Only from a sense of marital obligation did she consent again on the nights that followed, so it was something of a surprise to both of them that soon after they returned to Vienna, Franzi missed her cycle. She was advised by her mother to visit a doctor, and when she emerged, she was so flushed at the news that she almost fainted as she boarded the streetcar for the journey home.

She gazed blankly at the people around her, all busy with their own lives, and was hardly able to comprehend who she was and what was happening to her. She'd been an eighteen-year-old virgin when she left for the mountains and now here she was, already an expectant mother. The vehicle lurched on its tracks as it crossed the iron bridge into Brigittenau, but if she sat very still, she thought she could actually detect the baby's tiny heartbeat—or was it just the pulse that was pounding in her temple?

She didn't know very much at all about pregnancy and that's what made her fearful, not just of giving birth but of all the years beyond, which seemed to stretch out to eternity. For Franzi, at that moment in time, it felt as if her life were over before it had even begun.

"How do you know all this?" I once asked Charlotte after yet another remarkably frank episode about her parents.

"Know all what?"

"Well, what your father did, what your mother was thinking. What they even said to each other."

"They told me."

"About their wedding night?"

She looked at me, as if not entirely sure how to respond. "You don't know how it was with my mother. Sometimes, she spoke to me but it was like she was speaking to herself, you understand? And my father . . . Maybe he felt bad, I don't know. It was like he needed to explain what happened, what went on between them."

"He needed to explain to his daughter?"

"Who else?"

"How about his sister? Didn't he talk to her?"

"Berthe? Sure, he talked to Berthe about certain things, but not about that. Never about . . . you know, sex."

I nodded, but in truth, I was surprised that Charlotte would even talk to me about it. She wasn't exactly progressive in her attitudes. Her everyday values were extremely conservative, to the extent that she often complained about contemporary girls showing so much skin in the street, with their short skirts and bare midriffs.

Yet she very much wanted me to know what had happened between her parents, even in these intimate moments, because she was convinced that it was their relationship that explained so much about the rest of her life.

Why me, of all people? The answer is that I'm really not sure. Trust was a major factor, plus the fact that, even though we were in no way related, she regarded me as her adopted son and therefore part of her immediate family.

For Charlotte, though, it didn't really matter whether I fully understood her motives. She'd chosen to confide in me, to entrust me with her story.

For reasons of her own, she'd designated me the official inheritor of her secrets, the executor of her memory, so all I could do was pay her the simple respect of listening, whether it was about conflict, love, or anything else.

3

On a bitter evening in mid-February, a baby daughter was born to Jakob and Franzi and given the name Liselotte, or Liesl as an endearment. Only later in life would she choose to adapt that name to Charlotte.

A strapping, healthy infant who suckled all the milk her petite mother could provide, she immediately became the pride of the family and the focus of all attention, with every female more than ready to offer Franzi advice, whether they'd ever had children of their own or not.

This included Franzi's mother, sister, aunts, and cousins, as well as Jakob's sister, Berthe, the only in-law who was resident in Vienna. None of them left Franzi alone, taking turns by rote to help her along from morning to night. If she'd previously thought of herself as an angel, then she now took on the persona of a madonna, radiant and resplendent with babe-in-arms as visitors came to pay homage.

The couple had managed to rent a second-floor accommodation conveniently located on Staudingergasse, after the janitor, a big woman called Frau Graebner, had taken a matronly sympathy for Franzi and her youth.

This, along with a sizeable bribe from Jakob paid out of the wedding gifts, was enough to secure them the precious apartment ahead of others who also wanted it.

There was no running water, a major handicap, just a toilet and an all-purpose faucet between every two families. They did, however, have a gas supply into the kitchen to power the iron range, a luxury which allowed residents to heat water for general washing purposes, although a bath required a trip to the bath-house several streets away; and to use the basement boiler for laundry, they first had to make a reservation with Frau Graebner three days ahead.

On the plus side, labor was cheap, so a woman employed by the building owners came to clean every three weeks, and the location was central enough that certain staples like milk and bread could be delivered each week by horse and wagon.

In the meantime, the world beyond their front door was changing rapidly. The defeat of the Central Powers had brought about the downfall of three longstanding empires along with their ruling dynasties.

In Berlin, the Kaiser had abdicated; in Constantinople, the Ottoman reign was in turmoil and about to collapse; and in the Gutmanns' home town of Vienna, the Habsburgs had been dethroned after seven centuries in favor of a new republic.

All over, governments were in flux and economies were in a shambles, suffering the deprivations and forfeits of having lost a global war. While bankers discussed how to pay western demands in terms of reparations, the domestic populations tried in vain to cope with hyper-inflation, in which the value of money could be halved in a matter of days.

With minimal leadership and lax law enforcement, production output was all but abandoned. Factories were shuttered, returning troops couldn't find work to pay their rent, animals were slaughtered before they could complete their reproductive cycles, field crops were stripped bare, rivers and lakes were fished dry, and epidemics like influenza were rampant and went untreated.

It was a calamitous period in central Europe. They'd suffered millions of casualties in the war and now they were losing hundreds of thousands in the peace.

However, it wasn't equally bad for everybody and Jakob Goldberger thought he was smarter than most. He had no secret hoard or specialized knowledge, but he knew enough to figure that if he could buy a batch of something, whatever that might be, then sell it at even a small profit, he'd be ahead of the game, and if he could accomplish that enough times, he'd end up earning a living.

It was a basic, and some might say highly simplistic, business equation, but as long as he remained sufficiently disciplined to buy only what he knew he could sell, he believed it would work out.

The only problem was that he couldn't always operate in his own district and, sometimes, not even in the city. Often he'd have to travel, either across the country, or even across frontiers, in order to complete the deal.

It was tiring and occasionally risk-laden, but at least he was independent—no more army orders—and he knew, too, that his young wife and new daughter were surrounded by a family who wouldn't let him down. What he didn't realize, though, was how this perpetual motion was beginning to affect his relationship.

In many ways, Jakob had fulfilled his original promise to Franzi that he would not affect her life too much; that things would remain much as they were.

Of course, the baby had interrupted that master plan and was a great amount of work for an inexperienced young woman, even with family to help: an endlessly repetitive cycle of feeding, changing, washing, then feeding again.

Yet her very youth was also an advantage, with its natural reserves of energy, and at certain times, especially during the long evenings when the infant was asleep, she did indeed find time to read her books and study her languages.

She couldn't practice her cello the way she once did, but each day, she tried to find at least a few minutes to play one of the softer airs from the works of Bach or Brahms, which served as lullabies and actually seemed to comfort the child.

Unlike many wives in a similar position, she didn't have a husband coming home each night, so that many of the heavier chores, like multi-course meals and volumes of laundry, were removed from her life. The necessity of frequent sex, the bane of many women, was also eliminated and some told her to her face how lucky she was in that regard.

So, although her husband was away a great deal, that didn't make for an unpleasant life and when he did at last come home, he was as nice as he said he would be, thoughtful and caring and undemanding. He didn't drink or smoke, at least not when he was home, and even when he was away it was only the occasional beer or cigar just to keep a business colleague company.

He never raised his voice to her, not even once, and while it was true that money wasn't exactly plentiful, especially in the first year or two, there was enough to live reasonably, and he was always so grateful for her small efforts to economize that when he did have a few extra coins, he would put them into a special cash box just for her. In that way, she could purchase for herself the private things he knew a woman needed, as well as the occasional new dress or book.

In so many ways, Jakob could not have been a better husband, fulfilling every obligation, and Franzi possessed enough intelligence to realize how fortunate she was. Nevertheless, there was something missing, and that feeling was starting to become ever more perceptible.

Although Charlotte's father was an irregular figure in her life, her early childhood was spent in a loving and nurturing environment. She was an ebullient child, open and trusting and gregarious, who often created her own bits of mischief, not through any malicious intent but just because it was in her nature to have fun.

Often, she was led in this direction by her best friend, Trudi Hart, the daughter of their immediate upstairs neighbors, and the two children would sit together for hours on the steps or the landing, making dolls and doll clothes out of anything they could find: newspapers, broken bricks, wood chips, even chicken feathers. Then, at some point, Trudi would have an idea for a prank and they would start to giggle at the very thought of it.

One day, as they were packing their makeshift toys away, Trudi came up with something different, a trick to play on her friend, and this she didn't reveal.

"Go down to your place and stick your head out the window," she said suddenly. "I've got a surprise for you."

"What kind of surprise?" replied the gullible Charlotte.

"Just do it, you'll see. Go on, hurry up."

Charlotte did as she was told. She ran quickly downstairs and before her mother could ask the reason, she'd dashed across to the window, opened it wide and leaned out as far she could. That's when she heard Trudi calling from immediately above her.

"Hey, Charlotte, up here!"

She turned her face upwards only to have a wet blob of Trudi's spit land on her cheek, followed from above by raucous laughter.

Charlotte was furious but it was an important early lesson in the dangers of deceit. Unfortunately, she couldn't heed it because such suspicion simply wasn't in her character. She needed love from everyone around, absorbed it like a sponge, then poured it back out with friendship and generosity.

Indeed, she was glad to give away anything she had if someone else wanted it, and more than once, she was scolded for losing something of value in that way: a comb, a handkerchief, or some other item that would have to be replaced.

At these times, Charlotte couldn't live with her mother's annoyance and for hours afterwards, she would try to appease her by tidying up or running errands. She also promised on her word of honor never to give away anything again but she always did, because that was just her way.

At the age of six, Charlotte and Trudi began attending classes together at the same school, the public primary on Treustrasse. It became a good outlet for their childhood energies, and Charlotte, in particular, discovered much to enjoy.

In contrast to her mother, she was tall for her age with a robust physique: not as broad as her father but possessing enough strength and stamina to make her a natural candidate for any kind of outdoors activity.

She also had a competitive spirit which helped her excel at all her endeavors, whether sporting or academic, and this brought her early scholastic success, as evidenced by her term reports.

Her favorite teacher was a woman whom the class unflatteringly called an *"altesfräulein,"* an old maid. Freda Ifshitz was her name and although her students made constant fun of her, they actually liked her because her teaching methods relied more on encouragement and participation than criticism and obedience.

As a generalist, she taught them most of their lessons: mathematics, history, geography, grammar, and even some French, the most international and prestigious language of the era. The main exception was religious hour, when the Jewish minority was separated out for instruction at their own parents' request.

It was here that Charlotte, prompted and prodded by Trudi, misbehaved the most. Since neither of her parents believed much in the faith, she didn't really see why she had to study it, and although she invariably received passing grades for her work, her attention in class was sometimes marked down as unsatisfactory.

Her father, especially, wasn't pleased. "I didn't like the army, either," he told her firmly, "but I always behaved myself." Then he asked her a strange and somewhat embarrassing question. "Do they ever strike you?" He could see that either she didn't know how to answer or didn't wish to do so. "I asked you a question. At school, do the teachers ever strike you?"

"No"

"No? Is that the truth?"

"Yes."

"Well, you tell me if they do, all right?"

"Yes."

"You will? You promise?"

"Yes."

The reason for Charlotte's initial hesitation was that the school did indeed allow their staff to strike pupils on occasion. It all depended on the teacher, the child, or the mood of the moment. If, for example, it was a particularly difficult class with frequent interruptions, there might be a need to establish clear and visible authority; or it could just be that a particular teacher's normal patience had worn thin due to stress or headache and he or she simply felt the need to lash out.

The only moralistic code in these situations was that male and female teachers were never allowed to rap pupils of the opposite gender on the legs or buttocks, just on the palm of the hand. Yet with their own gender, they could do almost as they wished, from a single stroke with a wooden ruler to a full beating with the marks lasting for days.

As Charlotte said truthfully, it had never happened to her, but she'd seen the punishment applied to others in religious studies and it had terrified her. The teacher of this class, an older, orthodox man, could be especially severe.

Now, though, despite the fact that her father hadn't specifically spelled out what he would do in such a circumstance, his implied threat had somehow helped make her feel more secure.

She'd heard stories of his army days and in her child's mind, she saw him charging in to her rescue, rifle at the ready, and that mental vision served to establish a fundamental belief: even though he was absent from home for weeks at a time, he would always be there to protect her.

Ironically, far from discouraging mischief, his words sometimes had the opposite effect by boosting her confidence, allowing her to take ever bolder risks, like the time Charlotte was scheduled to go swimming at the public baths with Trudi.

Their mothers had given them money for the return journey on the Stadtbahn, but the two girls had spent the money on licorice, so between Charlotte's charm and Trudi's guile, they managed to talk their way into a ride back on a local coal wagon. Not only did they arrive home late, they were filthy, and Charlotte's one good coat was ruined.

The incident brought a major admonishment but at least it occurred in summer when the evenings were long. A far more serious and potentially dangerous truancy occurred late one January afternoon, when the weather was frigid, several degrees below freezing, and the light was already fading.

Twice a week, after school, Charlotte took one-hour piano lessons with Gisella Kerte, an acquaintance of her Aunt Paula, but one Tuesday she just didn't show up. For forty-five minutes, the woman waited, but the eight-year-old Charlotte failed to arrive and Fräulein Kerte became alarmed. It had never happened before.

After another fifteen minutes, she put on her coat and boots, then tramped her way through icy slush to the Goldbergers' apartment on Staudingergasse. Nobody was home. She knocked louder but there was still no answer, not from Franzi and not from Charlotte. Did they have a previous appointment and forget to tell her? Was she worrying for nothing, or was the child really missing? If so, where was her mother?

Gisella Kerte had no idea what to do, but like most of the community, she felt a sense of shared responsibility, so she made her way back into the cold, this time to find her friend, Paula, who was still unmarried and still living with her parents in the same apartment on Wallensteinstrasse. Dusk had already fallen but there was light from inside.

It was Paula herself who answered the door. "Gisella? What are you doing here? What's wrong? You look terrible."

"Is your niece here? Or your sister?"

"No, neither of them, why?"

"Oh my God, Paula, I didn't know what to do."

"Well, the first thing is to come inside."

After a hurried and somewhat frantic explanation, it was Paula's mother, the inherently bossy, but ever competent, Frau Gutmann, who took charge of the situation. Immediately, she ordered Paula to go wait at Franzi's apartment in case Charlotte showed up. They possessed a key just in case of such emergencies.

Then she asked another favor of Gisella Kerte: if she wouldn't mind going to the school on Treustrasse to check if Charlotte had been kept behind for some reason. Finally, she hauled on her outerwear, wrapped a hand-knitted woolen scarf around her neck and hurried several blocks to the Brigittenau police station on Pappenheimgasse in order to report the missing child.

She was hoping that the only Jewish officer in the district, the same man who'd attended the wedding, would be on duty. Unfortunately, he worked the day shift, so he wasn't there at that hour and she didn't receive the sympathy she would have liked, but she was nevertheless treated politely by the desk sergeant and asked to fill out a report, with the assurance that the matter would be investigated.

"When?" she asked.

"In due course," he replied dryly. "Officially, we have to wait twelve hours to act on a missing person file."

"But she's just a child, eight years old."

"Yes, I understand. But you also claim you don't know where the child's mother might be, isn't that correct?"

Frau Gutmann was obliged to acknowledge the point.

"In that case," said the sergeant, "don't you think there's a good chance they might be somewhere together? Calm yourself, Frau Gutmann. I'm sure everything's all right."

"And if it's not?"

"Then we'll take the necessary action, like I said, in due course."

There was nothing else to be done, so Frau Gutmann trudged back the way she came, highly unsatisfied and even more anxious now that darkness had settled in.

Instead of going directly home, she decided to check in at the apartment on Staudingergasse.

As it happened, by that time Franzi had returned from her card game at the Café Reclame on Obere Donaustrasse and was already into a major argument with her sister, Paula, who was accusing her of being stupid and irresponsible. Before Frau Gutmann could break up the fight, or even remove her coat, Charlotte herself appeared at the doorway, ruddy-faced with her skates flung casually over her shoulder, wondering what all the fuss was about. She'd merely skipped her piano lesson to go to the rink with Trudi.

For several seconds, she just stood there grinning, looking from her mother, to her grandmother, to her aunt, and that's when her happy expression faded away to nothing as she saw their fierce eyes and their gaping mouths.

Of all of them, it was her *bubbe*, her grandmother, who seemed most annoyed. Frau Gutmann had made a fool of herself at the police station and, for a family concerned with status, that was a serious matter. This time, Charlotte knew she was in serious trouble—worse than any mischief in religious class, worse than the ride on the coal wagon, worse than anything she'd ever done before—and she found herself wishing, even praying, that her father could magically appear to protect her.

For his part, Jakob heard nothing of such misdemeanors while traveling abroad. It was partly because Franzi didn't want him to think that she was a bad mother but also because he moved around so much that she rarely had a fixed address to which she could write.

At the time that his wife and daughter were causing the minor furor back home in Brigittenau, he was on his way from Brno in southern Czechoslovakia, with twenty gross of stored raincoats that he'd purchased cheap during the summer drought, to Padua in northeastern Italy, hoping to make it in time for the big spring rains.

When he arrived, he settled himself in a cheap rooming house to await the wet weather. Unfortunately, he'd miscalculated. The rains were late that year, so he was obliged to remain longer with the coats unsold, knowing he'd be able to elevate the price considerably once the need was more imminent. Meanwhile, he was stuck with little to do but wander the ancient streets and take in the wondrous sights of the chapels and the piazzas, as well as the Renaissance artwork that he knew his wife would have enjoyed if only she were there.

An especially impressive equestrian bronze statue by Donatello made him recall their daring entry into the Hofburg arena to see the Lipizzaner horses. However, as much as he tried to appreciate these sights, he was essentially an entrepreneur with business always on his mind, so he decided to forgo vacation pleasures and inquire into the local glassware industry, for which the area was renowned.

After visiting one particular manufacturer, he wired a contact in Warsaw who occasionally imported such merchandise and asked if there was a market for an overstock of water tumblers which Jakob claimed he could get his hands on relatively quickly. That's how it went for Jakob: a negotiation here, an opportunity there. Of course, each transaction required painstaking organization and endless paperwork, coupled with the necessary diplomacy with which to carry it through.

Sometimes it required even more than that because, in addition to basic freight and travel expenses, there were many intervening people in the process, from clerks to customs officials, who couldn't move quickly unless they had an incentive to do so. In the end, all such bribes had to come out of Jakob's ultimate margins, so what appeared be a promising deal could all too easily descend into unprofitability if he wasn't sufficiently careful.

All-in-all, it was a life that suited his self-reliant spirit but it was far from easy and there was an enormous penalty to pay, even larger than he realized. As the years went by, he was absent far too long from his wife and child.

He'd already left, for example, when Franzi was able to announce to elated relatives that she was once again pregnant, and he was still away two months later when she suffered a sad miscarriage, a loss that depressed and weakened her for weeks.

He was gone, too, when the municipality, on the initiative of the progressive Burgermeister Zeitz, finally installed electricity in their building; also when the Jewish soccer team, Hakoah, which played at Prater Park in nearby Leopoldstadt, won the Austrian national championship, thereby setting off a round of celebrations throughout the community. He was away when his mother died in Krakow, failing to get back in time for the funeral, or even to sit *shiva*, the customary seven-day mourning period.

He was away when Franzi's sister, Paula, became engaged to a refined young man who worked as an apprentice curator at the prestigious Palais Rothschild on the Währinger Gürtel, and he was away at the end of the decade when the Viennese stock market suddenly collapsed along with the entire overstretched economy, forcing a credit crisis and many subsequent bankruptcies—including that of the insurance company at which Herr Gutmann had spent his entire career.

It was the crash in Austria that began the global contagion. The wild run on financial institutions in Vienna first spread to neighboring Berlin, then on to Paris, London,

New York, and Chicago, ultimately initiating the period of stagnation that became known as the Great Depression. It didn't put Jakob out of business, he'd become too agile in his dealings to be severely affected, but it did cause disruption in the Gutmann family where the worry had become palpable.

"How's Papa?" Franzi asked Paula.

"Not good, not good at all."

They were meeting at the Kaffeehaus Landtmann, right opposite the Burgtheater, and once known to be a favorite haunt of the likes of Mahler and Freud. They couldn't possibly have afforded to frequent an establishment like this on their own, but this was where Paula's husband brought suppliers of the Palais Rothschild for coffee and he had an ongoing expense account, so occasionally the sisters liked to pretend, if just for a short while, that they were ladies of leisure.

On this day, though, the topic of conversation had dislodged any joy they might have felt from their escapade. After their father had been summarily dismissed from the bankrupt company, he'd learned that he would receive no severance and all the money he'd so carefully invested week by week in the employee savings plan had been frozen by corporate creditors.

Adding to that, the impossibility of finding equivalent work under the current circumstances made it a blow to his self-worth, as well as his income. A naturally proud man, he was taking it very hard, and recently, he seemed to have caught one cold after another, trapped in a downward spiral of doubt and despondency.

"Is he still sick?" asked Franzi.

"Still coughing a little," replied Paula. "He's taking the syrup, but he doesn't eat much. Why don't you go see him? You haven't been for a long time."

"I've been busy."

"Busy? What busy? We're all busy. Are you still playing cards?"

"No . . . Well, sometimes. So what, it's harmless. What's wrong with it?"

"It's a waste of time."

"Oh, and I suppose you're too high and mighty now to do something as low class as playing cards."

Paula didn't answer. She didn't want this to develop into a full-blown argument the way their conversations did so often lately. All she wanted was a pleasant morning in the city, away from the drudgery of home life. Although her husband worked for a grand family, he was merely an aide with a junior ranking and she still could not afford to hire any household help.

Meanwhile, Franzi used the lengthy silence to glance around the tables at the other customers: lawyers, accountants, merchants, society women; a clientele which seemed to represent a cross-section of Vienna's professional middle-class, or at least those who could still claim such status in this wretched state of affairs.

It made her think of the war years and the Café Grössenwahn where Jakob had first talked of marriage— not a proposal at that time, more like a suggestion—and she recalled how overawed she'd been by the fashions and the sophistication, dreaming that if they were together, somehow it might always be like this: coffee in the morning, dancing in the evening and, in between, satisfying hours spent in libraries and galleries.

Then there would be the trips, to Paris and Rome, with whole new worlds of music and culture to explore. How young she'd been; how stupidly, ruinously naive to imagine how an immigrant from Krakow would ever provide her with such a romantic life.

"Any news from Jakob?" asked Paula, interrupting her thoughts.

For a moment, Franzi was startled at how her sister seemed able to read her mind. "I think he's still in Italy . . . Padua, or Venice, somewhere like that. Then he's going to Warsaw, or so he says. I never really know."

Franzi gave a sigh that she couldn't totally hide. Mostly, she didn't say very much to anyone about her husband's prolonged absence because she was expected to be the dutiful wife, as her mother kept reminding her, grateful that her man was still able to provide in such times.

Jakob continued to send funds back on a regular basis, and from all reports, was faithful to a fault with never so much as a hint of anything untoward: no foreign mistresses or whores, not like some men who traveled. On that score, Franzi didn't have to worry at all. Her only problem was that she was lonely, sometimes desperately so.

Far from the angel of her adolescence or the madonna of young motherhood, she now thought herself to be more like an auburn Rapunzel, the forlorn woman in the Brothers Grimm fairy tale who was imprisoned in the tower.

"And my niece?" asked Paula. "How's my niece?"

Yet again, Franzi brought herself back to reality. "Oh, you know. Busy running around, here and there."

"As usual."

"Yes, as usual."

This was another element adding to Franzi's sense of isolation. Charlotte was now eleven years of age and out of the apartment for long hours almost every day, fully occupied with school, sports, music lessons, and her youth club. Franzi didn't begrudge these activities.

On the contrary, she was proud of her daughter's accomplishments, even a little envious of Charlotte's sheer enthusiasm for life, and secretly wished she could borrow some of it. For Franzi, the worst times were the nights just before she fell asleep when she was surrounded by the emptiness, lost in her own drifting thoughts.

What expectations did she have of her life? What cause for optimism could she possibly envisage? Was there any potential at all? At times, she even began to wonder if she wasn't going a little insane, but of course, she would never confess any of this to her sister. They just weren't that close and it would be too embarrassing.

The fact was that they'd each made their respective choices in marriage and now they had to stick with them, whatever came to pass. Paula's husband was home every night but insecure about his job, while her own man seemed sufficiently capable of providing an income but was forever absent. Which was better? She didn't know but she was still thinking about it, even as Paula had started to natter about more domestic trivialities, something about a bedspread she was trying to buy wholesale from a vendor in Leopoldstadt.

That's when the waiter arrived to take their order. He was youngish and slim with slick black hair and Franzi couldn't help but be distracted for the moment, at least until she caught herself looking at him and pulled her gaze back. That would be the last thing she'd want her sister to notice.

Another responsibility on Franzi's narrow shoulders was the upcoming matter of Charlotte's Bat Mitzvah—her daughter's formal passage into Jewish womanhood.

For boys, a Bar Mitzvah at age thirteen had always been compulsory, but for girls, the so-called Bat Mitzvah at twelve was an American concept, adapted from Roman times and recently re-introduced back into Europe. While traditional families still shunned it, some of the more reform-minded parents embraced it as a form of religious emancipation.

While neither Franzi nor her husband cared much for symbolic faith rituals, they did both feel that the gesture might be valuable for an active modern girl like Charlotte, and since Jakob was away so much, Franzi had been entrusted with organizing the entire affair, as well as with supervising Charlotte's extra studies in preparation. In each case, it was a struggle, causing her a great deal of stress.

Regarding the arrangements, the problem was that she'd ordered too many clothes from the seamstress: generous bespoke dresses for her mother and sister, as well as for Charlotte and herself, all of which had to be worked and re-worked several times, with spiraling costs. This left too little in the budget for the synagogue and she'd been forced to arrange a private meeting with the rabbi in order to plead poverty and hopefully obtain some kind of price discount.

By contrast, the issue of the Bat Mitzvah lessons was far simpler, just an act of rebellion by a child who thought she was already an adult. It was an attitude born of a recent day trip hiking into the mountains with her club when Charlotte had begun to menstruate for the first time. It was therefore not her mother but the youth leader, a blonde Catholic girl of eighteen, who had taken Charlotte aside and helped her, gently alleviating her embarrassment and, as a result, magnifying Charlotte's sense of independence from maternal influence.

"I'm already a woman," she insisted to her mother. "Why do I need to go through this stupid Bat Mitzvah to prove it?"

"Why? Because your father and I decided, that's why," replied Franzi curtly.

"My father doesn't believe in religion. He told me so. And neither do you."

"Well then, do it to respect your grandparents."

"I don't see why I should."

"You'll do as you're told, now that's enough. I don't want to hear any more."

Franzi had raised her voice louder than she had intended and the silence that followed only heightened the tension between them.

She understood enough to realize that her daughter's obstructive behavior was only partly to blame for the animosity and that it was mostly her own self-inflicted pressures which were causing the negative reaction. In theory, with both Jakob and Charlotte gone so much, this should be a time of freedom, when she could go back to her books and her cello. She should be rejoicing at the possibilities but all she felt in her soul was self-pity.

Her sister-in-law, Berthe, had even tried to find her a job just to get her out of the apartment each day, but nobody was hiring any more, including the government. Yet even if the miracle happened and her husband came home and settled down, she knew she'd still be miserable. She'd given up her youth to him and that was a debt which could never be repaid. The resentment ran deep.

The night of their argument, Charlotte went to bed hurt and upset. She'd always been susceptible to her own emotions and, on this occasion, felt strongly that her mother just didn't have the right to speak to her in that manner.

She tried to sleep but it was difficult with all the thoughts running through her head. At one point she even had the idea to run away, to live with her Aunt Paula, or even to ask her long-time friend, Trudi, if the Hart family would take her in.

These were just fleeting ideas, however, and even in her unsettled mood, she knew that they just weren't practical. Eventually, she heard her mother's door shut, so she turned on her tiny light and did the only thing she could think to do. She ripped a page from her homework notebook and wrote a private letter to her father.

As she began, the words just poured out of her and she couldn't seem to write fast enough. She wrote of how she missed him and how she loved him and how difficult her mother had become and how she wasn't being respected and how none of it was very fair.

Then, a few minutes later, when she paused to take stock of what she'd written, she tore the paper into tiny shreds, ashamed of herself and distressed that her mother might somehow discover the evil that she'd set down. For a long time, she just sat there, propped up against her pillow and letting the stray tears fall where they might. After that, she felt a little better but still had the urge to act, to do something to dissipate her turbulent feelings, so she ripped out another sheet of paper and started again.

The second version was still addressed to her father, but this time, it was more carefully composed, more conservative and more in line with what her father would expect. After all, she told herself, if she wanted to be treated like a woman, she had to behave like one. She therefore requested in the most respectful High German that, if it were at all possible, she would consider it a personal kindness if he could manage to return home in time for her Bat Mitzvah. At the end, just before she signed her name, she added special greetings because the last day of the year was her father's birthday and she was calculating that the letter might not reach him until then.

When she was finished, she folded it neatly and then tucked it into the pocket of her school pinafore dress. She would need an envelope and a stamp, plus her father's current address, but she knew that he'd recently written to his sister from somewhere in Germany and that, if asked politely, Aunt Berthe would keep this personal request for information to herself.

It was past midnight before she was finally able to close her eyes with some sense of satisfaction. She'd proven her independence, at least to herself, and now it was time for sleep.

Jakob was staying in Nuremberg, northern Bavaria, when he found the letter from Charlotte waiting for him at the lobby of his small guest house. It was unusual. This was the first time she'd ever written like this and his first thought was that something bad must have happened.

He was in a rush, already late for a dinner appointment, but he ripped open the envelope immediately and began to read it while standing by the reception desk.

"I hope it's nothing serious," said the aging clerk, observing the look of concern on his guest's face.

Jakob came to the end of the letter and smiled. "No, no . . . It's just my daughter. She wants me to come home."

The clerk nodded his understanding. "In that case," he said, "you have to go."

Jakob acknowledged the wisdom. He already knew perfectly well that he must try to get back in time for her Bat Mitzvah, especially since he'd already missed so much of her life, yet he also wondered how he could possibly leave this deal on which he'd been working for so long. It was one of the largest he'd ever negotiated and the dinner this evening would be a critical step in the process.

The restaurant was in St. Lorenz, near the Fleischbrücke in the oldest part of the city. It was a traditional institution of the kind preferred by visitors, with medieval-style wooden tables and buxom waitresses who revealed considerable cleavage each time they cleared the plates and wiped the surface.

One of them offered him a generous greeting as he sat down to wait for his guest but he was under no illusions about how he might be treated if she knew his true ethnic identity.

This place was a favorite for the thousands who came from all across the country for the annual Nazi party rallies and, at such times, would be full to capacity with SA Brownshirts, SS *Schwarzkorps,* and party functionaries at every level, from filing clerks to *Gauleiters.*

If it became generally known to either management or staff that Jakob was Jewish, he might not be so welcome, especially after the recent electoral triumph.

Just three months previously, the party had gained a breakthrough in the Reichstag, the German parliament. Although in numbers of delegates they were still second to the long-ruling Social Democrats, they'd managed to increase their representation nine-fold, from just twelve seats to one hundred and seven, and had garnered well over six million votes.

The size of their success had surprised all of Europe—but not so much Jakob, who had learned something of politics on his travels. As he knew well enough, the key element for most ordinary people was not ideology but the economy, and the financial crash had hit Germany exceptionally hard.

Under the conditions of surrender in 1918, the Weimar government was still struggling to pay reparation debts from the war and now, with all the bankruptcies, there were over three million unemployed.

According to Jakob, there were only two parties to whom the population could gravitate, the Communists and the Nazis, and it was the latter who appeared to have the momentum at this point in time.

They were more nationalistic, more organized and they tended to dominate the running street battles, in which thugs from left and right were frequently pitched together, some paid, some voluntary. Jakob was only too aware of the dangers and wouldn't even be in the country now but for this venture. It was just too good an opportunity to miss.

After several minutes, he looked up and saw the young man he was due to meet striding over towards him. He was of average height and build but had a dashing, energetic air about him.

Jakob got to his feet. "Herr Grundig, good to see you."

"Sorry I'm late," said Grundig. "Trying to finish everything before year-end."

"I understand."

They shook hands warmly, then made themselves comfortable at the table as the friendly waitress hurried to bring them a couple of large steins.

Max Grundig was a partner at a local electrical store, Fuerth, Grundig & Wurzer, whose sales catalogs also included a number of radio models. One of their more profitable arrangements was ordering in bulk direct from one of the principal manufacturers, Mende, based in the city of Dresden, in order to obtain a substantial cost benefit.

The agreement that Jakob had negotiated was to include his own purchase with the store, thus making him eligible for the same volume discount. The only item left to be worked out was the personal commission for the youthful Max Grundig, and that was the reason for the dinner.

The waitress brought back the beer plus two menus, but this time, she leaned in closer to the younger man until her cleavage was just a few centimeters from his face.

Jakob didn't mind. Why would he want a woman like this, he told himself, when he had his sweet Franzi at home?"So, what do you recommend?"he asked, deliberately keeping his eyes focused on the menu. "All right, don't tell me, let me guess. The bratwurst."

Nuremberg was well-known for its bratwurst and Grundig laughed good-naturedly at the cliché. "It's good here, trust me." He ordered for the two of them, then opened up his brief case, pulled out a thick package, and handed it across the table. "For your birthday."

Jakob was a little embarrassed. "For me? How did you know?"

"You think I don't know my business partners?"

"I don't know what to say."

"Maybe you should open it before you thank me too much."

Jakob tore open the brown paper and saw that it was a book, but not just any book. This was the complete two-part edition of *Mein Kampf*, the manifesto Adolf Hitler had written in 1924 while imprisoned at Landsberg. "And you're giving me this, why?"

"It's something I think you should read."

"Really?" Jakob had to be careful what he said in a place like this. "I presume you know my background?"

"With a name like yours, Herr Goldberger, it's really hard to miss. You should think about changing it."

"Yes, perhaps. One of these days. But I still don't understand . . ."

"You haven't read it yet, have you?"

Jakob just shrugged.

"You should."

"Why? I mean, apart from general interest."

"Oh, that's not just general interest for a man like you, believe me, Herr Goldberger. I gave you that gift for a reason. Seriously, that's what it is. A gift."

"I don't follow."

"Just read it. Not easy, I know. Actually, to tell you the truth, I myself found it almost unreadable . . . but there are some sections which are, shall we say, very relevant to someone such as you. Well, to your entire tribe."

Jakob glanced at the young man but chose to ignore the derogatory statement. In a place like this, he decided, discretion was a far better strategy. "How relevant?" he asked.

"He says he's going to use gas. It's right there, page three hundred and eighteen, volume two. I marked the page."

Jakob didn't open the book. He knew what gas could do, he'd seen the results during the war. He just looked at his dinner guest and then forced some kind of a smile.

"Herr Grundig, everywhere I go there's another crazy story about this man and what he's going to do. He's going to invade Poland, he's going to invade France, he's going to kill the old people, kill the handicapped . . ."

"I'm not talking about any of that. That's not why I bought you the book."

"You're worried about the Jews?"

"Not in the slightest. I bought it because it's your birthday."

"Thank you. Very generous."

Up to this point, Grundig's expression had been casual, even amused, but now he turned serious. "Herr Goldberger, you may not realize it but I did you a favor. This is the best gift you ever received. What he says in there, it's not just propaganda. He means it, every last word, and if I were you . . ."

"If you were me? What, Herr Grundig? If you were me, what would you do?"

"Do you have, by any chance, family in the west?"

Jakob hesitated. It was none of the young man's business but there seemed no harm in answering. "I have a brother in England."

"Good, so go to England. Take your family and go now. That's my advice."

"Go to England? We live in Vienna."

"Hitler is Austrian. You think he doesn't want to go home a hero, the return of the native son?"

Jakob accepted the logic and could only shrug—but move to England? What would he do in England? He hadn't seen his brother in years and he didn't even speak English very well, at least not by his own standards. Besides, he felt Austria was different than Germany in many respects. It was smaller and more cultured, more sophisticated in its attitudes. That there was a Nazi party he couldn't deny, but so far, it was just a fringe element.

"I think we're all right for now," he replied, "but I appreciate your concern."

Grundig nodded, as if he wasn't at all surprised. "Herr Goldberger, I'm going to tell you something, but I only tell you this because I like you. You're a fool."

Jakob took a slow sip of his beer. "Perhaps."

"Why don't you leave? I don't understand. Why don't you all leave? It would be better for everybody."

"Everybody?" Jakob tried hard to control his reaction. He couldn't afford to get upset, but he still felt the need to get his point across. "Herr Grundig, tell me, why should we leave our homes, our lives, everything we've known? Why should we panic? When the time comes, we'll decide, but for now . . ."

He left the sentence unfinished and all the other man could do was shake his head. A minute later, the waitress arrived back with their first course: plates of steaming potato soup and thick, dark bread. Once they were eating,

Grundig said, "All right, you want to do business, let's do business."

By the time they were on to dessert, they'd figured out a percentage compromise for which neither were happy, so they both were. They shook hands on the deal and, as far as Jakob was concerned, that was as good as a signed contract. He'd built his reputation around Europe on being hard but fair and, as a point of principle, was always as good as his word. It meant he could now go ahead and organize the transit, delivery, and final sale of Mende radios in Vienna. Even with all the expenses, plus this commission to Grundig, he felt he should make enough profit on the transaction to cover all his liabilities, including the extra money spent by his wife.

He might even have enough to add to his growing savings account, and it was this, rather than any escape plan, which had become his insurance policy. Next to him on the table was the book he'd just received as a gift and he decided to keep it and read it, as Max Grundig had suggested, just so he'd know what was in it. Yet he couldn't help but appreciate the irony of distributing radios.

Hitler, he knew, was one of the most ardent supporters of new technology and insisted that all his hundreds of speeches each year should be broadcast as widely as possible to all German-speaking peoples, which certainly included citizens from his country of birth, Austria. In effect, it meant that by bringing these appliances to the Viennese middle-classes, Jakob the Jew would be inadvertently helping the evil to spread.

Whether it concerned her parents, herself, or just life in general, Charlotte was something of a fatalist. She believed that actions were pre-determined and claimed to have proof of her theories based on the powers of astrology.

She wasn't a fanatic by any means, but she did like to study the newspaper horoscope every day, and she often used the reading of the stars to explain the unexplainable. For instance, she told me that despite the generational difference in our ages, we were mutually compatible because we were both born under the sign of Aquarius. In her view, it was only natural that we would get along.

In the same way, the reason that her mother was more compliant towards her father's initial advances than her Aunt Paula was the fact that Franzi was an accommodating Libra, while Paula was a stubborn Taurus. Furthermore, her father was a Capricorn, and that sign's romantic interest in Libra can apparently be overwhelming.

In Charlotte's mind, this was point proven. For her, it was as if the stars had magically aligned the moment her father first set eyes on her mother, and this, in turn, set the course for Charlotte's entire existence. She was of the definite opinion that the emotional devastation she would later suffer had been ordained from the start and nobody could have convinced her otherwise.

She even thought that Chinese astrology supported her beliefs. Once, when I returned from that part of the world, I brought her a book on the subject. We scanned its contents together over lunch and learned that, according to that culture's sixty-year lunar cycle, her sign was an Earth Sheep while mine was an Earth Ox. To her, the fact that we were both Earth signs, irrespective of the difference in the animals, was yet more confirmation.

Of course, it would have been far too easy to point out all the other inconsistencies in both western and eastern versions of the Zodiac. As an example, I discovered the outlandish coincidence that, like me, Adolf Hitler was also an Earth Ox, but I let it go because I didn't want to spoil it for her. If she wished to believe that destiny had guided her life's story, who was I to argue?

4

Charlotte was astonished when her father walked through the door. He'd promised to return for her Bat Mitzvah ceremony, and like a stage magician, suddenly there he was.

Excited and impulsive, she couldn't wait to tell him about everything he'd missed: about school and sports and music, about what she'd been up to with her youth club, even about her mischief with Trudi.

She bubbled about everything, but what she didn't tell him was the state of her relationship with her mother, which had frayed considerably since the night she wrote him the angry letter. It wasn't that she didn't love her mother, it was that she didn't really understand her.

Some girls her age might have chosen to confide in a long-time friend like Trudi Hart, or an empathetic teacher like Freda Ifshitz, but not Charlotte.

Whatever she felt about her mother was put aside when she needed help, advice, or just a pair of arms to hold her when things became too much.

That's why, in the end, she didn't tell her father about her mother. Besides, she didn't wish to start any arguments in the house when she knew her father would only be there for such a short time.

That same weekend, Charlotte's Bat Mitzvah took place on schedule in the same Klukygasse synagogue as her parents' wedding. However, it was a much smaller occasion due to the economic situation and the Goldbergers' new budget restraints.

While the women of the family were elegant in their new attire—Charlotte thought her own robe in strawberry pink was magnificent—fewer people attended, and the social affair afterwards was far more restrained. This time, no Hasidim showed up with their madcap celebrations. They weren't invited and wouldn't have come anyway because they didn't yet believe in the Bat Mitzvah ritual.

The afternoon was therefore modest in tone, the highlight being a brief speech by Jakob to his daughter in appreciation for her loving character, her devotion to her family, and his own hopes for her future.

Unlikely as it was to those who knew him, he even invoked the Deity, just because he was on religious premises and it was one of the rare times that he actually wore a yarmulke on the back of his balding head.

"May you live your life in peace, love, and prosperity," he concluded, speaking the words directly to his daughter. "And we thank the Lord for giving you everything you need in life. A good heart, a good brain . . . and hopefully, one day, a good man to be your partner."

At this, the guests offered a warm round of applause and raised their glasses with shouts of *"mazel tov,"* a combination of good luck and congratulations, as well as *"l'chaim,"* the traditional toast to life.

Then it was time for Jakob and Franzi's gift to their daughter. It was large and weighty, all wrapped in brown paper and neatly tied on top with a pink bow, specially to match Charlotte's dress. Jakob placed his hand on the package.

"Education," he said solemnly, "is the foundation of knowledge, and this, I hope, will help educate you about the world around you. Use it in good health."

He leaned over to give her a kiss on the cheek, then stepped back to allow her to unwrap the parcel. Charlotte had no idea what it could be. Her father had arrived home with it along with his baggage, then kept it in a cupboard, warning her that if she peeked early, he'd take it right back to where he got it.

That would have been an impossibility, because he wasn't about to go back to Nuremberg, but she didn't know that, so she kept her distance even if she was in a continual state of anticipation and curiosity.

A surprise gift, in addition to a beautiful new dress, plus best of all, her father back home—this Bat Mitzvah business was turning out to be far better than she expected and maybe even worth all the effort to learn her section of the Torah.

When she'd finally torn off half the paper, enough to see what was underneath, she gasped and rushed to hug her parents, first her father and then her mother. The people at the tables applauded, too, craning their necks to see it and amazed by the generosity. How many other children, at any age, received a brand new radio?

As a heartfelt gesture of thanks to her parents, Charlotte allowed her prized radio to be kept not in her own room but on the main bookshelf for use by the entire family. Although it used electricity, which was expensive, and required an annual fee for the government license, all agreed that it was an indulgence they could ill afford to waste.

There was only one local station, Radio Wien, but the broad waveband also provided service from Berlin, Zurich,

Warsaw, Prague, Budapest and elsewhere, all of which were more or less understandable by parents who were natural linguists.

Apart from the daily news bulletins, however, the true glory of the service was the morning-to-night music, reflecting Vienna's own great heritage in that regard, with symphonies and concertos by the Philharmonic, classic themes and arias from the State Opera, as well as the popular waltzes of the Strauss family.

There were also contemporary piano recitals by the famous team of Rawicz and Landauer, a local duo who always brought vibrancy to their broadcasts with accomplished renditions of the more popular themes, like Khachaturian's dramatic *"Saber Dance"*, Charlotte's personal favorite, and Debussy's romantic *"Claire de Lune"*, which her mother loved.

In fact, it was Franzi who often referred to the appliance as a godsend. With her husband once again away on his travels, she was consigned to the apartment, mostly alone.

Once a week she indulged her whim by going out to play cards, and very occasionally, she met her sister at the fancy *kaffeehaus,* but otherwise, she passed her days with a monotonous round of food shopping, household chores, and catering to whatever needs her daughter might have.

At least she now had this miracle of radio but while it helped her daily existence, she could see how it was nothing but a noisy drug of distraction, allowing her to submerge her dreams and to set aside, if only temporarily, her long list of regrets.

"Vati, why don't they like us?"

It was a year after Charlotte's Bat Mitzvah that the question arose as if from out of nowhere and from the comfort of his armchair, Jakob looked across the living room at his daughter, now a young lady of thirteen. As her *vati*, her daddy, he felt it was his responsibility to explain about the Nazi party.

However, he also knew that Franzi tended to frown on the idea, holding strongly to the opinion that their daughter was still too young, that they shouldn't disturb her too soon with such ugly realities. Childhood was so short, she told her husband. Why not keep it sweet for as long as possible?

It was a valid argument which Jakob had chosen to accept, but this time it was different. This was no longer a question of whether to tell Charlotte, because it was she, herself, who was asking the question. Didn't she, therefore, deserve an honest answer? Wouldn't she learn the truth anyway, at school, or from friends? Wouldn't it be better explained by her own parents?

They were listening to the radio at the time, a discussion about the new election that was still underway in neighboring Germany. Since the last vote just eighteen months previously, the disruptions had multiplied with ever more violent street clashes between the orchestrated militias on each side of the great divide: Fascists versus Communists.

For this new campaign, the Nazi party's chief of propaganda, Joseph Goebbels, was promoting a provocative slogan that challenged the population to choose once and for all. "*Brown or Red! Berlin or Moscow! Hitler or Stalin!*" It was designed to make the answer obvious to any true German: vote for the forces of national patriotism or be forever controlled from outside the country by a Soviet agenda.

Obviously, the strategy was devised to make the election all about repelling the Socialist influence—and much of Europe was prepared to believe that—but Jakob knew better, believing that this particular thrust was merely to take advantage of the moment.

He still had the copy of Hitler's manifesto, *Mein Kampf,* that he'd received as a birthday gift from Max Grundig in Nuremberg and had actually read enough of it to understand the author's most dire intentions.

Hitler planned to restore Germany's pride by rebuilding the military, despite the signed conditions of surrender, to cease the reparations which had ruined the economy, to avenge the humiliation by France, England, and Russia, and most relevant to Charlotte's question, to exact retribution for the "backstabbing by Jewish traitors and speculators" who, Hitler claimed, had caused Germany to lose the conflict in the first place.

It was the worst kind of vindictive rant, yet it offered a heady attraction for a suffering population, which needed not just hope for a brighter future, but also someone to blame, the forces of "International Jewry," for the defeats of the past.

The appeal of Hitler as some kind of Teutonic messiah seemed to have gained an irresistible momentum, as today's election results were beginning to show. By the time all the news had trickled in, the Nazi party had gained as many as a hundred and twenty-three seats, making them by far the most dominant force in the Reichstag, now almost twice as large as the second-place Social Democrats.

For Jakob, it was highly disturbing news but the current question still remained: how to explain it all it to a girl of thirteen who was full of life and fun. How could she ever comprehend? Nevertheless, he felt he owed her a response.

After all, he was the one who'd given her the radio with a wish to broaden her education, to help her understand the world around her, so how could he now deny those words, especially on this topic, the most important of all?

"*Vati*," said his daughter again, "why don't you answer me?"

For a moment, Jakob looked over at Franzi in the kitchen. She was almost imperceptibly shaking her head, as if willing him not do it, not to disturb Charlotte's innocence, but Jakob was torn. He loved and respected his wife, yet he felt responsible, even obligated to educate his daughter.

Eventually, he said to his daughter, "I need to think about it, *liebste*, maybe do a little research. You wouldn't want me to give you the wrong answer, would you?"

"I just want to know why they don't like us."

"I know, I know."

"Is it something we did to them?"

"No . . . not really."

"Not really? What does that mean? Does it mean we did?"

"No, of course not, it doesn't mean that at all. Listen, it's complicated, that's why I need to think about it, all right? Will you allow me to do that?"

"When will you tell me?"

"Soon, *liebste*, soon."

"No, you'll be going away again soon. You'll forget."

"Maybe your *mutti* can tell you better."

"No, it has to be you."

"Come on now, don't be such a baby."

"I just want you to answer me before you go away."

Jakob was trapped. Again, he glanced at his wife and saw that her expression had changed from a negative to merely a shrug. He took it as a sign of approval.

"All right," he said to his daughter, "before I go away, I'll tell you."

"Promise?"

"Yes, yes, I promise." Then he ended the conversation with the old imperative familiar to all parents, everywhere. "Now, go get ready for bed, it's late, you've got school tomorrow."

The following day, Thursday, Jakob took a lunchtime stroll with his sister, Berthe, in the small park near her municipal office. It was warm, and although formal tradition frowned on a man removing his jacket in public, on this occasion he gave himself permission to walk in just his shirt sleeves.

Next to him, Berthe was wearing her work attire: a neat white blouse, perfectly ironed, and her usual mid-calf skirt. She'd gained just a little weight, as had Jakob, obviously a family failing, but she looked well enough.

It was after several minutes of talk about nothing in particular that Jakob said, "While we're here, there's something I want to ask you."

"Of course there is," replied Berthe, in that offhanded tone she sometimes adopted. She wasn't being quite as sarcastic as usual, because out here in public, they spoke no Yiddish, only German. Then, to Jakob's questioning look, she smiled and took his arm in hers. "Tell me something," she said, "when was the last time we met in the middle of a weekday?"

He responded by raising his eyebrows, caught at his own little game. "I think you know me too well."

"I'm your sister, in case you'd forgotten. So what did you want to ask me about? Is it about Franzi?"

"Why do you say that?"

"I don't know, just a guess."

"See? You don't know me as well as you think you do. Actually, it's about Liesl."

"Liesl? What about Liesl? Is she sick?"

"No, no, relax. She's not sick."

"So, what then?"

"I need to tell her about the Nazis."

"Excuse me?"Berthe turned to look at him, just to see if he was serious.

"She doesn't know and she's asking, so I need to tell her."

"So tell her."

"Franzi thinks we shouldn't spoil her childhood too soon with all this ugly truth."

"And you don't think she's right?"

"Who knows anymore? What should I do? What would *you* do?"

Berthe nodded but remained silent as she gave the matter some thought.

Around them were many people trying to enjoy a few minutes of sun before they had to head back to their offices. Everyone always complained about work, it was like a national sport, but those who had it were grateful for it.

Eventually, they sat down on a bench not far from where a shaggy man was attempting to harangue anyone who could be bothered to listen into believing that the world would soon be ending. It seemed somehow appropriate, thought Jakob, for the discussion they were having.

"So?" he asked at last.

"I don't know, Jakob. Tell her or don't tell her. She's your child, not mine."

"I know, but I was hoping . . ."

"You want my opinion? All right, I'll give you my opinion. Whatever you do, don't lie to her. You shouldn't lie."

"I know that," said Jakob. He'd already figured out such simple morality on his own and had a ready answer. "But you could say that not telling her is a lie in itself. Legally, that's called lying by omission."

"That's true, too," agreed Berthe. "In that case, maybe you have no choice but to tell her."

"But how? What do I say?"

"You tell her the truth."

"What? That they're going to come and gas all of us?" Jakob suddenly glanced around to see who might have heard but nobody was paying attention to their conversation. They were all far too busy inside their own little worlds.

"You really think that's what they want to do? I mean, really?"

"It's what he says in his book."

"And you believe everything you read?"

"It's right there, in black and white."

"Sure, written by a madman. He'll say anything."

"Maybe . . . but that still doesn't answer my question."

"Well, whatever you do, don't tell her that. You don't have to give the child nightmares. Tell her the truth but in a balanced way. On the one hand, this. On the other hand, that. You don't have to lie, but you don't have to be cruel, either."

"No . . . No, I suppose not."

"You're actually worried about this lunatic, aren't you?"

"Haven't you been following the elections? Every time he runs, he gets more seats."

"Jakob, take it easy. I read the papers, too . . . and they tell me he's a long way from gaining any kind of real power. Let him rant and rave, what's he going to do? Overthrow Hindenburg? Take over the army?"

Paul von Hindenburg was president of the German Republic, a tough old giant with massive public approval, and the traditionally-minded army establishment openly looked down on Hitler as a low-class nobody. In fact, the whole scenario sounded ridiculous when she put it in those terms, even to the cynical Jakob.

Yet he couldn't help watching the man on the other side of the grass verge, stopping people to say it was all coming to an end, that they should mend their ways, otherwise God would rain fire down upon their cities and their houses and He would surely destroy them all.

From where he sat, Jakob watched and listened and couldn't seem to avoid the obvious thought: what if the man were right?

The morning he was due to leave again, Jakob walked Charlotte to her high school, an older building on the southern side of the Augarten.

"The world, well, it's like a big schoolyard," he was telling her. It was his prepared presentation. "You've got some children who are nice, like you, and you've got some who are bullies."

"*Vati*, please. I'm not six years old."

"What? It happens. Isn't that how it happens?"

"If you're going to tell me, just tell me."

Jakob sighed. He'd had a feeling it wouldn't be so simple. "All right, all right. You want the truth? I don't know for sure why they don't like us. We don't cause any trouble, we contribute as much as we can—to the economy, to the arts, to the sciences, to life in general. We do what we can, but still they don't seem to like us."

"Why?"

"Why? Who knows why? Probably just because we're different. We try to mix with others but we have our own ways, our own religion, so people are wary of us. Also, we tend to think that God chose us specially, which doesn't help."

"But you're not even religious."

"True . . . but I don't think I'm a typical Jew either."

"When did it start?"

"Good question. As far as I can see, it's been that way throughout history. Five thousand years, and still, people don't like us. You know, where we came from, I mean originally, there were always wars . . . invaders, conquerors . . .

"An unfortunate location, but that's how it was. So sometimes we won, sometimes we lost. And when we lost, we were scattered, and then we had to work hard just to keep from losing our identity. All over the world, there are Jews trying to remain Jews. I mean it.

"Everywhere you go . . . America, Africa, Asia, everywhere you go. Did you know there are still Jews in China?"

"Really?"

"Sure, I can even tell you which cities . . . Shanghai, Harbin . . . In India, too, in Cochin there's a famous community."

"Do they hate us there?"

"No, as a matter of fact, they don't. In some places, they actually like us. It varies, what can I say? With the Nazis, it's the opposite, that's all."

"Are you worried?"

Jakob tried to think before responding. This was perhaps the most poignant question of all. Berthe had advised him to tell only the truth and she was right, of course, but how could he answer this? Was he worried? Of course he was worried.

"We have to be strong," he said finally. It was the best he could do.

"You mean brave?"

"No, I don't think so, *liebste*. Brave is a good word but only in fairy tales. I saw too many brave men die in the war. No, strong doesn't mean brave, it means . . ." He paused, not really able to think of a suitable definition, and he could sense her waiting for him. "We must be strong, but careful."

"I'm not sure . . ."

"I know, I know, it's hard, but that's how we've got to be. The world is complicated, *liebste*. If it were simple, we could be brave, or even cowardly if it came to that. Things would be easy, we'd know what to do, how to behave. Attack and fight like a lion, or turn and run fast like a rabbit. You see? Easy. Both work. But the world's not like that, not the human world anyway, so we must be strong. All the time, we must be strong. Strong and smart . . ."

"And careful."

"That's right, and careful. Will you be strong and smart and careful, even when I'm not here?"

"I'll try."

"That's all I ask," he said to her. Then he repeated it as he squeezed her hand to show how proud he was. "That's all I ask."

To Charlotte, it seemed like her fourteenth birthday in the February of 1933 was like a loud alarm bell, awakening her to new realities, both political and personal. There was her future to consider.

When the family got together at the Gutmann parents' apartment to celebrate the day with coffee and a comically bad sponge cake that Paula had attempted to bake for the occasion, any pretense at light conversation quickly descended into a stirring debate about Charlotte's prospects.

She was due to leave high school but to do what, to go where, and to what end? Everyone had an opinion. The most ambitious in the family was Franzi, ably supported by her mother, who engaged freely in talk of university admission and how best to achieve that lofty goal.

At the other end of the scale was Berthe, as down-to-earth as ever, who'd heard through departmental gossip that the government was now considering the idea of taking on school leavers as volunteers. Successful entrants would have to live at home, work for no pay and if genuine employment ever became available, they would receive first consideration.

When asked what kind of work that would entail, Berthe had no answer. Would there be real training involved, or was it just running errands and emptying the garbage?

Again, she had no idea but was forced to concede that it would most probably be the latter. It was as if the discussion was reaching new highs and lows with each minute that passed.

One end of the spectrum saw Charlotte glowing with achievement in the study halls of academia, while the other had her grateful to be sweeping floors when there were now so many unemployed.

All this time, Jakob had been sitting patiently, coffee in hand, content to let it all play out. He knew from experience that none of them would be satisfied until they'd had their say.

Finally, it was the rapidly aging Herr Gutmann, his face sallow and his hair gray, whose hoarse voice invited Jakob into the conversation.

"And what does the father think? Jakob, you're too quiet, give us your pearls of wisdom."

Jakob put down his cup and waited for the hubbub to subside. "Glad you asked," he said in Yiddish, with a trace of his familiar humor. It was his own way of reducing what had already developed into an adversarial tone.

"I'll tell you what I think . . . I think I should ask my daughter what *she* thinks. So, *meineliebe* Liesl, you've heard all this? It's your future we're all so busy talking about. What's in your heart?"

Charlotte glanced around the room, uncomfortable at being singled out, even though the discussion was all about her. "I don't know," was all she could think to reply.

"You don't know? Really? Come on, don't be shy. You must have some notion of what you want to do."

Again the same response but this time, it was just by a single shake of her head. While she understood her mother's wish to see her at some grand university, she just couldn't visualize it, and if she was being honest with herself, she had little desire.

At both primary and high school, she'd received generally good marks, but she knew, somewhere deep inside, that she just didn't possess an academic brain, and the concept frightened her. To be more accurate, the idea of failure frightened her: the thought that she might somehow not live up to expectations.

She just couldn't bear the thought of disappointing her parents like that. At the same time, she could hardly reject the idea of university outright in front of her mother, who appeared to want it so badly.

In the meantime, she could see her father looking at her, waiting for a more positive reply, but she was unable to provide one. She refused to give an opinion, because she just couldn't bring herself to admit her fears.

Eventually, he signaled her to come over to him, so she did as she was told, crossing the room self-consciously to squat down on the floor next to his chair. She felt his broad hand on her shoulder, solid and confident, still protecting her, even now.

"All right, *liebste*," he said softly, "I know it's a big decision, too much to think about. If anyone had asked me at your age what I wanted to do for the rest of my life, I wouldn't have known either."

Then he looked up, as if including the others while somehow continuing to speak to her alone. "Listen, I've got a suggestion. I don't know what you're going to think about it, but I hope you'll tell me, all right?"

In the gentlest way, he squeezed her shoulder, demanding some kind of response. "All right," she said hesitantly.

"Good, good, so listen. What I think is that everyone's right. You should have an education, that's the best thing we can do for you, but it's also true that jobs don't grow on trees. So let's look at what we've got here.

"The first problem, the universities these days, they're not like they used to be. The professors, the students, they're most of them sympathetic to the Nazis, am I right?" He checked around, but nobody demurred, not even his wife. She, too, read the papers, listened to the broadcasts, and she knew he was essentially correct in his assessment.

"And forgive me, Berthe, but this government plan you're talking about . . . If it were a real job, I'd say let's go, *seitgesund*, wonderful. But it's not real, is it? You want my opinion, this idea they've got, it's no better than slave labor. We did that once in Egypt, remember? Didn't work out so good."

He was talking about the Biblical tale of the Israelites under the Pharaohs, as told each year on Passover, and the way he said it made everyone smile, thereby softening the blow of criticism to Berthe's suggestion. "So where does that leave us, eh, *liebste*?"

Charlotte looked up at him, expectantly. His question had been rhetorical and she was now waiting for him to provide the answer, to hand down the pearls of wisdom that her grandfather had requested.

"You need to study," he continued, "but in a good atmosphere. And you also need to know that at the end of it, you'll have work, an income, a little independence from your parents, am I right? Of course. So what we need is the best of both worlds."

"So tell us already," said Berthe.

Jakob shrugged, as if his solution were completely obvious. "Technical college," he said simply. He waited for some reaction, but there was little, so it was left to Berthe.

"What kind of technical college?"

"All depends."

"On what?"

"On what she wants to do. I made some inquiries, there's one not far from here, she can learn many trades."

"Such as?"

"I don't know exactly. I think they've got cooking, hairdressing, sewing . . . How about sewing, *liebste*? You could be a seamstress. Always plenty of work for a seamstress. Making, adjusting, repairing. People get fat, they get thin, young people grow up, old people shrink down, they always need clothes. What do you think? You like to sew, don't you?"

Charlotte nodded, an acknowledgment of the skill she'd already developed to some extent on her own. It had begun with doll's clothes, playing house with Trudi Hart.

Then she'd borrowed accoutrements from her mother and began attaching bows and ribbons to her own clothes to dress up the pockets and hems. More recently, she'd also become interested in different types of stitching.

Even Franzi had to admit that her daughter showed some aptitude in that area, but a seamstress? Her expression suggested she wasn't sure about that at all. It was so much lower than her expectations that she really didn't know how to react, so she remained silent.

Again, it was Berthe who was the first to respond. "Not bad," she said, but the shrug that followed seemed to say even more.

It was the only comment of any sort, but it appeared set the general tone. While nobody was wildly enthusiastic, they couldn't actually see anything wrong with the suggestion.

It wasn't really the best of both worlds, as Jakob had said, it was more like a compromise and they all knew it, but who could afford to be so fussy these days?

For the sake of change in our Friday lunchtime routine, Charlotte and I would occasionally head out for a baguette and coffee at a local bistro. This was only in the summer, of course, and only then when it was warm and dry.

While she would make her painfully slow way with the walker as best she could, I would dawdle alongside, carrying her things and holding up traffic at the intersections with my arm outstretched like a school crossing guard.

Sometimes the traffic backup caused gridlock, but nobody seemed to get annoyed or blare their horns. It was as if the entire world stopped dead in its tracks for those few moments, with everyone waiting for Charlotte.

Along these few blocks, everybody seemed to know her. She was like a living icon of the neighborhood, a human landmark, and they'd all ask her how she was doing in whichever language they were most comfortable.

"Comment çava, *Charlotte?*"

"Come sta, *Charlotte?*"

"Wiegehts, *Charlotte?*"

In response, she'd just smile her acknowledgment, content that people still knew her, still remembered her. There was always something of the narcissist in her nature, so be-

ing the local center of attention was an attitude which came easily and I believe she quietly reveled in it.

Yet, as always, it didn't take much for the inner torment to burst through, causing its shockwaves of turbulence, and on one day in late August, the target for her wrath happened to be the Hasidim, the Jewish ultra-orthodox.

They hadn't hurt her, they hadn't even spoken to her, yet she loathed them with an illogical fury. We were driving back from lunch through the district's grid of narrow streets when we came across a member of the Lubavitch community whose vehicle was blocking the road.

He was a hefty man in shirtsleeves, with a major belly, a thick beard and side curls dangling from under his broad-brimmed hat, and he was standing next to his kosher food delivery van, hand on hip, while engaged in conversation with another man perched up on a balcony.

There was nothing aggressive or even rude about their attitudes. It was the kind of thing that happens in every neighborhood, just people being people, and I was prepared to be patient, assuming the man would move his van soon enough, but not Charlotte.

She was at my side in the passenger seat and I could see her becoming upset, silently fiddling with her purse and becoming ever more agitated. Before I could say anything to calm her, she lowered the window and began screaming at the man, a mouthful of verbal abuse. Shocked, he turned to see who could possibly be swearing at him in Yiddish.

This was a peaceful community where the majority spoke French. For a long moment, the man glared at Charlotte, and I wasn't sure what his response might be. As it turned out, he wasn't sure how to react because this was so far outside any of his normal parameters.

He could hardly blame it on age-old anti-Semitism, since he was being accosted in his own language by someone of his own ethnicity, nor could he yell back, because she was an elderly woman to whom he was expected, by his own moral standards, to show respect.

There was really nothing he could do to defend himself from this unprovoked onslaught, so without saying a word and with no expression on his face, he just climbed into his van, slid the door shut and drove away.

Long after, when we were already back at the apartment, Charlotte still hadn't recovered from the incident. "Why do they have to be like that?" she asked me.

"Like what?"

"The way they dress, the way they behave."

"They mind their own business. What's wrong with that?"

"They make me sick."

That was her answer, and she refused to elaborate. There seemed to be no motive for her attitude, at least none that I could figure out, but I knew from experience that with Charlotte, I had only two possible alternatives in a situation like that: either to wait for the sorrowful reaction to set in, or to change the topic and make her laugh.

To me it was no choice at all, so I retrieved from the depths of my memory an old joke I'd been saving, something about a rabbi going into a bar. I deliberately gave her the long version, extending the story for as long I could.

Even before the end, she was chuckling. The crisis had passed, the tension was lifted, and I was able to brew some coffee while we chatted away amiably about other things.

So why did the ultra-orthodox cause that response in her? Was it that she blamed such people for calling attention to themselves, for not fitting into the societies around them and thereby bringing down scorn upon all Jews, or was it less obvious than that? What if she couldn't tell me why it happened because she really didn't know?

I've been told by those who study such things that reaction to early-life trauma can often be unpredictable and can therefore manifest itself later in many forms. It can be direct, based on reminders of the actual cause, but it can also be fairly random, triggered subconsciously by vague clues or perceptions.

These tricks of memory are powerful enough to affect the entire nervous system, causing it to malfunction and provoke a severe emotional response. This certainly appeared to be the case with Charlotte, and for me, it explained in more clinical terms what I'd already begun to understand.

5

Apart from the decision about college, the year of 1933 was important to Charlotte on a broader scale. Now that she'd learned—and was continuing to learn—about the Nazis, she could begin to comprehend the electoral earthquake that was currently taking place in Germany, just two weeks after her fourteenth birthday.

Although she was as self-absorbed as any other adolescent—and perhaps more emotionally-driven than most—she was neither silly nor frivolous concerning the world around her and always tried very hard to live up to her father's expectations in this respect.

If, for him, the politics of Germany was of deep concern, then it was for her, too, and she listened with interest to the radio bulletins as the returns were announced.

This was the third such ballot in three years, the climax of a violent period of upheaval that had left the economically-depressed population angry, anxious and no further ahead.

Finally, seeking some kind of order out of the chaos, they turned to the Nazis, propelling them into power with a massive majority. Those on the right declared it to be a free and fair result.

To those on the left, however, it appeared as if the Nazis had engineered the victory by setting fire to the Reichstag, the central parliament building, and then blaming it on the Communists as an act of treasonous anarchy.

However blatant such an outrageous ploy might have seemed, it achieved its aims. Opposition was reduced to a minimum, the outcome was declared, and the aging President Hindenberg had no choice but to allow it to stand. It meant that after so many years of agitation and provocation, the Nazi movement had finally seized control.

Hitler was now in power and the essential levers of state were at his disposal. Within government walls, the acclamation had given him the necessary legal credentials, while out on the streets, he still had the intimidating presence of his Brownshirts, now several million strong.

He couldn't yet exert the complete control he craved because many in the establishment, especially in the senior ranks of the army, still thought him to be a low-class rabble-rouser, but he now had sufficient momentum to advance further towards his openly declared goal of a thousand-year Reich.

Fortunately for the Jewish community of Vienna, listening to the news from Berlin was a little like eavesdropping over the backyard fence while rowdy neighbors argued amongst themselves.

Despite pockets of Nazi support in *völkisch* rural areas like Styria and Carinthia, and despite the vast number of unemployed, the party's rise in Austria wasn't nearly as rapid as it was in Germany.

Here, ultra-nationalist factions like the Heimwehr splintered the right-wing appeal, and although Nazi headquarters in Munich had sent in its own man to sort things out, the situation hadn't changed enough to make a major difference. There were some minor skirmishes in the streets, but these were mostly between the Socialists and the Christian Democrats with both adversaries, for various reasons of their own, being essentially anti-Nazi in attitude.

Altogether, it meant that while the political developments in Germany were deeply worrying, it was of no immediate concern in Austria. On this side of the border, it was economic hardship which remained the most immediate concern, and even more reason why it made sense for a robust girl in good health to learn a useful trade.

So it was that in the month of September, Charlotte began her classes at the Dreijährige Fachschule für Damen, the three-year technical school for ladies, with the objective of becoming a competent and employable seamstress.

Her period of training was to be the full three-year course, followed by an optional year of apprenticeship and, ultimately, acceptance into the guild.

She was permitted by her parents to continue with her piano lessons, as well as her physical activities if she so wished: skating or swimming or hiking with the *Socialiste Arbeitsjugend*, the labor youth movement of which she'd recently become a member.

However, her professional development was now the main priority, and her days at the technical college were considerably more arduous than anything she'd experienced at high school.

Sometimes, by the end of the afternoon session, her back, arms, and fingers ached from the strain, her eyes blurred from the continual focus, and her head pounded from the time pressures involved with every exercise.

For the first year or so, she found it rigorous, even grueling, but she refused to disappoint her parents and she overcame these initial difficulties by digging deep into her resources of energy and good humor. Besides, she felt proud and grown-up to be attending such an institution—the baby of the family no longer.

The only things missing at this all-girl college were boys. She met many at her youth club, but somehow, she didn't feel ready for any kind of relationship, not even for an experimental kiss. It might have been that an athletic environment simply wasn't romantic enough for someone as emotionally influenced as Charlotte, or it might simply have been the conservative and socially naive side of her character.

Either way, even though her mind and body were developing, she restrained from flirting or flaunting the way some of the other girls did, and as a result, the boys just didn't seem to be aware of her. It wasn't that she was spurned or deliberately ignored. It was more like she was just one of the crowd, someone who joined in the fun but never shone brightly enough as an individual to be appreciated.

She worked, she played, but she didn't get involved with any of the boys, and there was no one special until after she turned sixteen. Then, just as the snows were beginning to melt on the distant peaks, she bumped into Hugo.

"Oh, I'm sorry, excuse me," said Charlotte.

"No, no, my fault," said the young man.

It was a simple accident, a case of pedestrians not looking where they were going, but for Charlotte, it was more than that. Something inside her chose to awaken from its dormancy, and just before she turned the street corner, she felt an involuntary compulsion to glance back—just in time to see him disappear into the doorway of a watch repair shop, a minuscule place she'd never really noticed until now.

She'd never noticed the young man before, either. Was he a customer, or did he work there? She didn't know and had no time to investigate further. If she didn't move fast, she'd be late for her first class.

The incident happened quickly, just a brief moment in a busy day, yet she found herself thinking about him for hours: during darning, buttonholing, textiles, machine finishing, and other lessons, but especially while she was eating her sandwich lunch.

At one point, her mind was so far away that her friend, Magda, with whom she shared several classes, had to speak to her twice.

"Hey, dreamy-head, I asked you a question. You're not even listening."

Charlotte shook herself awake. "What? Sorry . . ."

"I said do you have any more of those pencils?"

"Pencils?"

"Things you write with."

"Why, you need some?"

"My brother. Give me ten, if you have."

Charlotte picked up her large bag from the floor and searched around for the beige carton, still full of the pencils. She hadn't sold too many yet. It had been her father's idea, presented to her at the time of her most recent birthday.

"Now you're going to college," he'd told her, "you should learn a little about money, about business." He'd brought back several gross from Prague as part of a deal with a supplier. The man couldn't pay what he owed, so he sent boxes of pencils instead, two thousand of them, and now Jakob was stuck with them, trying to sell them in order to get at least some of his money back.

That's why he'd engaged his daughter, asking her to sell as many as she could to students at her school, or colleagues at her club. Any money she collected, she could give to her mother as a contribution to household expenses.

For Charlotte, it was an inconvenience, and it wasn't very polite, she felt, to be selling pencils to her friends, but she could hardly refuse her father's request, not when he worked so hard to pay for her studies.

She counted out ten, handed them over to Magda, and put the proffered coins into her purse.

Magda, however, wasn't finished. "So who is he?" she asked with a smirk.

Charlotte had already bitten into her sandwich of cream cheese and pickles. "Who is who?" she managed to say with her mouth full.

"Your boyfriend."

"I don't have a boyfriend."

"Yes, you do, you can't fool me."

"No, I don't."

"You're a liar," said Magda, in a teasing, sing-song voice. Then she began poking Charlotte in the shoulder with her forefinger. "Liar, liar, liar."

Inevitably, Charlotte started to blush, which only made matters worse. "Magda, stop. I told you I don't have a boyfriend."

"And I told you I don't believe you. You know, friends are supposed to share with their friends." Magda waited but received no answer, so she tried another approach. "If you don't tell me, I'll spread it around."

"Don't you dare."

"So you'd better tell me."

"You'll spread it around anyway."

"No, I won't."

"You will."

"I give you my word."

"You promise?"

"I just said that." By now, Magda was sitting opposite, gazing across the table, enthralled, while also having fun at her friend's embarrassment. "Come on, out with it."

Charlotte looked around, but there were only the two of them at the table. Even so, she lowered her voice to a semi-whisper. "I only saw him for a few seconds. I just . . . I just bumped into him. You know, on the street."

"I bet it was deliberate."

"It was not." Charlotte was shocked at the thought. A trick like that would never have occurred to her.

"So what's he like?"

"I don't know."

"Of course, you do. Was he tall or short?"

"I don't know . . . maybe average."

"Blond or dark?"

"Blond, but not really."

"Not really?"

"Like a sandy blond. A dark sandy blond."

"A dark sandy blond?"

"Well, medium dark."

Magda smiled again at Charlotte's difficulty. "So, we've got a medium, dark, sandy blond of average height. And his eyes?"

"His eyes?"

"What color were they? Blue? Brown? Green? Pink?"

The jokes were annoying but there wasn't much that Charlotte could do about any of it. She actually believed that Magda would indeed spread it around and she'd have done anything to avoid that. "I didn't see his eyes, I told you. I just bumped into him."

"Are you going to bump into him again?"

"I didn't do it deliberately."

"So you say."

"It's true."

"You haven't answered me yet."

"Answered what?"

Magda gave a mock sigh. "Will you go back and see him?"

"No . . . I don't know."

"You should."

"You think so?"

"Better than sitting around here daydreaming. You should go tonight, on your way home."

"He might not be there."

"He might, he might not. You won't know unless you go." Magda got to her feet. It was time to head back to class. "I'll expect a full report tomorrow."

In response, Charlotte offered a weak smile, but this time, she didn't answer. She'd said enough for one day.

The problem was that she just wasn't sure she had the courage to do what Magda suggested. How could she just show up and introduce herself, she wondered? That was no way for a young lady to behave.

She might be mistaken for one of those women who sell themselves for money; not that she'd ever met any, but her mother had warned her that female intentions could be easily misunderstood.

Don't dress improperly, don't unfasten any more than the top blouse button, don't wear too much makeup, don't laugh loudly, don't engage men in conversation, don't linger in the street—these were the rules of conduct that her mother had given her, and they were unbreakable.

Charlotte's school day usually ended at five, but that afternoon, they concluded a few minutes early due to an after-class teacher conference. Normally, she would have headed directly home, her habit being to have coffee and do her homework while her mother prepared an evening meal for the two of them.

That afternoon, however, Charlotte's mother had traveled a little farther to go shopping for flour, matzo meal, and certain other commodity items she could purchase cheaper at a bulk dealer down near the canal, so the plan was for Charlotte to meet her at the nearby Café Reclame at six in order to help carry the heavy bags home.

Charlotte paused at the exit to her school, not sure what to do. If she walked fast, it would take only forty minutes or so to the café, which meant she had at least a quarter of an hour to spare. For several long seconds, she hesitated while the other students filed out past her.

For some reason, she was hoping she wouldn't see Magda. The lunchtime taunting had done its work and she now had it in mind that if she didn't go back to the watch repair shop, she'd be seen as weak and cowardly.

Her father told her that running away like a rabbit was an acceptable strategy and that the huge rabbit population was testimony as to how well it worked, but that wasn't how she felt at that moment. She was afraid and it was only the shame that drove her forward, down the school stairs and on to the street.

People, wagons, vehicles—she didn't see any of them, and even when she did notice that a horse had turned its head to look at her, a weary gray horse with a scruffy mane and chafed fur, all she could see in its eyes was accusation.

"Hussy," the horse was saying. "You're nothing but a hussy." Still, she kept walking, but by now, she was busy trying to reason with herself, asking what harm could there be to go in that direction? The little shop was only a block out of her way and would probably be closed anyway.

However, that's when her subconscious mind came up with an idea on its own. Her father had told her how sometimes it happened to him. If he had a difficult problem, he'd just let it stew like a *cholent* for a while, and it would often solve itself. That was the expression he used: "stew like a *cholent*."

It referred to the heavy concoction of lesser cuts of meat, low grade potatoes and thick gravy that strict Jews kept simmering on a low light right through the Sabbath so they wouldn't have to break any commandments, either by lighting the stove or cooking the food.

In this case, the problem that had been stewing inside Charlotte's head was how to begin talking to the mysterious stranger without appearing to be the kind of hussy her mother—and the horse—had warned her against. Suddenly, the solution came to her of its own accord, and she could see nothing wrong with it.

On the contrary, the idea was startlingly obvious, and she now found she was stuck with it, almost obliged to carry it through. What a terrible, traitorous thing the brain could be, she thought. When she arrived at the street corner, the same place she'd bumped into the young man that morning, her heart began to pound.

The lamp inside the little store was burning, which meant somebody was still inside, still working. In theory, it was the moment to choose whether or not to enter, but Charlotte knew the decision had already been made.

Her brain had thought up a way to do it, and now her nerve was forced to subjugate itself and obey. She walked as far as the door and then stopped again to take several deep breaths. She still wasn't sure who was in there.

For all she knew, the boy she had seen that morning had merely been a customer and all she would find would be a wizened old man repairing watches. She waited a little longer but she was very conscious of the time slipping by. She still had to meet her mother by six.

Tentatively, she pushed open the door and heard the tinkling of the tiny bell. Inside, the narrow space was dusty and dark. On one side was the wooden counter, with scales and several ledgers. On the other were floor-to-ceiling shelves stuffed with household and office items: wall-clocks, radios, flashlights, typewriters, and many others, all undoubtedly in need of repair.

The shop's main illumination came from a small glass-fronted booth at the back and, by its yellow glow, she could make out the same young man. On seeing her, he put his tools down, got to his feet, and emerged to attend to the new customer.

Charlotte thought her chest might explode and what a mess that would make.

"Good evening," she said, hoping her words would come across more confidently than they sounded to her own ears.

"Good evening," he replied. He had a pleasant voice, as if he were just content to see someone, anyone, after working here alone for so long. "May I help you?"

Charlotte tried a smile, not a big smile, just a normal, friendly smile. "You don't just repair watches?" She wasn't sure why she even said that, except that it seemed like a good way to start.

"No, not just watches." He raised his hand casually to point out the shelves.

"All kinds of objects."

"Ah . . . I thought it was just watches."

"No."

"That's . . . good to know. In case, you know, I ever have something to repair."

"You don't have anything to repair?"

Charlotte shook her head. "No, I don't, I'm sorry." She knew he was about to ask again how he might be able to help her, so she jumped in first. "No, it's just that I'm going around the district . . . selling pencils."

The young man looked puzzled. "Excuse me?"

"I have some pencils, very good pencils. My father . . . he bought them in Prague, so now I'm trying to sell them. Well, not all of them, of course, just the ones he gave me."

"You have them with you, these pencils?"

"Yes, yes, in my bag. Would you like to see them?"

He shrugged slightly. "If you wish to show me."

Hurriedly, she lifted her bag to the counter, rummaged through and brought out her carton of pencils. She removed the lid, so he could see for himself.

He picked one out to inspect it, turning it this way and that, feeling the weight and the balance of it in his hands. "The Czechs make good pencils," he said gently.

Was he teasing her? Charlotte suspected as much but didn't know for certain, so she just replied, "Yes . . . yes, they do."

"And you're selling them?"

"Yes, that's right."

"For a good price, I imagine."

"Less than you could buy elsewhere."

"All right, I'll take some."

"You will?"

"You're a good sales person."

"I am?"

"Very good."

"Really?"

"You come in, you don't waste my time, you show the product, you don't try to exaggerate . . . and you have a nice smile. What more could anybody want in a salesperson?" Charlotte could feel herself blushing again, far worse than at lunchtime with Magda. It was just as well, she thought, that the light in there was low.

"You think I have . . ." She stopped herself in time, but he'd already guessed what she was going to say.

"Yes, a very nice smile. I'll take twenty."

"Twenty? Really? You don't have to. I mean . . ."

"Now, please, don't prove me wrong. You've made the sale, so it's time to remain silent and carry out the transaction. Only when you've got the money in your hand and I can't take it back should you speak again."

At this, she couldn't help but be amused. "Yes, you're right. Of course. I'll remain silent. From now, I mean."

He grinned back and they completed the sale. While she counted out the pencils, he opened up a small cashbox and counted out the coins. Then they exchanged.

"I can speak now?" she asked him.

He laughed, not a big laugh but a soft, throaty sound. "You learn quickly," he said. "I think you're going to go far in life."

This was the kind of advice normally dispensed by an elder relative and she immediately began to wonder about his age. He was older than she was, certainly, but by how many years: two, maybe three? It was hard to tell in this light. In addition to his age, she would also like to have known the color of his eyes, if only because Magda had asked her, but she couldn't see those too clearly either.

"I was going to ask you why you need so many. Pencils, I mean."

"Why? Because I like to keep a good stock of everything. Tools, spare parts . . . Why should pencils be any different?"

"I suppose." There was really nothing else she could add, so she told him the truth. "I have to go meet my mother," she said, as she packed up her bag.

In response, he reached out. "Well, Fräulein . . ."

She paused to shake his hand and felt the warmth of his fingers. Then it dawned on her that he was waiting for her name. "Goldberger," she replied.

"Well, it's been very good to meet you, Fräulein Goldberger."

"Thank you . . . for buying the pencils."

"Thank you for selling them."

Now, she knew for sure that she was being teased but she didn't mind, because he did it in such a nice way.

"I have to go."

"In that case, I wish you a very good evening."

"You, too."

As she was about to open the door, he called after her.

"Fräulein Goldberger?"

She turned anxiously. "Yes?"

"If you ever need anything repaired, you know where to come."

She nodded. "Yes, yes . . . thank you."

Then she hurried out, with that little bell tinkling once again just above her head, but almost as soon as her feet trod the sidewalk, she felt like an idiot. She'd told him her name but she hadn't asked for his. Now Magda would definitely make fun of her. She'd also completed the sale, so she had absolutely no reason to return.

Why hadn't she held back some of the pencils, she asked herself? She could have said she only had fifteen to spare right now, the others were already promised to another customer—or something like that. It would have been a lie and she didn't like lying, nor was she very used to it, but it would have served her purpose. Now she had nothing, no reason at all to go back.

She strode all the way to the café by the canal, exhilarated that she'd been so daring and that he'd told her she had a nice smile, but also disappointed that she had no further excuse to see him. Maybe, she thought, if left alone, the answer would again come to her.

In style, the Café Reclame was far removed from the classic coffee houses of the Altstadt. There was no vaulted ceiling, no *sachertorte* served with silver-plated forks, and no great figures of music or art had ever gathered there.

This was more *heimisch* in character, more homely, with frayed tablecloths and chairs that wobbled on the uneven floor.

The coffee was good, though, and so was the strudel if purchased on the same day it came from the bakery. Afterwards, they'd still serve it, but it really wasn't worth eating.

Charlotte had been here before and knew that the only reason her mother frequented the place was to play cards with her friends; also because the aging manager didn't mind them being here for as long as they wanted, no matter how little they ordered.

She knew, too, that the game they played was thirteen-card rummy and that, simple as the game might be, they usually played it with some intensity.

She'd seen the excitement it generated and even witnessed serious arguments, especially when there was money on the table like today: small piles of ten-groschen coins in front of each of the four women.

After the post-war inflation bubble, ten thousand kronen had been replaced by one schilling which, in turn, was divided into a hundred groschen, so they weren't playing for very much.

Sometimes her mother won, but on this occasion, she didn't seem to be so fortunate, and Charlotte watched silently until the hand ended in yet another loss.

By this time, her mother had very few coins left, hardly enough to pay her debts, so she turned to her daughter and whispered a request: "*Liebste*, do you have any money on you?"

"Of course," said Charlotte proudly. "I sold thirty pencils today." There was no reaction from her mother, who was busy shuffling the cards.

It was as if she hadn't even heard that last part because all she said was, "Give it to me, would you?"

Charlotte hauled out the bulging purse, handed it over and watched her mother tip all the money into her lap. The ten-groschen coins she placed on the table in front of her, the fifties she put back, but she didn't give the purse back to Charlotte, she just tucked it into her own bag.

As Franzi began dealing the cards, the portly woman opposite her, whose name was Mathilde, had begun telling some humorous story, but Charlotte was no longer watching or listening.

Thoughts of the young man she'd met at the repair shop had been temporarily banished from her mind, replaced by the disbelief at what had just happened.

She'd sold thirty pencils in one day, six times more than she'd ever sold before, and there'd been no congratulations, not even a word. Worse than that, her mother was now gambling with the money Charlotte had earned, which seemed neither fair, nor appropriate.

"*Mutti*?" she said, trying to get her mother's attention.

"I won't be long, *liebste*. Sit if you want, I'll just play one more hand."

In the end, Franzi lost that hand and also the one after. Only with the third did she win, and that's when she finally made her excuses to leave, getting up from the table while her friends continued to play.

There were several sacks of shopping, which she organized between herself and her daughter. Then, they said their goodbyes and left the establishment for the long walk home. For a while, they paced along in silence. Charlotte had already grown a centimeter taller than her mother, but with her physique and youth, she was considerably stronger, and she found herself slowing her stride a little so her mother could keep pace. Eventually, it was Franzi who spoke.

"So, *liebste*, how was your day?"

Charlotte glanced at her mother, not sure what to say, or even whether to answer at all. In truth, it had been an astonishing day and she was thrilled at what she'd managed to accomplish. She'd bumped into a young man, a genuine accident despite Magda's assertions otherwise, she'd invented a way to speak to him and found within herself the courage to do so, and on top of all of that, she'd sold thirty of her father's pencils. If he was here, she knew he'd have been very proud.

Yet in reply to the question, all she said was, "My day was fine." She'd been longing to blurt it all out, to share the adventure, but she was disgruntled by what had just happened, so she kept it all to herself, bottled up and tightly corked.

Tomorrow, she said to herself. Tomorrow she'd tell Magda about it, but not this evening, not to her mother. She just couldn't bring herself to do it.

As usual when she was in a bad mood, Charlotte slumbered fitfully, drifting in and out of sleep until, at just after three in the morning, she decided she couldn't take it anymore. She crept out of bed, anxious not to wake her mother, and padded barefoot through to the living room.

It was almost totally dark and she had to feel her way around the furniture until she arrived at the sideboard on which the radio had been mounted. Feeling for the large tuning knob, she wedged the tips of her fingers in behind it and pulled. It wouldn't give, so she tried harder—two, three, four times—until, with a slight crack, it finally came away in her hand. She paused, wondering if her mother had heard the sound, but all was still.

That should do it, she thought, and felt her way back through to her room.

Predictably, after such a restless night, she slept late and had to be shaken awake. She washed in cold water, as usual, dressed in her school clothes, and arrived for breakfast, only to hear the question she'd been expecting since she opened her eyes.

"Do you know what happened to the radio?"

Charlotte pretended to be surprised. "It's broken," she replied.

"I know it's broken. I asked you if you know what happened?"

"No. No idea." This wasn't a harmless evasion or omission, this was a direct and outright lie. Charlotte couldn't ever recall doing that before, but today, she just didn't care.

"You didn't touch it?"

"No."

"If it was an accident . . ."

"I told you, I don't know anything about it."

"Please, *liebste*, don't take that attitude. I'm only trying to find out what happened."

"Well, it wasn't me."

"All right, all right."

Her mother went back to what she was doing, washing and putting away some dishes. A thoughtful look remained on her face, but she didn't say any more about it.

It was fifteen minutes later, once Charlotte had finished eating, that she said, "I know a place we can have it repaired."

The radio was both heavy and awkward to carry, especially with her school bag draped over her shoulder, but she made it to the small store without problem, pushing the door open with her elbow. Once again came the pleasant sound of that little bell.

This morning, the young man was already behind the counter, drinking tea from a tin cup as he worked on his ledgers. "Well, hello again. More pencils to sell?"

"No, no, the radio broke." Charlotte placed the appliance down in front of him, glad to unload the weight. Her arms were aching. "The knob fell off."

He nodded. "Yes, I can see that."

"Can you fix it?"

"Is that all that's wrong with it?"

"Yes. At least, I think so."

"Shouldn't be too much problem."

"The only thing is . . . Can I ask you a special favor? Is it possible to do it today? Only you see, my mother likes the radio, it keeps her company during the day. She likes listening to music and . . ." Charlotte stopped. She could hear herself and she recognized the signs. The guilt was already starting to get to her. "Would it be possible?"

"What time can you come back?"

"After school, maybe about five-thirty. Would that be all right?"

"If it's only the knob, I can get it done."

"Good, good. Thank you."

Charlotte wasn't sure whether to leave.

"Was there something else?" he asked her.

"I don't even know your name."

"It's right outside, right above the door . . . Kohn. Actually, the first name there is my father's, Herman."

"What's yours?" Charlotte couldn't believe she was even asking such a question, but somehow, yesterday's incident with her mother had changed her. She now broke things with equanimity, lied about doing so, and asked strange young men for their names. She saw him smile again, this time so broadly it seemed to spread to his eyes, which she noticed for the first time were a deep shade of indigo.

"I'll tell you mine if you'll tell me yours," he said.

"All right."

"Hugo. My name is Hugo Kohn."

"And my full name is Liselotte Goldberger, but most people call me Liesl."

"Well, I'm very pleased to meet you . . . Liesl."

He shook her hand again, more extravagantly than the previous afternoon when they'd simply been completing their business deal. Yet for Charlotte, it served the same purpose and, once again, she was able to feel his touch.

This time, she left the shop with a totally positive attitude. Despite all her devious manipulations, she was extremely pleased with herself. She felt like she'd struck a real blow for her own sense of independence, and as a bonus, when she met up with Magda at lunchtime, she'd have all the necessary details to relate.

As it happened, Charlotte didn't share everything with Magda that day, or any day afterwards, because she just didn't feel like doing so. When Magda scoffed and once more threatened to spread the word around, Charlotte replied that she didn't care—and it was true.

Why should she be ashamed, she argued to herself? Even if her mother did somehow find out, it wouldn't matter, not any more, not after what had happened at the café.

Instead of Magda, her regular confidant became Hugo himself, and two or three times a week, she would stop in on her way home to chat, to drink tea, and to talk about the things that mattered in her life. Most times he continued to work as she spoke, sometimes in his little booth, sometimes at the counter, but he always kept an attentive ear and seemed to understand every nuance of her issues, her problems, or anything else she wished to discuss.

Even after a few weeks, she still wasn't sure if he genuinely liked her or was just happy for the company in his lonely trade, but it didn't matter. They'd become friends. Perhaps for Charlotte, they were even more than friends, because he was now the only person in the world with whom she could really talk.

Her father was away all the time, and as for her mother, Charlotte still loved her, but there just wasn't the same level of respect as before. There were many like Magda whom she called her friends—at school, at her club—and she still saw her childhood friend, Trudi, occasionally, but none of them were the same as Hugo.

Her few minutes with him were special and she began to look forward to them, counting down the hours until she could see him again.

"Are you a Socialist?" asked Charlotte. It was a more direct question than usual, but she had an ulterior motive.

"No, not really," Hugo replied. "My father used to be but not me."

"So what are you? A Nazi?"

Hugo laughed at the idea. "No, I'm not a Nazi either." Then he felt the need to add, "I suppose I'm nothing really. How about you?"

"Me? I'm nothing, too, but I do belong to the *Socialiste Arbeitsjugend*." She was referring to the Socialist youth club, which she'd joined on leaving high school. "But it's nothing to do with politics or anything," she added hurriedly. "They just have sports and so on."

This caught his interest. "What kind of sports?"

"I take part in the skating and the swimming . . . Well, skating in the winter, obviously. And swimming, you know, in the summer. But they also have other things. Hiking, if you like. Running, too."

"Football? I like football. Do they have that?" He was referring to the English-invented game, also known as soccer, that had become extremely popular all over the continent.

"Yes, as a matter of fact. Would you be interested?"

"Well, I don't know. It's been a while since I played, what with work and everything."

"Because if you want, I could introduce you. Of course, it's up to you, but there's a meeting soon. Well, it's more like a kind of a dance, really, but everyone will be there. All the leaders, the members, everyone . . . but like I said, it's up to you."

"A dance?"

"Kind of a dance. It's like an annual event, you know? They hold it every year."

"Yes, I suppose they would if it's an annual event."

Charlotte was embarrassed again, sounding silly, even to herself. She'd thought she would be mature enough to ask him and had even thought up a way of doing it, by mentioning the sporting angle first. She thought she'd been very clever, but it didn't appear to be working at all.

That's when he said, "I don't dance very well."

The comment surprised her because, in those few moments, she'd almost convinced herself that she'd failed. "So you'll go? You'd like to go?"

Hugo shrugged. "Do you think it would be all right? I mean, if I came as just a guest. I don't really want to make a commitment."

"No, no, I understand. You don't have to commit to anything. It's just to meet people. So you'll go?" she asked again. "I mean, it's only if you want to."

"Fine."

Charlotte couldn't believe it, couldn't get over her own audacity. She'd invited him, and he'd accepted, and although she took enormous pains not to display her emotions, inside she was euphoric.

It was with a sense of pride that she accompanied Hugo to the dance. It was the first time she'd seen him out of his work clothes. His hair was combed, and he was wearing a jacket and pants, not matching and not new, but his open white shirt was freshly laundered, and he looked very presentable.

For her part, she was wearing a new dress that her father had brought her from Sardinia: an unusual style in brighter colors than she normally wore—hues of cream and beige, with yellow trimming—and it somehow made her look more fashionable, even a little exotic, or so she liked to imagine.

A middle-aged trio provided the music, mostly waltzes that were very relaxed, for which Charlotte was thankful. It was true that Hugo wasn't especially talented at dancing but the easy rhythm helped him get used to the movement.

As for Charlotte, it just felt wonderful to be moving around the floor with him, in his arms, while her friends watched and wondered who this newcomer might be.

Half-way through the evening, after she'd introduced him around to various groups, she broke the news.

"My father's coming later . . . to pick me up. I'm sorry."

"Why are you sorry?"

"Well, you know . . ." Charlotte felt awkward. She'd had it in mind that Hugo would walk her home.

"Where's he been?"asked Hugo, trying to help her out.

"The Mediterranean. That's where he bought me this dress. Do you like it? You didn't say."

"Yes, it suits you, the color and everything. Is he coming to meet me?"

"No, not really. It's just that we see so little of each other, you know how it is. Don't worry, he won't bite."

Hugo nodded but didn't seem reassured, and when they paused to take refreshment, soda and cake that had been provided by the club, she found that their conversation had dried up a little.

Afterwards, they danced some more until not long after ten o'clock, when the music came to an end and the event wound down.

As arranged, her father was waiting by the door, which caused her to take a long breath.

"Hello, *liebste*," he said when he saw her. "You look so beautiful this evening." It was at that moment he looked over and saw Hugo, who was hovering a pace behind her.

"*Vati*, this is Hugo," she said, encouraging the young man to step forward. "Hugo, this is my father."

"I'm very pleased to meet you, Herr Goldberger," said Hugo, politely extending his hand.

Jakob didn't take it. He just gazed for what seemed to Charlotte like an eternity, his expression changing as he turned back to her. He'd been jovial, genuinely happy to see his daughter, but his mood had darkened considerably. He lifted his hand, and without any warning, he brought it down on the side of her face.

It was more of a tap than a true slap but it was the first time he'd ever struck her and Charlotte recoiled from the sheer shock. Her face went red, not from the blow but from the embarrassment, the worst she'd ever felt. Next to her, Hugo was open-mouthed, and all around, she felt people were looking, staring.

"That's for lying to your mother," her father said softly.

Then, without waiting for a reply, he turned and walked out, leaving her alone with the tears already starting to fill her eyes, smudging her carefully applied makeup.

She didn't need to ask him what she'd done to deserve such an accusation. She knew perfectly well. She'd told her mother that Hugo was Jewish, but he wasn't, and her father could tell instantly.

It wasn't even the fact that Hugo was Christian because, in the end, her father just didn't care that much about religion. No, it was solely because she'd lied about it, both to her mother and, by implication, to her father as well.

That's what had made him so angry and that's why she was in such a wretched state, running from the venue with her handkerchief to her face, with Hugo following behind, neither understanding, nor knowing what to do.

"Was it my fault?" he asked when he finally caught up to her.

She shook her head.

"I'm sorry," he went on, "if it was my fault . . ."

She looked at him with her streaked face and managed to find some pity. "No, no, it has nothing to do with you."

"But—"

"Are we still friends? Just tell me we're still friends."

"Yes, of course we're still friends."

That's when she kissed him for the first time, not on the lips but on his cheek, leaving traces of her lipstick. When she tried to wipe it off with her tear-soaked handkerchief she made it worse, causing her to laugh a little.

It made her feel better and she held his hand as they continued on their way. What would happen when she arrived home didn't matter to her, because she and Hugo were still friends, and he was walking her back, just as she'd wanted.

To take her mind off what had happened, she forced herself to chat, asking Hugo what he had thought of the dance, the music, the people, and anything else she could think of.

When they reached her building entrance, all talk stopped and they just looked at each other. Charlotte felt as if she must still resemble a circus clown, but she wanted to kiss him, properly this time.

She might have done so but that was when Frau Graebner appeared in the hallway, going about some late evening business with a large ring of keys in her hand, so the opportunity was lost. Instead, they just smiled at each other, more amused than frustrated by the situation, and thanked each other for the pleasant evening.

When Charlotte got inside, there was no yelling or screaming. To her surprise, everything was normal. Her mother offered her some hot cocoa, and her father said "good night, *liebste,*" as if nothing at all had happened.

While she was content that the incident hadn't alienated Hugo, she nevertheless felt miserable, as if the guilt was fully on her for having betrayed her parents, especially her father.

By the time she'd washed off her makeup and crawled into bed, the tears had once again welled up and that's how she fell asleep.

Even later in life, Charlotte's emotional nature seemed to be forever at odds with a deep-rooted need to prove her independence.

For example, although she could hardly walk, she insisted she could drive. She couldn't even get into the passenger seat without someone helping her lift her feet in, yet she genuinely believed she was capable of operating a vehicle on the busy streets.

On a day-to-day basis, it was Claude, the building janitor, who ferried her around, taking her to the mall, the shoemaker, the pet store, and every other place she needed to go. In return, since he didn't possess a vehicle of his own, he was also permitted to use Charlotte's small car for his own errands.

It was an amicable arrangement, and logically, it meant she didn't need a driving permit at all. However, every couple of years her permit came up for renewal, and each time, she refused to give it up. She wrote the check and sent the forms because, for her, to lose that small piece of paper in her wallet would have been like surrendering her freedom. As a gesture, it was more symbolic than practical, but it was real enough to her.

Then one summer, Charlotte took it into her head that she was actually going to get behind the wheel and she asked that I accompany her. Of course, my preference would have been to say absolutely not, under no circumstances, but I was torn.

If I'd given her an outright "no", she might well have accepted it because of the trust she had in me, but I knew I would be destroying an essential part of who she was. On the other hand, there was a serious responsibility involved.

With Charlotte at the controls, we'd be endangering not just ourselves, but everyone and everything out there, from stray cats to stray children.

Everybody I consulted said I shouldn't do it, that it would be criminal even to try. Yet I couldn't bring myself to break her spirit like that, nor did I want to be the villain who had to tell her that she was no longer fit to drive. I therefore devised a scheme which I hoped would achieve the same goal without hurting anyone, either Charlotte or the rest of the world.

First, I made her a promise. I told her that the following Friday, weather permitting, I'd take her out driving, but I said no more than that. When the day came, it was fine and clear, so I arrived an hour early for our usual lunch.

"We're going?" she asked me, hardly able to believe it.

"Sure, we're going. Would I break a promise?"

Her car was parked tightly in the building's underground garage, so I suggested that I take it out and drive her to a suitable location, at which point she could take over. She agreed, but she wasn't fooled.

Within a few minutes, she'd guessed where we were heading and what I had in mind. However, instead of being upset, I saw from her wry smile that she was fine with the idea, and that she actually thought it was a neat solution.

I drove for about fifteen minutes until we reached Mount Royal, essentially a large round hill which represented the city's central green space. About halfway to the summit, there was a spacious car park, but on a weekday like this, I knew it would be mostly empty. Here, I turned in and brought the car to a standstill, leaving the engine running. It took several long minutes to ease her out of the passenger seat, then for me to help her around the car to the driver's side.

This was a challenge all its own. I had to shift the seat back to its fullest extent, then once I'd tucked her legs and feet in, I had to push the mechanism forward again with her in it, not an easy maneuver. At last she was settled, hands positioned on the wheel, feet accessing the pedals, eyes in line with the mirror.

"Just take it nice and slow," I said to Charlotte, trying hard to prevent my voice from betraying my anxiety. "Agreed?"

"Why, you think I'm going to go racing?"

My major concern was whether she'd be able to shift her right leg quickly enough from the gas to the brake in case of an emergency, and I must admit, I had an ugly premonition of the car lurching forward and careering out of control.

Even large, empty car parks contain hard objects like lampposts and pay booths. At least in this location, I had reasonable confidence that we couldn't actually kill anything— unless, of course, some negligent squirrel chose the wrong moment to cross the asphalt.

I needn't have worried. Charlotte kept her word, and with a surprisingly light touch, she managed to steer her way around at no more than ten miles per hour. She repeated the circuit several times more until she was fully satisfied.

Even then, I was afraid she might ask me if she could now drive back to her building, but that didn't happen either. She just came to a stop and pushed the shift into park.

"All right, I'm done," she said simply.

It was over. She'd had her fun, renewed her sense of independence, and I must confess, I didn't try to encourage her to go any farther. I merely replied "Good for you," and left it at that. We changed places again, and I drove us back for the lunch that was still waiting.

As a result of our outing, she never asked to drive again. I didn't have to tell her she wasn't capable of handling a car in traffic, because she was nobody's fool, and our brief session had been a convincing demonstration.

Yet the decision now belonged to her and no one else, enabling her to keep that vital spirit of independence intact.

6

On turning eighteen, Charlotte would have become eligible to vote—if there had still been any democracy in the Republic of Austria. Unfortunately, the right of suffrage had already been banished by Chancellor Dollfuss when he declared himself dictator, instituted his own brand of Austro-Fascism and loudly proclaimed it to be the only viable countermeasure to Hitler's rise in Berlin.

It was hardly a propitious course of action. Within months, Dollfuss was assassinated by Nazi agents and succeeded by one of his own ministers, a relatively youthful forty-year-old with the grandiloquent name of Kurt Alois Josef Johann Edler von Schuschnigg.

On achieving power, Schuschnigg found his political inheritance difficult to manage. In addition to a near-bankrupt economy, he had to maintain a precarious balancing act between the popular Socialist agenda and the increasingly aggressive pro-German factions, and between the paramilitary rabble that threatened Vienna's civilized streets and his inadequate security forces, who were strictly limited in both numbers and weapons by the 1918 armistice treaty.

In response to this environment of tension and almost continual crisis, he governed as best he could. Economically, he attempted to work out some arrangement with governments in Paris and London to ease Austria's debt, but all his efforts were in vain. Then, diplomatically, he tried to appease Hitler by signing a treaty, which tied him closer to Germany's policies and left him with even less independence of action.

It's possible that neither outcome was his fault, since Schuschnigg had little leverage with which to negotiate, yet he seemed to compound the problems with his own well-intentioned but somewhat delusional domestic policies based on nothing but pretense.

In effect, he sought to shore up the nation's morale by hearkening back to the previous era, a symbolic resurrection of Viennese pride in which he encouraged all citizens of means to restore the cultural *joie-de-vivre* that had been one of the defining features of the old Habsburg monarchy. He, himself, did his part by sponsoring lavish affairs like the full-dress ball at the State Opera to which he invited four thousand guests.

Some of the more courageous news editors likened the situation to playing music on the deck of the sinking *Titanic*, but Schuschnigg dismissed such criticism with his firm belief that a great country needed to act great or lose its own self-respect—an opinion many of his fellow citizens were only too willing to share.

It was within this apocalyptic atmosphere of denial that Franzi had begun to attend the afternoon tea dances which were once again in vogue. Even more than playing cards, these outings had become an opportunity to forget the workaday, to leave behind the drudgery and the scarcities, in order to glide and swirl and ignore, if only for an hour or two, all reality.

Whenever such events were held on a Sunday, she would take her daughter along with her. By this time, Charlotte towered over her mother by several centimeters, and it was frequently assumed when the two strolled arm-in-arm that they were sisters, especially by the young men who approached them requesting the next dance.

The highlight of the season was a unique affair held at the Café Theater on Praterstrasse, for which Franzi had obtained a pair of invitations through her brother-in-law, courtesy of the position he still managed to hold at the Palais de Rothschild.

Several prominent guests from the world of entertainment were to be honored that day, including Fritz Lange, director of the silent classic *Metropolis*, and Peter Lorre, the actor who first gained fame by starring in Brecht and Weil's infamous psycho-drama *M,* in which he played the macabre central role of a serial child killer.

However, despite the long-standing arrangements to attend the function, neither of these luminaries deigned to appear. The only Fritz who bothered to show was the cabaret artist, Fritz Grünbaum, direct from his own spectacle at the Kabarett Simpl just across town.

For the award presentation to Grünbaum, Charlotte edged her diminutive mother closer to the stage and it was Franzi's unusual auburn hair which caused the celebrity to notice her. After the brief ceremony ended and the music was once again underway, the flamboyant Grünbaum stepped forward and, with courtly charm, asked her to dance.

Naturally, she was delighted to accept, leaving Charlotte by herself at the side of the room, a statuesque figure in her gown of *eau-de-nil*, but nevertheless intimidated by this society crowd.

Not since Hugo Kohn, the watch repairer, had there been anyone special in her life. After that embarrassing evening when her father had arrived at the club dance, her brief flirtation with Hugo just seemed to disappear of its own accord. She still viewed him as a good friend, still called in to his little workshop to chat, but there was no longer any relationship and she would never have invited him to a place like this.

It was as she stood there, a forlorn figure thinking nostalgically of Hugo, that the miraculous happened.

A tall individual with burning eyes, straight black hair, and a fashionably elegant suit appeared in front of her and begged her to allow him the privilege of a dance. He held out his hand in invitation and then waited. It was a confident, almost arrogant challenge, and she had little option but to accept; not that she would ever have thought of refusing.

He was perhaps the most handsome man Charlotte had ever seen, like a hero from the pages of some gothic fiction, and she could hardly breathe as he swept her around the dance floor. He was very certain of how he was leading her, never missing a beat, never putting a foot wrong. When the music drifted into a slower tune, he didn't let go, he just held her differently: a little closer, but also looser, so she wouldn't feel pressured.

There was a significant age difference between them, possibly as much as ten years, but for Charlotte that didn't matter. It was intoxicating to be with a man so sure of himself.

"May I be permitted to ask your name?" he asked, his voice redolent with old-world chivalry.

"Liselotte. My name is Liselotte."

"In that case, may I say, Liselotte, that you are very beautiful."

Despite her lack of experience, Charlotte knew well enough that it was just a line, a casual compliment that didn't mean very much. Yet nobody had ever called her beautiful before, even as a superficial gesture.

"Thank you," she said, hoping her blush couldn't be seen in this light. "And you're a very good dancer."

"*Merci, mademoiselle.*"

The French, too, was an affectation, but he was so smooth he made it work, and she didn't mind at all.

"And what's yours?" she asked. "Your name, I mean."

"My name is Karl, and I'm pleased to make your acquaintance."

"Likewise. Is this where you come, to tea dances, you know, to meet girls?"

"Sometimes," he said confidently.

She liked the fact that he was direct and hadn't even tried to lie. "I see," she replied, for want of something better.

"Does that bother you?"

"I don't know."

"Have I been too forward?"

"No, not at all. It's just . . ."

"We have such an age gap."

"How did you know that's what I was thinking?"

"Because it's what I was thinking, too. Look, I'm sorry if . . ."

She could tell he was about to stop dancing, to leave her right there in the middle of the floor, and that was the last thing she wanted.

"No, no, you've done nothing wrong," she insisted. "It's just—It's just that I'm a little shy, that's all. You'll have to forgive me."

He smiled at her with his impeccable white teeth. He didn't appear to have a blemish anywhere, a perfect specimen of a man who had just appeared out of nowhere. Perhaps this was all a dream, she thought airily, then realized how much like a silly schoolgirl that seemed.

For heaven's sake, grow up, she told herself, as the music continued to play and they continued to dance—a waltz, a foxtrot, a quickstep, then another waltz—until she heard a voice coming to her from nearby, at the side of the room.

"My goodness, *liebste*, will you ever stop?"

That's when she did stop, nervously tidying a strand of hair which had escaped. "*Mutti* . . . I forgot."

"I can see that."

"What time is it?"

"Time to go, I'm afraid. Aren't you going to introduce me? Where are your manners?"

"Sorry, sorry . . . Karl, this is my mother. *Mutti*, this is Karl . . . I'm sorry, I don't know your second name."

"Schneid . . . Karl Schneid," he answered. Then to Franzi: "*Enchanté, madame.*"

"Very pleased to meet you, too."

"Would it be a terrible imposition if I were to call on your daughter again sometime?"

"Well," said Franzi, "perhaps you'd better ask her that."

They both looked at Charlotte, who nodded her assent, a deliberate attempt to restrain herself. It didn't look good to be too forthcoming.

"Excellent," he said in response. Then he waited again. "I apologize, but may I obtain your family name? Would that be possible? Otherwise, it might be difficult, you know, to arrange anything. Also a number, too . . . if you have a telephone."

"Yes, yes, of course," said Charlotte. In fact, they'd had a phone installed just the previous month. It was expensive, just like everything else, but her parents had both felt it necessary so that her father could keep in touch on his travels if ever there was some emergency.

Charlotte proceeded to spell out her name and number, while he copied it all down into a small notebook.

While he was writing, Franzi asked: "And what is it that you do, Herr Schneid?"

"Please, call me Karl."

"Very well, what is that you do, Karl?"

"Import-export," he said flatly, without elaborating.

"Ah, really? My husband is also in that line of work. Do you travel a great deal?"

"A little." A shy smile. "Actually, no, not a great deal. But I've been to Paris on two separate occasions. I love Paris. Have you ever been, *madame*?"

"No . . . no, I haven't."

"Such a romantic city."

"Yes, so I believe." At that point, there was a slightly awkward pause in the conversation, so Franzi took her daughter's arm in preparation for leaving. "Well, good to meet you, Karl."

"Yes, and you, *madame*." He turned back to Charlotte, bowing very gently. "And you too, *mademoiselle*. I enjoyed dancing with you. Thank you."

"I, too, enjoyed it."

"I hope to see you again."

"I look forward to it."

"In that case, *au revoir*."

Charlotte allowed her mother to lead her out of the café but as soon as they were on the street, the questions began, and Franzi wanted to know everything: what his age might be, whether he was of their faith, how he'd asked her to dance, what they'd talked about.

"I don't know," Charlotte kept replying. Her head was too full to recall much of anything specific, but she did have one, all-important question of her own. "*Mutti*, do you think he'll call me?"

"He said he would."

"I know . . . but do men really mean what they say? Magda says they never do. She thinks they're all liars."

"Is that what *you* think?"

"I'm not sure."

"Well, we'll just have to wait and see."

"*Mutti* . . ."

"I know, I know, *liebste*. You hope he calls you. I hope so, too, for your sake."

That night, Charlotte couldn't help herself. She cuddled her pillow and tried to imagine what it would be like kissing Karl, not on the cheek but on the lips like adults—no, like lovers. She was certain, one hundred percent certain, that he would know exactly what to do, precisely how far to go. She'd never felt this way before, not even with Hugo, who was wonderful as a friend but no more than a boy in comparison to Karl. This was something totally new and she didn't even care that he was so much older. In fact, that was a vital part of the attraction.

Was it possible, she thought, to fall completely in love so quickly, so easily? She'd read about it, of course, and some of the girls at the college talked about nothing else, but to feel it, to experience it in reality, was like a revelation. She couldn't imagine that any man could possibly be so dashing, so prepossessing. He was the very essence of the fairy-tale prince, and here in her bed, she imagined herself to be some pristine Sleeping Beauty awaiting that first embrace.

She was fully cognizant of the fact that it was highly premature to be thinking like this, but she was incapable of resisting the powers of her own imagination. It was as if something unworldly—some sylph or perhaps some demon—had taken hold of her consciousness, and once again, she shuddered as his image appeared within the color swirls of her closed eyes.

Just before she fell into sleep, she came to a decision. This time, she wouldn't talk about her feelings to Magda, or to anybody else for that matter. She definitely wouldn't drag Karl along to any youth club dance, as she had Hugo.

From now on, she admonished, it would be tea dancing only, and then, perhaps at a later date, dinner at a chic restaurant, followed by the theater, or even the cabaret. In the meantime, all she could do was wait and hope and try to contain, at least while at school, her chronic tendency to daydream.

The day after a tea dance often found Franzi trying to maintain the lyrical lightness of mood as she did her chores. There was always so much to be done, even with just the two of them. No inside faucet meant that every cleaning task, whether washing dishes, or clothes, or floors, required going outside to fetch a bucket of water then waiting as it heated on the stove.

Since she could never afford the best detergents, she was obliged to use old-fashioned bricks of soap, which never generated enough suds. That in turn, meant extra scrubbing. Then there was the cooking, trying to stretch the food money as far it would go by preserving or salting or pickling, and the shopping itself, which took forever as she went from one store to another, several streets away, looking for the best value.

Just a few groschen made all the difference. Charlotte, with her training, could help her with the sewing and mending—she was fairly skilled and fast, too—but she had her homework to complete in the evenings, and afterwards, she needed her sleep. So Franzi worked and did the best she could, but she found budgeting to be stressful, and the daily rigors were hard on her fragile physique.

Worse, though, was the intense monotony of it all, with rarely any company to relieve such tedium. Sometimes, she felt that her brain was stultifying from lack of interest, yet there was nothing she could do. Her husband was away, she had a daughter to look after, and the work needed to be done.

This was her responsibility, and although she'd never been one to shirk her duty, either to her parents or to her husband, she sometimes found herself wondering if she'd made the right choices in life. She'd accepted to marry Jakob because it was the right thing to do. Her parents had said so and she'd wanted to be a worthy daughter, not like Paula, as haughty as a Habsburg aristocrat, too good for anything put in front of her. Yet here she was, Francesca Goldberger née Gutmann, no more than a servant in her own house and a lonely servant at that. This was the reward for her faithful obedience. Sometimes, she became so filled with regret that it simply overwhelmed her.

That was why she liked to play cards, just for the escape, just for the momentary thrill. She especially liked to dance, because when she danced she was transported, not just while she was being held and twirled, but also for a day or so later, as the memory and the magic remained in her soul. On these following days, when Charlotte was at school and she was alone again, she'd turn on the radio and float around to the music, and somehow, the chores didn't seem quite so heavy. With the iron, she would sway to a waltz, then with the broom, she'd slide into a foxtrot.

On this day, she had the additional inspiration of that one word: Paris. It was that good-looking young man who'd danced with Charlotte who had mentioned it, and now she couldn't get the thought out of her mind.

As she drifted around, her head was overflowing with thoughts of baroque architecture and spacious galleries replete with paintings she'd only ever seen in pictures.

She loved the classic romanticism of Géricault and Delacroix, the brilliantly colored primitivism of Gauguin, but most of all, she adored the Impressionists. From the recesses of her mind, she conjured up the ballerinas and the bistros of Dégas, the gardens and the regattas of Monet and the sun-dappled, erotically suggestive afternoons of Pierre-August Renoir. She saw men in straw hats laughing casually at some secret pleasantry and voluptuous women sitting on the grass with ripe breasts shamelessly exposed.

What kind of indulgent love would follow, she wondered. *Would it be in the open air surrounded by the delicate scents of jasmine and lavender, or in some loft studio bathed in light with tall windows overlooking the rooftops?*

As the radio played, Franzi's mind created ever more fanciful scenes until, eventually, her vision became blurred with tears at the sheer frustration of it all.

A week passed, but Karl Schneid had failed to communicate with Charlotte in any way. There was no call, no note, no message of any kind. It was as if he'd never existed. She understood that girls of her age were prone to crushes, she saw it clearly enough with others at her school, but she had profoundly believed that what she was feeling was far too deep, far too intense, to be like that.

Her stomach twisted into knots at the sheer thought of him, and she was giddy at the idea of just being with him; of strolling with him and dancing with him, wrapped in his arms, listening to his whispers. Yet gradually, over the days and weeks, her ambitions began to fray. She stopped asking her mother on her return from school each day if anyone had called, stopped perusing the mail delivery to check if she'd received any personal letters. All she could conclude was that her friend, Magda, had been right.

Charlotte didn't necessarily think that all men were liars, because her father was a man and he'd never lied, not as far as she could recall. Hugo, too, could be considered a virtuous example, but in this case, with Karl, she was starting to believe it might just be true.

She was despondent, depressed, and it was during this period that Charlotte felt as close to her mother as they'd ever been. Throughout her childhood, she'd always been more her father's daughter, even though he was hardly ever home, yet after that one afternoon at the tea dance,

Charlotte felt there was more of an understanding than there'd ever been before and it was the only redeeming factor of the distress she was suffering. They'd never really been confidantes but they were now able to talk about more than just homework and chores.

There was now a certain complicity, and at last, Charlotte began to learn things she could really only learn from her mother, not just about physical and biological changes, but about the many emotional stages of life and what each of them meant.

She knew all too well that her mother had little practical experience in these matters but there was now a sensitivity to their conversations and an instinctive empathy that proved to be of comfort in Charlotte's ever deepening despair.

Eventually, events of such magnitude forced their way into Charlotte's life that any lingering thoughts of handsome young men and tea dances were pushed aside, forced into frivolous insignificance. It began with a Sunday morning call just three days before her nineteenth birthday.

Charlotte's heart still jumped a little when the telephone rang but this reaction was just an instinctive residue. She didn't expect it to be Karl and, of course, it wasn't.

It was her father, but his voice sounded perturbed. Instead of congratulating her and wishing her happy returns, he asked if he could speak immediately to her mother.

The conversation went on for a long time but Charlotte had already gone back to her homework and didn't hear much of what was being said. When her mother finally put the phone down, her face was pale.

"*Mutti*?"

"That was your father."

"I know."

"He's in Prague . . ."

"What's wrong? Did something happen? Is he all right?"

"What? Oh yes, he's fine . . . but things are not good."

"What things?"

Franzi didn't answer. She just poured herself another cup of the coffee she'd brewed for breakfast. It was nearly cold but she sat and sipped it anyway, just to steady her nerves a little.

"*Mutti*?" Charlotte repeated.

Finally, Franzi pulled herself together enough to speak. "It seems Schuschnigg met Hitler again yesterday. It didn't go well."

"Why? What happened?" Charlotte was only vaguely aware of recent political undercurrents. She often listened to the news bulletins with her mother, but for past few weeks, she'd been too full of her own problems to pay much attention.

"It was a surprise. Hitler gave him an ultimatum."

"What's an . . ."

"Ultimatum? It's when somebody tells you to do something and threatens consequences if you don't."

"So Hitler threatened him? How?"

Franzi looked at her daughter but just shook her head, still trying to guard her daughter against life's uglier details. "It doesn't matter how. Enough you should know your father thinks it's serious."

"How serious?"

"He asked me . . ." Franzi was finding it hard even to say it.

"What? What did he ask you? *Mutti*, please . . ."

"He thinks we should start planning to leave."

"To leave? To leave where? The apartment?"

"Vienna . . . Austria. He says now's the time . . . but how can I leave?"

"Where would we go?"

"He doesn't know yet. He says we should arrange things quickly and go meet him in Prague, but I told him, I said that's impossible. How can we just go to Prague, just like that?"

"Did you ask him?"

"Your father says he's thinking of us. He says he only wants to protect us."

Charlotte nodded. That sounded like the father she loved. She knew from her high school geography that Prague was one of the closest of the European capitals, situated in neighboring Czechoslovakia, just a couple of hundred kilometers northwest of Vienna. That didn't seem too far.

"So maybe . . ." she began.

"No, *liebste*, it's impossible. My whole family's here. It's all right for him, his family's in Poland . . ."

"Aunt Berthe lives here."

"Not for long. She's already planning to leave, to go back to Krakow."

"Really?"

"That's what he says."

"So why don't we go to Krakow?"

"*Liebste*, please, you don't understand."

"But *Mutti*, if *Vati* says—"

"That's enough."

Charlotte could object and argue all she wanted but her mother had shut down. Franzi didn't want to hear any more, didn't even want to consider discussing it. She'd made up her mind.

For several days, nothing happened. Charlotte attended school, and while there was some minor political talk along the corridors, it usually dissolved soon enough into more pressing daily concerns. Her birthday came and went, but apart from good wishes and some fancy biscuits in her lunchbox, nothing special happened.

In the evenings, she listened with her mother to speeches from Berlin and Vienna, and although the level of the rhetoric had risen sharply, the citizens of Austria had heard vitriolic words many times before in the national discourse and it didn't seem to mean that much.

As a way to shore up support, Schuschnigg announced that he would hold a plebiscite on German demands, but then he set such onerous voting restrictions and phrased the question in such a biased way that Hitler became infuriated, demanding that the vote not only be cancelled, but that Schuschnigg be removed as Chancellor and replaced with his own nomination, Arthur Seyss-Inquart, current Minister of the Interior.

Under the Austrian parliamentary system, the only way that could happen was for the constitutional head-of-state, President Wilhelm Miklas, to validate the action. When the president point-blank refused to do so, Hitler openly announced that he would send his armies across the border to take control the following day.

Jakob had already called back several times, with each conversation more strident than the last, but as soon as Hitler's threat was made public, he begged his wife to reconsider.

"Franzi, please, take Charlotte and leave now, today. Just put what you can into a bag and go. Never mind the rest. Once the Nazis cross into Austria, that's it. They'll close the border."

"They won't do that. My father says it's all just talk."

"Please, for the last time, just pack a bag and get on a bus. We can discuss it here. All right, all right . . . if nothing happens, so much the better, you can go back. But what if I'm right?"

"Jakob, I can't leave, I told you a hundred times. I can't leave my father, my mother. My sister's still here, you think her husband's an idiot? He works for the Rothschilds and he's not running so quickly."

"So he works for the Rothschilds, very nice. I don't have that privilege, so I'm telling you now to get on the bus."

"No, Jakob, I can't."

"My God, you're stubborn. So send Charlotte."

"Charlotte? She's got school. How can she leave school right in the middle?"

"Franzi, Franzi . . . what are you talking about?"

"When are you coming home?"

"Home? You think I should come home?"

"Well, of course."

"Franzi, listen to me, listen to me carefully. If they close the border, then we'll both be trapped."

"That won't happen, it's ridiculous."

"Why? Because your father says so? Because Mr. Bigshot at Rothschilds says so?"

"Because everybody says so."

"And what about me? You don't trust my judgment?"

"I think . . . I think you travel, you hear talk and . . . I think you panic, Jakob."

"Panic? Panic? For the love of God . . ."

"Don't swear at me."

"Why not? I can't seem to talk to you."

In anger and frustration, he hung up, but Franzi calmly replaced the receiver before turning to Charlotte. "Your father's in a panic," she stated flatly and went back to making supper.

That evening, they listened to the radio broadcasting continual updates on the crisis. Finally, just after midnight, when Charlotte was already asleep, her mother came tiptoeing into her room and shook her shoulder.

"It's all right," said Franzi softly. "It's all over, everything's back to normal."

"We don't have to leave?"

"No, we don't have to leave."

The announcement had been made on the stroke of midnight by President Miklas. He told the nation that Chancellor Schuschnigg would volunteer his resignation and be replaced, as Hitler wanted, by the minister, Seyss-Inquart.

In this way, Miklas—and all of Austria—believed that the tension had been resolved and the direct threat of invasion had been averted.

What they didn't yet know was that the President's decision hadn't mattered at all, because several divisions of the German Wehrmacht had already crossed the border. They encountered no opposition whatsoever.

By daybreak, the news was widespread, and when the first battalions arrived in the city of Vienna just before midday, their commanders were astonished at the level of popular support.

The troops were given a heroic welcome by the massive crowds, dozens deep, who'd turned out in the streets to wave swastika flags and cheer enthusiastically.

As the first order of business, President Miklas was summarily dismissed, Chancellor Schuschnigg was arrested, and Seyss-Inquart was named Governor, reporting directly to the Führer.

The *Anschluss*, the total annexation of Austria by Nazi Germany, was underway with the people's overwhelming approval.

In Prague, Jakob took no solace at all in having been proven right. He'd known it would happen, was absolutely convinced in his own mind.

Back in Nuremberg, Max Grundig had even warned him to get out while he could. He should have listened and had the argument with his wife much earlier. Now it was too late. He had no contingency plan for her blind refusal.

For several hours, he paced his hotel room, listening to the bulletins, full of guilt, full of remorse. He should have gone back, he kept telling himself. Perhaps he could have somehow persuaded her if only he'd gone back. Already there'd been word around the hotel lobby that the Austrian borders had been closed at the main crossing points and would soon be sealed.

It meant that he couldn't return, even if he wished to do so, nor could his wife and daughter travel here to join him. If they'd only taken the bus the night before, they might have made it. Now, it would be all but impossible.

Once again, he tried calling, but the switchboards were all out of service, so he continued to pace the room, back and forth, trying to think up a course of action. He went down to buy a newspaper and discovered to his shock that, as a result of thousands of instant refugee applications, the immigration ministries in most of the major capitals were refusing to issue any more visas until the current state of affairs had settled and a new policy could be formalized.

This was serious and getting worse by the hour. If he didn't decide what to do soon, he'd be stuck here in Prague, using up his funds with no means of going anywhere. He sat on the narrow bed, then transferred to the tiny armchair. Then he stood by the window, which looked out upon the uninteresting courtyard where they kept the garbage.

Late one night, he'd seen several large rats running across. Today, however, there was no life at all to be seen, not even a bird. Above the roofline, a severe weather front appeared to be moving in, yet another obstruction to bar his escape.

It was the cloud formations which gave him the idea. He opened his wallet to count the cash he had left, subtracted the remaining expenses in his head—primarily his hotel bill—and figured they might just be sufficient. For another hour, he debated his emerging plan back and forth, finally arriving at the conclusion that he had no choice, none whatsoever.

He'd made up his mind. With great deliberation, he refastened his tie before putting on his coat, hat, and gloves. He took a last look in the mirror, not to check his appearance, but to confirm to himself, to his own face, that he'd made the right decision, then descended to the lobby and strode purposefully onto the street.

It was a three kilometer walk to Wenceslas Square, the long central boulevard which fronted the city's most prestigious real estate. Here were the foremost stores and showrooms, their windows full of the kind of merchandise he could never afford—handcrafted shirts, Swiss watches, and the most opulent automobiles—but he didn't have time to admire any of it, because he was on his own self-appointed mission.

Eventually, not far from the classic facade of the Hotel Europa, he spotted the familiar crown trademark he was seeking: the central sales office of KLM, Royal Dutch Airlines.

For a brief moment, he paused outside to gather himself, then swung open the door and stepped inside as if he were a millionaire. At the counter, he peeled off his gloves, unbuttoned his coat, and while he waited to be served, he placed his hand impatiently on his hip with the air of a busy executive with no time to waste.

It was an excellent portrayal, and very soon, a smart young man in a blue jacket and crested tie came scurrying over.

"Yes, sir, what can I do for you?"

"Yes, I'd like to book a flight to London. If I'm not mistaken, the connection is in Rotterdam, am I right?"

"You are indeed. And when would you like to travel?"

"As soon as possible."

"I understand, but I'm afraid you've missed today's flight."

"Then it will have to be tomorrow."

The young man pulled out a reservations ledger and proceeded to flick through the pages. "Yes sir, we're in luck, still some seats available . . . DC3 service departing for Rotterdam, Waalhaven at 8:20, connection to London, Croydon at . . . let me see . . . Ah yes, 4. 45 in the afternoon."

"Fine, I'll take it."

"How many passengers?"

"Just myself."

"And your return date?"

"One-way, if you don't mind."

"Yes, sir. If you'll give me a few minutes, I'll have your ticket prepared."

It was done. Normally, Jakob would never have thought of flying, mainly because air travel was so costly. For most of his travel, he relied on train and ferry, or he just took the bus like in his old army days. However, he figured that if he arrived in England by air, they'd treat him more like a gentleman and be less likely to suspect him of being a refugee.

He wouldn't try for any kind of immigration visa, because he knew in advance that it would just be a waste of time under the current political circumstances, gentleman or not. Chances were, they'd just refuse and deport him right back. His alternative was to request a tourist visa, nothing more complicated than that.

He would tell them he was there simply to see his brother, Herschel. No, wait, he'd have to say Harry, the English version of his brother's name—and if they asked him how long he'd be staying, his reply would be vague: a few days, or perhaps a few weeks, depending on his schedule.

Yes, he thought, that might conceivably work, and even while he was waiting for his flight ticket, he tried to get the story straight in his head. In order to pull it off, he would have to appear completely natural when he arrived, and he didn't have long to practice.

Once in London, he'd try to organize things from there. First would be the immediate wire transfer of his own funds, which should be enough to last him a while. Fortunately, he had a standing pre-signed procedure to this effect with his Viennese bank, a necessary arrangement in his line of business.

Then he'd have to apply for permanent residency for himself, his wife, and his daughter. This was not obvious at either end. In England, he was hoping that if he was already there, the political climate would be sympathetic enough that they wouldn't, in all good conscience, send him back. As far as Austria was concerned, he was hoping that after a few days, once the Nazis had consolidated control, the borders would re-open and some kind of normality would resume. Assuming all that, he'd then have to transport his family and their belongings to London, while at the same time, finding a suitable home into which they could settle.

Later, he'd need some way of generating income since his savings wouldn't last forever, and also language lessons for his wife and a school for his daughter so she could continue her education.

As he stood at the airline counter, the list of tasks appeared to rise ever higher, and even for a man of the world, well-used to life's complexities, it seemed like a vast undertaking. The only way to accomplish anything, he knew, would be to focus on one step at a time, and the first order was to make sure he got himself safely on that morning flight out of Prague.

Three days later, Charlotte was called from machine class into the principal's office. She walked nervously along the corridors, and as she tapped on the door, she was still searching her mind for what she might have done wrong.

The principal, Herr Beck, was a graying man, with a deeply lined face and round glasses perched on his nose, who seemed perpetually overwhelmed with work. When Charlotte stepped in, he barely looked up from the pile of papers on his desk.

"Telephone. They say it's urgent . . . from England."

"England?"

"Take it there."

He indicated a chair near the corner of the desk where the phone was off the hook, but Charlotte didn't sit down. She lifted the receiver immediately to her ear.

"Hello?"

"*Liebste*? Is that you?"

"*Vati?*"

"Oh, thank God."

"Are you all right?"

"Yes, I'm all right. How about you?"

"Yes, fine."

"And your mother?"

"Fine, everybody's fine. Where are you? Why are you calling me here?"

"Listen, I don't have much time. I'm in London, in a government office. They're very nice to lend me the phone but I might be cut off at any time. I had to say it was an emergency just to get the line. I couldn't reach you at home, I was worried."

"You're in London?"

"Yes, yes, it's a long story. I was in Prague but I had to leave. I'm staying with your Uncle Herschel. Now listen, you need to tell your mother something."

"Of course."

"Tell your mother it's what I feared. The borders are all closed and it's hard to get a visa to anywhere. You got that?"

"Yes . . ."

"I'll keep trying, but what she's got to do, what you've both got to do, is to start applying for a visa. You go to any embassy you can . . . England, Switzerland, France, America . . . anywhere you can go. You ask questions, you stand in line, whatever you have to do, all right? But you must try to get out of Austria. Have you got that?"

"I think so."

"Yes or no?"

"Yes, *Vati*, I've got it. Apply to the embassies for a visa."

"Tell your mother. I don't want any arguments."

"What about you? Are you coming home?"

"No, *liebste*, I told you. Now concentrate. The Austrian borders are all closed. Nobody gets in or out. I can't come home, that's why I came to England. They've been very nice to me, the people here, the officials. They're allowing me to stay for the time being, but bringing you over won't be so easy. They say you must apply to the embassy there, so that's what you'll do. You try from your end, and I'll keep trying from mine. Now please tell me you understand."

"I understand."

"Tell your mother I'll try to wire some money. The bank said they would help."

"Yes . . . yes, I'll tell her."

"Are you still there?"

"Yes."

"The line's bad. *Liebste,* I want you to do something for me . . . you, yourself. You remember I told you to be strong?"

"Strong and smart and careful."

"Good, you remember, very good. So that's what I need you to be. Strong and smart and careful. You have to take care of your mother. I'm counting on you, all right?"

"Yes, *Vati.*"

"*Liebste*, you're a wonderful girl. I just want you to know . . . I'm so proud of you."

"I'm not a girl any more, *Vati*, I just turned nineteen."

"Can I be proud of you anyway?"

She smiled, but before she could respond, her father continued with a little more urgency in his voice.

"Listen, there's someone here telling me I'm talking too much. It's my big problem in life. Will you remember everything?"

"Yes, I'll remember. *Vati*, you're all right?"

"Yes, yes, never better. I'm just worried about you. Now please do everything I've told you. I've got to go. Goodbye, *liebste*, I'll keep trying to call, but if I don't get through, don't worry, all right?"

"All right."

"I love you. Bye for now."

"Bye, *Vati*."

Charlotte heard a click and then a buzz, so she slowly placed the receiver back in its cradle. Then she glanced up, suddenly conscious that Herr Beck had been watching, his weak blue eyes gazing at her over the rim of his glasses.

"Your father's right," he told her quietly. "You should leave before it's too late."

For a while, Charlotte didn't respond, she just looked back at him sitting there behind the clutter of his desk. At last she said, "May I use your phone again? To call my mother."

Herr Beck considered the request as seriously as if she were asking for a better grade on her term examination, then gave his permission with a single nod. When she was finished, she said thank you, left the office, and walked slowly back towards her class, but she didn't enter right away. She was still thinking about the call from her father, so she just sat down on a bench in the empty corridor.

What she'd told him was true. She and her mother were indeed fine because, so far, while the German authorities were establishing themselves in the city's center, little had happened in their small neighborhood of Brigittenau.

She'd heard there were some fresh Nazi daubings on Jewish store windows down near the canal, anti-Semitic slogans and insulting caricatures, but nothing any closer to home. Yet she understood why her father had said what he did about leaving, and she understood, too, why her mother was still hesitant. Still, it was strange to think about it. Like her mother, Charlotte had lived here in this district, Bezirk 20, all her life, and the idea of just packing up to go somewhere else was a little overpowering. That evening, as she arrived home, she happened to meet her long-time friend, Trudi Hart, in the stairwell.

"Have you heard?"asked Trudi.

"Heard what?"

"Hitler's coming to Vienna."

"He is?"

"He's in Linz already but they say he'll soon be here. Want to go see him?"

"Who? Hitler?"

"Who else are we talking about?"

"Why would I want to see Hitler?"

"Because everybody does. That's what they're all talking about at school."

Trudi was at a teacher training college and Charlotte knew that many of the self-styled young intellectuals were in favor of Nazism.

"So?"asked Trudi again.

"Is it safe?"

"Are you scared?"

"No, I'm not scared. I'm just asking."

"There'll be thousands of people. Who'll notice us?"

So typical, thought Charlotte. *The world's upside down and here's Trudi, still looking for mischief.* "You're still crazy, you know that?"

"Last chance," said Trudi. "I'm going anyway. You coming with me or not?"

Charlotte shrugged. "If you like," she said.

After the first few days of the occupation, the situation in the Austrian capital began to change rapidly, and the number of citizens targeted by the Nazis seemed to be getting larger by the day, comprising a broad cross-section of society.

This included key political opponents; high ranking members of the administration or bureaucracy who had, for whatever reason, uttered negative comments; and anyone known to sympathize with the left, especially members of the Communist party.

There were also entertainers or celebrities known to have mocked the Nazi cause, either through performance, statement, or humor, as well as people thought to be homosexuals, whether known, rumored, or perceived. Many of the victims were degenerate or homeless.

Then, of course, there was the ten percent of the Viennese population who were ethnically Jewish, whether Hasid, Orthodox, Conservative, or Reform, as well as those who believed they were totally assimilated.

By the end of the second week, a total of over seventy thousand had been questioned or arrested. By contrast, the rest of the two million citizens tended to support these measures, choosing to accept what the mass media was now telling them: that those seized had been a danger to society and that the evil had to be purged to restore order and guard the purity of Austrian life.

The staff at the main broadcasting authority, the government-owned Radio Wien, had been redirected to offer such propaganda.

While the main newspapers were still in private hands, they had also begun to censor themselves in favor of the new regime, either through their own ideological support or, for those with a conscience, through fear of reprisals.

In Brigittenau, the disruptions to daily life were becoming especially heinous. The Brownshirt thugs with their swastika armbands, known officially as the *Sturmabteilung*, or SA for short, were not only more prominent, they were also becoming more arrogant as the regular police found themselves powerless to prevent, or even intervene, in the most violent activities.

Jewish store windows were crudely painted with admonitions not to buy at those establishments, the old and the bearded were physically taunted on the sidewalks, and women who looked Jewish were accosted according to whim.

While such behavior was formally encouraged due to Nazi doctrine, most of the day-to-day incidents occurred for the sake of mere amusement, with the instigators flaunting their enjoyment by laughing and showing off.

This meant that for Charlotte and Trudi, an adventure into the city center had turned into a dangerous proposition. Their destination was the Heldenplatz in front of the Hofburg, where a crowd of two hundred thousand was gathering to listen to their new Führer, the native son of Austria who was now being hailed as a liberator.

Fortunately, Trudi had been right. Nobody took any notice of them as they edged their way forward. Indeed, the two girls managed to get so close that Charlotte spent most of the time gazing at the intensity in Hitler's eyes and the bombastic nature of his gestures, twin fists pounding the air, arms raised and lowered to emphasize his intonations.

She didn't really listen to the speech because she didn't actually care what he was saying, and anyway, she'd heard most of it before on the radio.

What did amuse her a little, however, was when he invoked God as his reason for returning to Austria. She knew well enough he was just favoring the Catholic crowd, but it nonetheless struck her as ironic, and she wondered what her father would have said about that.

After an hour, she'd had enough, and when the crowds around her began to respond with repetitive chants and stiff-armed salutes, she began to tug at Trudi's sleeve. It was time for them to slip away and they were able to leave as inconspicuously as they'd arrived.

Hitler's speech had been well-timed to inspire a national plebiscite scheduled for the very next day, designed to provide international legitimacy to the new state of affairs.

Since the vote was controlled by the Nazi party, it was organized as an open, not a secret, ballot with all the intimidation that such an arrangement implied. Who would ever mark no to the *Anschluss*, the formal annexation, with the Brownshirts looking over every shoulder?

A further restriction was that Communists and Jews were banned from voting but that didn't matter. The decision was pre-determined, and when the result was announced with over ninety-nine percent in favor, nobody was very surprised

Since the nations of the world preferred to choose acquiescence over confrontation, the engineered verdict thereby became an established fact, a *fait accompli* in the international language of diplomacy.

After less than two decades of its existence, the independent republic of Austria had simply ceased to exist.

The territory was officially re-named the province of Ostmark and completely absorbed as a contiguous part of the Greater German Reich.

On the same day that Charlotte skipped school to go with Trudi to the Heldenplatz, Franzi paid a visit to her mother in the old apartment on Wallensteinstrasse. Ostensibly, it was to see her father, who wasn't doing at all well—both his physical condition and his mental state had seriously deteriorated—but in reality, she needed some advice. Next to her at the small kitchen table sat her mother, her slim fingers rubbed raw as she made the traditional *helzel.* It involved stuffing the skin of a chicken neck with flour, *schmaltz* and fried onion, then sewing together the opening with a stout needle and thread.

"Jakob is nagging me to leave," Franzi said, as she blew on a scalding glass of tea.

"You should," replied her mother.

As Franzi sipped at her drink, she glanced across at her father in his armchair, coddled in blankets and wheezing slightly, his expression vacant. "How can I leave when he's like that?"

"You can't worry about us. That's what I told your sister and now I'm telling you, too. It's not good here and it's going to get worse. Get out while you can."

Franzi didn't know what to say. She knew that Paula and her husband were already making plans to cross the border into Switzerland, if not legally, then by other means. However, it was easier for them. They had the great Rothschild organization to help them out. For Franzi, it meant applying to the embassies like everybody else and already the lines were stretching for blocks.

"I don't know, *Mutti*. I just don't know."

"How can you talk like that? You have a child. If you don't know for yourself, how can you ignore your child? She's young, she's got a life to live. What kind of future does she have here, can you tell me that?"

"But what about you? What about *Vati*?"

"I told you, we'll be all right. When Paula gets to Zurich, she'll pull some strings. She'll get us out."

"You think so?"

"You just take care of your daughter. That's your responsibility now."

Franzi looked around at her father, at this apartment where she grew up, at the table under which she'd been quietly reading the day Jakob first arrived. Her parents had been highly respected back then and her life had been stable. How could it be, she wondered, that such a safe world could be so turned upside down?

The husband she'd never loved had basically abandoned her to live his life of travel, and now she'd been left alone in dire circumstances, with the Brownshirts and the Gestapo around every corner, and the responsibility of a grown daughter of her own. How had this happened? By whose authority? In her own mind, it was all so unfair.

Each time Charlotte told me another chapter of the story, I had dozens of questions. What were certain individuals like? Where did they live and what did they do? How did they behave? How did they dress? What did they eat? What did they say? What was the reply? What else happened on that day, that week, that month? How did the newspapers or the radio describe it at the time?

It was always interesting, often fascinating, and I wanted to know the background context as much as the main story, the more details the better.

At first, I developed the notion that her anecdotes were like a living history, the recollection of a key period enriched by personal perspective. However, over the years, I came to change that point-of-view, and it only happened when I began to realize that the questions she found easiest were the basic facts of everyday existence: the streets, the food, the politics—especially the politics, for which she seemed to have an intuitive grasp.

She may have forgotten a few aspects, and sometimes her descriptions were a little vague, but she had no problem attempting a response. What she found far more troubling was when I tried to delve into motivations, especially when it concerned her mother.

Why did she do this? Why did she say that? Occasionally, there seemed to be no logic to any of it, but when I tried to probe further, Charlotte would give me the same reply.

"I don't know, it's not a movie."

Of course, in her own way she was trying to tell me that people are not one-dimensional. They're unpredictable and it's impossible to know what they're thinking, how they're framing events and how they choose to justify their actions, even to themselves.

However, in this instance, I think her mother's state of mind was so confused that any attempt at understanding was bound to fail, especially for a nineteen-year-old girl. Like mothers and daughters of every era, theirs was a complex relationship, but the most fundamental aspect was that while Franzi was struggling to cope with the predicament in which she found herself, Charlotte was striving just as hard to comprehend her mother.

From all of this, I learned to appreciate that the narrative I was hearing wasn't so much historical and factual as psychological and emotional. The fact that it was set against a unique and increasingly desperate backdrop of circumstances was not nearly as poignant as the central relationships involved.

In the end, what drove Charlotte to tears in those conversational sessions of ours was not how she suffered from hardship or privation, but how her foundation of trust was so devastated.

7

While Jakob was scurrying all over London from one government office to another, Franzi began dutifully lining up at the embassies as he'd suggested: one night here, another night there.

The problem was not in achieving a simple yes-or-no answer to obtaining a visa, it was the lack of any kind of answer at all. The speed at which events had transpired in both Germany and Austria meant that the great democracies were undecided about what to do. Governments everywhere were deeply divided and their policies in a state of flux.

Many of the individuals in authority were privately in favor of Hitler's racial laws, and it meant that formulating some kind of solution for the millions of would-be refugees was unattainable.

So while the debates were raging, the various ministries and departments charged with the responsibility opted for a safe middle course, which would neither tilt the balance, nor accomplish anything of consequence.

In practice, this meant that embassies were instructed to register all applicants for asylum as a way of portraying sincere goodwill, but without actually processing any such requests.

However, the would-be claimants had no knowledge of this official subterfuge, and the mere fact that the doors were open to receive inquiries encouraged them to spend their days and nights in hope, patiently standing on the sidewalks in teams of two and three, so that one could leave to bring back sustenance for the others without losing their place.

Unfortunately, it also meant they became a convenient target.

The first evening, straight from school, Charlotte went with her mother by Stadtbahn to the British embassy, an imposing, neo-classical structure on Jauresgasse in Bezirk 3, south of the Altstadt.

Spring had already arrived in the city, so at least the weather was amenable, but they were shocked to see how far back in line they had to stand.

Worse, it appeared to be hardly moving at all, so all they could do was settle in and eat the cold supper of bread and salted fish that Franzi had brought, while shuffling along a couple of paces every fifteen minutes or so.

The trouble happened soon after seven. It began with a group from the *Hitlerjugend*, the Hitler youth organization which had grown substantially in just a few short weeks.

They were boys of sixteen or seventeen in their group uniforms, on their way to some rally and all in high spirits. While it appeared that they hadn't really targeted the waiting lines, that they just happened to be passing, they couldn't resist the urge to demonstrate their loyalty to the cause as well as their collective sense of bravado.

At first, it was pointing and jeering from the other side of the street, a random calling of the officially sanctioned epithets they'd been taught by the SA Brownshirts: *Untermenschen*, sub-humans; and *Die Jüdensindunser Unglück*, the Jews are our misfortune.

With all the noise and laughter, a crowd soon began forming to see what the disturbance was about. People came out of buildings and cafés, others leaned out of windows. This only encouraged the boys who now felt they were the stars of the show, so they began edging off the curb and out on to the road.

At this time of night, there was little traffic. Then, the one who seemed to be the leader pushed another all the way across and gave him a dare. For a moment, this other youth, younger and leaner with scruffy hair and wild eyes, looked around for encouragement.

When he received it in the form of cheers, he ventured forward, not far from where Franzi and Charlotte were standing, puckered up and launched a globule of spit towards the line. It didn't reach its target, but it brought out a round of applause from some of the bystanders and caused the people in line to shy away.

As for Charlotte, her immediate thought was of the time years back when her friend did exactly the same from the upstairs apartment, and she didn't take the attack seriously. To her it was more of a prank, but when she saw the look of agitation in the people around her, especially in the eyes of her mother, she instinctively stepped in front, using her body as a shield.

As an athletic nineteen-year-old, she was as tall, and probably as strong, as the boy facing her, and her movement challenged him to come any closer. For that brief moment, he stared at her, but then with a big grin, he scampered back to his friends across the street, as if his mission had been accomplished. At that point, Charlotte turned to find her mother visibly shaken, so she put her arm around those tiny shoulders and tried to calm her down.

"It's all right," she kept saying. "It's all right, I won't let them hurt you."

As the seasons changed from fresh to sultry, Charlotte and her mother spent at least two evenings each week lining up at the embassies. Only once did they even see a member of staff, when a junior American attaché stood on the steps to read a formal announcement.

By order of the State Department, they were shutting down their consular services in Vienna until further notice, and all future requests would have to be made through Berlin. The idea of applying to the heart of Nazi Germany was such a ridiculous notion that, for many in line, the frustration gave way to scorn and they laughed outright.

Then, one day, Charlotte arrived home from college at the usual time, ready to change and go out again, this time to the French embassy, but she found her mother at the table with her head in her hands.

"*Mutti*? What is it?"

Franzi couldn't answer. She just shook her head.

"*Mutti*? What happened?"

When her mother finally looked up, she seemed weary, as if it were all too much for her. Her complexion, pale at the best of times, now looked almost white.

"I tried," she said softly. "I tried."

Charlotte sat down next to her and stroked her hand. "Tell me what happened."

Franzi took a deep breath to try to pull herself together. "I had to go to the butcher. What we've got left, the *flanken* I was saving . . . It turned, you know, in the heat, so I had to go, but . . ."

"But what? What?"

"Twice I tried, but they were there, waiting."

Now Charlotte knew exactly what she was talking about: the SA Brownshirts, who'd taken to wandering the streets of local neighborhoods, deliberately making trouble and causing disturbance.

It was part of the overall plan to drive the Jewish population away, and it was working, too, except for the fact that there was no country which would take them. Meanwhile, the SA kept up their harassment, and the community of Brigittenau continued to suffer.

Charlotte glanced at the small clock on the mantel. Her father had brought it back from a trip to Switzerland as a household gift. "Want to go now? They might still be open."

"We were supposed to go to the embassy . . ."

"I know but we have to eat. Come on, let's try to get to the butcher again. I'll go with you. Which was it? Rosenbaum?"

Franzi nodded. "What if—"

"We have to eat."

Gently, Charlotte helped her mother pull herself together. Then they took their purses and baskets and descended tentatively to the street. Even at five-thirty in the afternoon, it was still exceptionally warm, and the pavement shimmered before them.

So far, though, so good. On Staudingergasse, there was no sign of any untoward activity, so they marched on, heading south on Treustrasse, past the primary school that Charlotte had once attended—it seemed so long ago—and on towards the canal area of Leopoldstadt. Here, the lanes and alleyways were narrow and interlocking, so they couldn't see very far ahead at any one time. All they could do as they turned each corner was hope that the next block would be clear.

"You see?" said Charlotte, when they finally reached Rosenbaum's. "It's fine, no problem at all."

They were there less than ten minutes, just enough time for Franzi to select a couple of cheap cuts, which was basically all that was left on the shelves. Here, too, the meat went off quickly, especially by late afternoon when the day's stock of ice had mostly melted.

It was just as Franzi and Charlotte were leaving that they ran into them: two Brownshirts leaning against a wall chatting amiably as if just out for some air. Franzi tensed but Charlotte had her arm tightly linked in hers. She encouraged her mother to keep walking, not to look at them, but it was too late.

The older of the two eased himself off the wall and wandered across to them. He was of average height and had thinning black hair but he affected a tough appearance, with a day's stubble on his chin and a vaguely red area on his neck, as if he'd been injured or burned as a child.

"Good evening," he said with a look of mild amusement. "Beautiful summer weather."

Charlotte could tell that his overly polite pleasantries were merely a contrived act for his own bored enjoyment, and she'd have preferred to ignore him, but she could feel her mother starting to tremble, so she had no choice but to speak up in response.

"Good evening," she replied, her voice wary.

"Your papers, if you please."

Franzi and Charlotte opened up their bags and took out their identification documents without saying anything. The man held out his hand, snapping his fingers until he received them, but still with that infuriating smile on his face.

"Frau Goldberger . . . and Fräulein Goldberger. Perhaps I'm mistaken, but these appear to be Jewish names," he said, feigning surprise. "Well, well, you're in luck. You're going to have the privilege of helping to keep our Reich clean." He began to copy their names and addresses into a small notebook.

"Tomorrow morning, both of you, nine-thirty sharp at Scholzgasse. We know where you live, so don't even think about not showing up, otherwise . . . Well, let's not get into that on such a beautiful day. Bring buckets, brushes, and soap, and be prepared to do your duty, understand?"

He looked directly at Franzi, but she seemed unable to respond, so once again, it was up to Charlotte.

"We understand."

He gave a single nod, then sauntered back to his friend, and they began talking again as if nothing had happened.

Charlotte hurried her mother away, walking at a rapid pace all the way back to the apartment. Once inside, they prepared the meal together in silence, with all thoughts of the embassy now gone. Every so often, while they were eating and then while tidying up the small kitchen afterwards, Charlotte caught Franzi gazing at the telephone, almost willing it to work just by looking at it, but their line had long since been cut, and even if it hadn't, there was nobody to call.

The police were no longer able to do their jobs with any sense of independence, and the one Jewish officer, the same man who'd attended Franzi's wedding, had somehow vanished. Even his family didn't know where he was, which meant he was either in a Gestapo cell block, or he'd been consigned to the hell of Dachau near Munich, one of the recently enlarged Kz camps run by the German Reich. Neither augured well for his survival.

At least the radio was still working, and both mother and daughter stayed up past midnight, with Franzi reading and Charlotte sewing while they listened to the melodies of Puccini's *Turandot* until both fell asleep in their chairs, exhausted from the nervous tension.

At daybreak, they were still fatigued, but they didn't dare disobey the order from the SA, so with some haste, they washed and dressed, then forced themselves to chew on some bread with *schmaltz* and drink a little tea before setting out.

It was embarrassing to be carrying buckets with soap and scrubbing brushes along the streets, because it meant that everyone knew where they were going and what they were about to do. Yet what choice did they have? They'd been told to report to Scholzgasse, and so just before nine-thirty, that's what they did.

There were others already there, about half-a-dozen Jews, none of whom they recognized, all in the process of filling their pails from a rusted spigot in the side-yard of a hardware store. Supervising them were three Brownshirts: one giving the orders; another holding a menacing wooden club; and a third, overweight, just watching lazily with his thumbs in his belt.

There were also bystanders, as there had been outside the British embassy and as there were on all such occasions, emerging as if from nowhere to applaud the public humiliation. Some must have been Nazi supporters even before the *Anschluss,* but most were neophytes, converted to the cause as if by some mass epiphany.

Previously, they'd been friendly and accommodating but now they suddenly realized that they'd never really liked their ethnic neighbors. Naturally, not all the Viennese population was like that.

Many felt guilty for what was happening, and a few still tried to help in their own limited way, but there were always enough of these instant party members on hand to form a jeering crowd at any street spectacle.

Charlotte and her mother filled their buckets like the others and were then ordered to get down on their knees and start scrubbing.

The task was to clean some Communist graffiti from the sidewalks, whitewashed slogans about Stalin and the working class, all essentially meaningless, but nevertheless, someone had insisted they be cleaned up so Jews had been rounded up to do the job. The harder they worked, they were told, the sooner they could go back to their miserable lives.

As the morning progressed, the sun grew stronger. Sweat was starting to dribble down Jewish foreheads but none of them could afford to relent. One heavy blow from that club could cripple their bones and consign them to life as a paraplegic.

The pressure to continue was intense and one older man in particular was feeling the strain. Franzi, on her knees next to him, offered him a few whispered words of encouragement, but one of the Brownshirts—the heavy one who'd had his thumbs in his belt—heard her and wandered over.

"You!" he said sharply, pointing directly at Franzi. "What were you talking about?"

She answered without even daring to look up. "Nothing," she said quietly.

That's when he began to take a closer interest in her, leaning over to touch her hair. When she recoiled, he grabbed hold of it, forcing her face upwards.

"Are you Jewish?" he demanded. "You don't look Jewish."

She said nothing, but she was visibly shaking.

From a couple of meters away, Charlotte tried to watch out for her as best she could, but there was little she could do. There was no resistance she could offer other than hurling herself forward, and even that would have been of little use.

Unlike the *Hitlerjugend* at the embassy, these weren't boys goading each other, they were street-hardened ruffians with no trepidation. Perhaps, in another existence, they'd be criminals or hoodlums, but here in the Greater Reich, they were given uniforms and armbands and an ideology declaring that force equals power, to which they could well relate.

Meanwhile, the man refused to let up. He seemed to be fixated on Franzi. "I asked you a question," he said to her, his voice taking on a threatening tone.

Once again, Franzi didn't respond, but instead of losing interest as she hoped, the Brownshirt just became even more annoyed and kicked at her thin wrist with the hard toecap of his boot. It wasn't severe, just a way to get her attention, but it caused her pain, and she had to muffle the cry.

"You ignore me when I'm talking to you? Maybe you'd like another duty this afternoon? Plenty of streets to scrub."

That was when the *kommandant* noticed what was happening and immediately broke it up by swearing at his own man, instructing him to back off otherwise the whole job would fall behind schedule. The graffiti paint was proving to be stubborn, and the cheap household soap was hardly adequate. Turpentine would have been far more effective, but there was none available, and anyway, that wasn't the point. The exercise was designed primarily as degradation.

When the allotted time was up, the task still wasn't complete, but the scrawled words were no longer legible, so the result was deemed sufficient and the detainees released. Slowly, Charlotte got to her feet. Despite her fitness, she found that her back and shoulders ached from the effort.

How much worse must it be, she thought, *for the others who were older and less able?* She wiped her forehead, straightened out her clothes with as much dignity as she could muster, and then turned her attention to her mother, whose wrist had turned red and slightly swollen from the kick. It might have been bruised, sprained, or fractured, there was no way to know.

The man responsible for the injury still wasn't prepared to let it go. "This afternoon," he said, "the two of you, report to the Gaussplatz."

It was Charlotte who dared to reply, "She can't do it, she's hurt."

"Hurt?" screamed the man. "I'll show her hurt."

He raised his hand high for the blow, but found his arm held from behind by the *kommandant* who demanded to know what the devil was going on, but no sooner had the explanation begun than he silenced it.

"Enough," he replied, without hiding his impatience. "At this rate, I'll never get any damned lunch." Then he looked at Charlotte. "She's your mother?"

"Yes."

"Get her out of here."

Charlotte would have been more than content to do so but she hesitated. "Gaussplatz is on our way home," she said. "If we're asked to work again . . ."

The *kommandant* sighed, but he seemed to have a bureaucratic mindset, and contrary to all expectations, actually paused to consider the problem. He felt around in his pockets, then pulled out a stubby pencil and a package of branded paper, the kind used for rolling cigarettes.

With great deliberation, he removed one of the small sheets, put the rest back in his pocket and proceeded to write a short note. At the end, he signed it. "If they stop you, show them that," he said.

Charlotte took the piece of paper she was handed. If she was surprised at this unlikely occurrence, she didn't show it. She just nodded her thanks before leading her mother away.

In London, Jakob returned from yet another futile trip to yet another bureaucratic department, only to hear his brother, Harry, ask the same inevitable question.

"Any luck?"

They were both still living under the same roof in Harry's apartment, located in the Jewish neighborhood of Whitechapel in the East End. Although Harry was in business for himself, restoring penny slot machines and redistributing them to amusement arcades in the Essex area, the economic depression had affected him, like everyone else, and his life hadn't substantially advanced in several years.

Jakob eased himself down in one of his brother's decrepit armchairs and shook his head. "*Bupkis*," he replied, using the Yiddish slang for "nothing at all." Literally, it meant "droppings."

In the time he'd been there, his initially limited English had improved considerably, to the point that he could now hold an adequate conversation with any junior civil servant and even pose the right questions, but he still sometimes lapsed into the comfort of Yiddish when he was here with Harry and his wife, Leah. They had a son, too, about Charlotte's age, a corporal in the British army, but he was rarely home.

"What will you do next?" asked Harry, his attitude sympathetic. Although he hadn't seen his brother for years before the latter's arrival, they looked remarkably alike. Both had added a few pounds around the waist as they moved towards middle-age, and both had lost the majority of their hair.

"*Werweiss*?" answered Jakob. Who knows?

"Did you try calling Vienna again?"

"Try? I do nothing but try. Every day, I try. What good does it do?"

Jakob had already assumed that his own home line had been cut, but for the last month, he hadn't even been able to call Charlotte at the school either because the principal there, Herr Beck, refused to put him through. When Jakob reminded the man he was still paying Charlotte's tuition, there were many apologies.

Herr Beck said he appreciated the problem, he really did, but he was under pressure from his board of governors, and there was nothing he could do. Charlotte was still welcome as a student, but he had to be far more careful these days and hoped that Herr Goldberger would understand the unfortunate position in which he found himself.

What could Jakob say to that? As long as Charlotte was in Vienna, she would need an education, and so far, there was no indication from any quarter that he'd be able to get either his wife or his daughter out of there. While his own status as a refugee was confirmed, insomuch as they wouldn't physically deport him, entry was barred to all others, even family members, until government policies were finalized—and, no, they didn't know when that would be.

They weren't in charge, they kept telling him. They were just civil servants. They didn't make the rules, they just followed them.

For Jakob, who understood how democracies worked, the excuse was reasonably valid, but he got so tired of hearing it, he wanted to scream.

Meanwhile, he gleaned information about the situation back home from wherever he could find it. He wrote avidly to Franzi but hadn't received any letters back for some time. From other émigrés and refugees, he tried to learn what was going on but it was difficult to separate truth from rumor.

He read the papers and listened to the radio, but while the BBC was reliable enough, there was never anything specific about the Jews of Vienna.

One time, he managed to reach Berthe in Poland and although she was able to assure him that his own family there in Krakow was fine, their aging father and their alcoholic brother, she'd heard nothing recently from what had once been Austria. Jakob was frustrated by the lack of definite news but he didn't panic because he was long past that stage. When he'd first arrived, he'd been frenetic, running all over the place, never able to sit for longer than a minute at a time, but now he was just weary, his energy dissipated.

Every day, he tried hard to keep going, to keep asking and searching, but he was fatigued from the sheer effort of it all and worn out from the constant anxiety.

There was another factor preying on his mind, too. Sometime soon, Jakob knew, he'd have to begin working to support himself and that would give him even less time to apply for documents or seek out news. His brother had been wonderful, taking him in and even promising to find him some kind of occupation, but Jakob didn't want to take advantage for too long.

That wasn't his way. He still had his dignity, and without that, he felt he might as well just give up.

By the time the leaves in the Augarten were turning, Charlotte could sense that Franzi was starting to worry about money. She saw her mother scribbling arithmetic on small scraps of paper, trying to eke out the funds that Jakob had managed to wire through, but they were steadily being depleted.

No matter how carefully they were managed, the sum would continue to diminish until it disappeared—and then what? Charlotte's grandparents, Herr and Frau Gutmann, were still receiving small amounts from Paula and her husband, who were already in Zurich, but nobody knew how long that could last.

Besides, there was no way Franzi could ask Paula for equal consideration. It wasn't her sister's fault that Jakob had departed for England, nor was it her responsibility.

Meanwhile, around the neighborhood, living conditions had deteriorated rapidly after the introduction in May of the Nuremberg laws, with each new rule, each further restriction, adding to the burden.

Jews were now denied access to many professions and guilds, and those already established were ejected, no matter what their standing or reputation. Citizens of Jewish origin were also denied voting rights, licensing permits, bank credit, and other aspects of statehood that most people took for granted.

Passports, certificates, qualifications, and other official documents were stamped with *J* for *Jüden*. They could only shop at certain stores, could only ride in the back of streetcars, and had to step off the sidewalk into the gutter whenever they passed a Brownshirt or other uniformed official in the street.

Worse than all of that, however, was the daily abuse, a continual plague of fear that damaged nerves and decimated civilized existence.

During this time, Charlotte tried to remember her father's words, "strong, smart and careful," but it was hard, sometimes exceptionally so.

She continued to attend the Drejährige Fachschule because her principal, Herr Beck, was willing to defy authority by keeping his Jewish pupils enrolled—it was a Jewish area and he would have lost half his revenue—but others amongst the staff and students made Charlotte's life there almost unbearable.

She was called disgusting names and deliberately jostled in the corridors, sometimes causing her to drop what she was carrying. Close friends like Magda tried to guard her as best they could by accompanying her to class and sitting with her, but they, too, found it awkward. To compensate, Charlotte still smiled along, still tried to have fun, but she wasn't sure how much longer she could bear the harassment.

Her only mental relaxation was at home in the apartment with her mother. There were endless chores, trying to put meals together and make do with the little they had, but at least while they were inside the front door, they could quietly listen to music on the radio and feel relatively safe. However, even that minimal sense of security was challenged one terrifying night in November when the Brownshirt packs were finally unleashed.

As usual, mother and daughter were alone together all evening. After dinner, Charlotte finished up a homework assignment, while Franzi allowed herself the increasingly rare luxury of reading just for the pleasure of it.

At about quarter past eleven, they switched off the music and were about ready for sleep when there was a knock on the door. It was Charlotte who went to answer it and found Frau Hart, Trudi's mother, in a highly agitated state.

She was wearing her good coat and shoes as if she'd just returned from somewhere, but strands of her hair were stuck to the perspiration on her face.

"Don't go out," she said, her voice filled with anxiety.

"It's late," replied Charlotte, "we're not going anywhere."

"Good, good, so lock your door. Make sure. They're going crazy out there."

By this time, Franzi had also arrived to find out what all the fuss was about. "What's going on?" she asked. "Who's going crazy?"

"The SA . . . My God, they're burning everything."

"What? Slow down. You want to come inside?"

"No, no, I've got to get home. Just lock your door."

She turned to run upstairs to her apartment, but Charlotte reached out and held on to her sleeve, intent on knowing what was happening.

"What are they burning?"

"Everything," said the woman. "I saw it. I watched. I couldn't believe it. I was lucky they didn't see me. They're everywhere, smashing and burning, with the police and the fire brigade just standing around, doing nothing. All the Jewish stores, the buildings, the *schuls,* too, with all the books. Anything they can get their hands on."

"The *schuls,* too?" said Franzi. It was Yiddish for synagogue, a language she never normally used.

"I told you, they're destroying everything. I've got to get home." She pulled her arm away from Charlotte and ran upstairs to her own apartment, almost tripping over the stairs in her haste.

It was Franzi who closed the front door. She was trembling again, just like when they were cleaning the street, but she made sure to fasten the lock. "Let's turn on the radio again," she said as she tried to steady herself. "Maybe there's some news."

They waited nearly forty more minutes for the midnight bulletin and that's when they heard it, the leading news item.

"Good evening, this is Radio Wien. Tonight, spontaneous public demonstrations are reported in many locations across the Reich, protesting against the cold-blooded assassination of the chargé d'affaires, *Ernst vom Rath, by the 17-year-old Jew, Herschel Grynszpan. Here in Ostmark, damage to Jewish property is extensive, and security forces have been put on alert. Authorities are asking all citizens to remain calm and to stay indoors."*

At its conclusion, Charlotte looked over at her mother whose face now seemed ashen. Then she got up and went over to the window, looking left and right in order to check what might be happening.

"Do you see anything?" asked Franzi.

"Not in the street, but there's a kind of glow in the sky, a red glow. You think Frau Hart is right? You think they're burning the synagogues?"

"I don't know. How can I know? Come away from the window, please."

"I think I see something. Some men on the corner."

"Come away from there, will you? Do as you're told."

A tremor had entered her mother's voice, so Charlotte obediently moved away while Franzi switched off the radio and turned out the light. The immediate darkness and the accompanying silence merely served to magnify the tension and intensify the amber glow outside. Sleep would be impossible on such a night so, instead of retiring to bed, they just sat there silently in the living room, fully dressed, as the time passed.

Then her mother stirred. "Do you hear something?"

They both listened intently to what sounded like noise in the street. It was low at first, then seemed to get louder as it came closer.

There were voices shouting, then something breaking, the smashing of glass, the splintering of wood. Charlotte moved to sit next to her fearful mother, putting her arm around Franzi's shoulders and wishing it would just all go away.

It was inconceivable that this could be happening here in their beautiful Vienna, city of literature and music and learning, as if half a millennium of cultural development was being blown away like smoke into that incandescent night sky.

They waited but the disturbance didn't pass. It approached the building until the noise reached the sidewalk just below the Goldbergers' third floor window.

Then, suddenly, there were men inside and Charlotte saw the expression of terror on her mother's face, felt the grip of those small fingers tightening around her own. The voices were in the hallway now and there were boots on the stone stairs.

"Quick," whispered Franzi, "run, hide yourself."

She tried to push Charlotte away but Charlotte wouldn't move.

"Hide where?"

Franzi glanced around frantically. "In the closet."

"What about you?"

"I'll be all right."

"No . . ."

"I don't look so Jewish, they said so."

"*Mutti*, there's a mezuzah on the door."

"So I'll tell them I'm the housekeeper. Now go, quickly."

"The housekeeper? What if they ask for your papers?"

Franzi was becoming ever more agitated. "*Liebste*, don't argue, just go."

"No," said Charlotte firmly. "Not without you."

She took her mother by the arm and led her over to the broom closet off the kitchen, a dark, cramped space where they kept the ironing board and the cleaning materials. Franzi was no longer able to form a rational objection, so she just nodded, and they both squeezed inside as best they could.

Then Charlotte pulled the door shut and they just stood there, with the strong stench of disinfectant tearing at their sinuses and their throats. They could hear the intruders coming closer, climbing each staircase, first the second and then to their own third floor. By this time, the two women were huddled so close that Charlotte thought she could feel her mother's heart pounding rapidly. They both closed their eyes and even stopped breathing in case it might be audible from outside.

A minute went by, then another.

The loud voices were right outside the door. Charlotte and Franzi waited, waited ... but nothing happened. There were no fists pounding, no locks broken, no wood shattering. The invaders had moved on, their boots continuing along the corridor, moving farther and farther away. It was as if some Passover angel had intervened to save them.

Only then did Charlotte allow herself to breathe. "Do you think ..." she began.

The words were so muffled they were almost unintelligible, but even that was too much for her mother, who put a single index finger on Charlotte's lips to indicate the need for continued silence as the men tramped heavily upstairs.

There were doors banging, men arguing and swearing, then cries of pain: a woman screaming, a man in agony; and this time it was Franzi who couldn't help muttering: "My God, the Harts."

All Charlotte could think about was her friend, Trudi; so full of fun and mischief that they had even gone to see Hitler together. She felt like charging up there to challenge the hordes, but managed to hold herself back.

Apart from the suicidal nature of such an attack, she couldn't leave her mother here like this, so she just remained in the darkness, ashamed that she couldn't do more. The dank smell made her want to vomit, but the real problem was inside her head, where her imagination was creating havoc.

For another hour or so, they waited. Then, when they were sure it was clear, Charlotte pushed open the closet door, a millimeter at a time, before stepping out. Yet, still, they didn't touch the lights, didn't play the radio; they just went to sit together as they had before.

Would the SA come back? They didn't know. Had they invaded the Hart apartment? This, too, they didn't know. After a while, Charlotte allowed her eyes to fall shut from nervous exhaustion, but when she woke again at some time close to dawn she saw in the dim light that her mother was still wide awake, her eyes fixated on nothing at all.

All was silent now, as if it had merely been some grotesque nightmare, and Charlotte's neck felt stiff from having slept in a bad position. To get some circulation going, she got up from the chair and went into the kitchen with the notion of making tea.

However, before she could boil the kettle, she heard a faint tap on the front door. Charlotte saw her mother look up, wide-eyed, so she gestured her to remain seated while she went to answer it.

Again, there came a gentle tap. It didn't sound like the SA, it was too gentle, too polite. Carefully, Charlotte opened the door to see the building janitor.

"Are you all right?" asked Frau Graebner, her voice remarkably soft for such a big woman.

"Yes, thank you."

"And your mother? How about your mother?"

"She's fine."

"Good, that's good. You know, I told them."

"Told who?"

"The men. I told them not to touch you. 'Don't touch the women in apartment eleven,' I said, 'otherwise I'll get my son on to you.' He's a *kommandant*, you know, in the SA."

"No, I didn't know."

"Just as well for you."

Charlotte wasn't sure what to say. "Yes . . . yes, I suppose so. Thank you . . . Thank you very much."

"You tell your mother not to worry. Where's your father these days?"

"He's out of the country . . . in England."

"England? Is that right? Well, you ask me, he should stay there. They'll be arresting lots of Jews today . . . the men, just the men, my son told me."

"Why? I mean, why would they arrest them? Why just the men?"

"Why? I'll tell you why, because somebody's got to pay for all the damage, that's why."

"But . . ." Charlotte was about to say that Jews were the victims, that it made no sense they should have to pay for damage caused by the SA, but she held back. After all, the woman had performed an act of kindness—and anyway, there was no point discussing Nazi ideology when her son was already a *kommandant* with the Brownshirts.

Such an argument would get nowhere, so Charlotte changed her tone. "Do you know, by any chance, what happened upstairs? Was it the Harts' apartment?"

"The Harts? No, no, it was that man next door to them, the new tenant there, Weisskopf. He said something to them."

"What happened?"

"What do you think happened? He said something he shouldn't and they taught him a lesson."

"Is he all right?"

"Who knows?"

Charlotte found it hard to understand this woman, but once again, she kept any reaction to herself. When the door was finally closed, she returned to tell her mother what Frau Graebner had done.

Franzi, too, had no explanation for the woman's actions. "That's just how it is," she remarked. Then she repeated it with a long sigh, as if summarizing the entire universe in five words. "That's just how it is."

In London on that same Thursday morning, a shocked and anxious Jakob read the news of what happened. Even with his limited English, he painstakingly read every story in the *Times*, *Telegraph, Mail,* and *Express* that related to the events in Vienna.

He listened to radio, talked to his brother, even spoke to strangers along Whitechapel if he was convinced they were Jewish. He tried to glean every morsel of information from every source, but he just couldn't uncover enough details.

Correspondents on the scene in Vienna had written that all the city's synagogues had been destroyed—"burned and pillaged," as one described it—but Jakob found it hard to believe that none were left standing. There had been dozens of them.

In addition to the temple on Klukygasse where he and Franzi were married and Charlotte had celebrated her Bat Mitzvah, he knew of others on Hubergasse, Leopoldgasse, Turnergasse, Humboldtplatz, Müllnergasse, Neudeggergasse, Siebenbrunnengasse, Zirkusgasse . . .

Surely, he thought, not all of them were gone. The papers also reported that most Jewish stores had been plundered and ransacked, that six thousand Jewish males had been arrested, either jailed or sent directly to Dachau, that some had been killed, beaten to death with wooden clubs or iron bars, and that a few had even committed suicide in despair.

He read it all, but Jakob tended to discount much of it as exaggeration, just a way to sell newspapers—or that's what he told himself. He recalled that during the Great War, nationalist propaganda had claimed that the enemy played football with babies' heads, but that turned out not to be true either.

That's why he kept asking people for information: to know what they thought, to find out if they believed it. From one man, he heard that it was now being called "*Kristallnacht,*" or "Night of Crystal", from the shards of smashed glass that were strewn across the streets, but Jakob merely scoffed at that.

How could anyone come up with such a poetic name, he wondered, for such an ugly episode? However, this reaction was just his frustration at not knowing enough details, magnified by the profound guilt of not having been there. He'd left his family to face it alone.

He'd thought he was doing the right thing, the wise thing, but now he didn't even know if they were alive or dead, or some horror in between.

He'd been making calls frantically every half-hour from his brother's office phone but hadn't been able get a line through. Either they were all down, or all busy.

The one time he did manage to connect, it was to Charlotte's school, where a female voice told him officiously that the principal, Herr Beck, was no longer employed at the institution. When Jakob asked if Beck had been arrested, he received a single word reply. "Perhaps."

For a brief moment, he thought of going to the German embassy to bang down the doors, to cause some havoc, to make his voice heard, but that would be pointless. That's what had given the bastards the excuse for the riots in the first place: that single boy, that brave young idiot who'd taken it into his head to gun down a German diplomat.

It was a stupid, futile gesture, but it had happened, and there'd be nothing to gain by any repetition. All Jakob could do was dash around, a cyclone of a man, buying up newspapers, asking his questions, and vainly trying to phone whenever he had the chance.

If there was any consolation at all, it was that the one night of savagery had finally woken the rest of the world to the true nature of life under the Nazis.

As the *Times* remarked in its uniquely upper-crust fashion, "*No foreign propagandist bent upon blackening Germany before the world could outdo the tale of burnings and beatings, of blackguardly assaults on defenseless and innocent people.*"

Less than a week later, after a lengthy debate and a desperately moving appeal from Jewish community leaders, the British cabinet under Neville Chamberlain launched the Refugee Children Movement, or RCM, in which the nation would admit unaccompanied Jewish children, organizing transport by train, and making arrangements for their reception in England.

When word leaked out about the program, Jakob, with all his new-found contacts, was one of the first to hear. Initially, he was overjoyed, then dismayed when he learned of the restrictions.

"Unaccompanied" meant that Franzi would not be eligible, and "children" meant school age, from five to seventeen years. Charlotte was already nineteen.

As always, it was Harry who tried to raise Jakob's spirits again over their breakfast toast. "Cheer up," he said from behind his newspaper, "it's a start."

"I know, I know, but . . ."

"What, but? How long were you in business? I'll tell you. Long enough to know there's no such word as 'but. ' All 'buts' can be fixed."

"Thanks a lot, boychik. If you're so smart, tell me how I fix this." Jakob had begun talking to Harry the same way he used to speak to their sister, Berthe, when he was on leave in Vienna, a conscious parody of their own Yiddish syntax.

Harry didn't mind. For him, it was a throwback to their youth together in Krakow, so he just shrugged and continued chewing.

He had no ideas about how to fix this particular problem. He'd restated the overriding principle—the entrepreneur's unwritten code that all obstacles can be navigated, all barriers overcome—which was all he could do.

A gap opened up in the space between them. Beyond Harry was his wife, Leah, a busy silhouette in front of the kitchen window, checking the larder and making out another of her endless shopping lists.

Jakob watched her puttering around, but his eyes were distant, his mind elsewhere. He'd had an idea building inside him for a couple of days, but now with this news about the RCM, he had a solid reason to act. Harry said fix it, so that's what he decided to do.

"What do you think of the Rothschilds?" Jakob asked his brother from out of nowhere.

Harry was surprised by the question and raised his eyebrows at the same time as he lowered his paper. "The Rothschilds? Powerful family."

"Even now, do you think?"

"Sure, even now. They don't like it here, they move there. That's how big they are. Why are you asking me about the Rothschilds?"

"You think they're big enough to help me?"

"No doubt, but why would they help a little *pischer* like you?"

Jakob ignored the jibe. "I don't know that they would. I'm just wondering." Then, faced with Harry's inquisitive gaze, he added, "Franzi's sister, Paula. She married a young man who works for them."

"Is that right? And where are they now, Paula and her young man. Still in Vienna?"

"No, they got out. Maybe in Zurich, I'm not sure. You think they could help from there?"

"Couldn't hurt to try."

Jakob nodded slowly. That was exactly the conclusion he'd reached himself, and calling neutral Switzerland would certainly be a lot easier than trying to get through to Austria.

He just wished he knew what was happening with his wife and daughter in the meantime: whether they were all right; whether they were still making ends meet in the apartment on Staudingergasse, or whether they'd been dragged off to . . .

No, he told himself. He couldn't afford to think like that. He had to remain positive, otherwise what did he have left?

It was on a chilly morning in December that Franzi heard a firm knock at the door. Her daughter was at school and she wasn't expecting any visitors. She'd been increasingly nervous ever since the night they were now calling *Kristallnacht,* but the rapping sound was insistent, and she thought it might be the janitor, Frau Graebner, or perhaps one of the tradesmen.

There was always some problem with repairs in the building, especially the dilapidated heating system.

When she opened the door, she found a bespectacled man with a large head, a thick neck, and a graying mustache, his bulky features masked by a fine, vested suit and a long overcoat, which hung open. He removed his gloves and raised his homburg slightly.

"Frau Goldberger?" The voice was a sonorous baritone.

"Yes? May I help you?"

"My name is Werner, Gerhard Werner. May I come in?"

"Well . . . if I might know what it's about."

The man pulled out his pocket watch and impatiently flipped it open with his thumb, as if time were passing, and he had none to waste. "Your sister and brother-in-law asked me to visit."

"My sister? Paula?"

"You have only the one sister, I believe."

"Yes, yes, of course. I'm sorry, I wasn't expecting . . ."

The man raised his hand to stem her apologies. "Please, I cannot stay long, I'm due in court soon."

"Yes, come in, come in. You're a lawyer?"

"I'm private counsel to the Rothschild family." He stepped inside and followed Franzi in to the living room but refused the offer to sit down. "Frau Goldberger, please listen to me carefully. I'm here to ask you if you will allow your daughter to leave the country."

"To leave the country? To go where?"

"Specifically, England."

"Her father's in England. Did he send you?"

"I know nothing of that. I'm here to tell you that the British government is sponsoring a system of children's refugee trains from Vienna, and I need to know if you'd like me to help organize passage for your daughter. No guarantees, of course, but I would like to be sure of your wishes before I proceed."

"Now? You need an answer now?"

"If she has any chance of acceptance, we need to file an application as soon as possible . . . so, yes, if you don't mind, I need an answer now."

"Are you sure you won't sit down? Can I get you some tea?"

"No, thank you. As I said, *meine Frau*, I cannot stay long."

Franzi nodded and tried to focus. In the confined space, the man towered over her, causing unnecessary pressure. "You said a children's train? Is that what you said?"

"Yes, unaccompanied children only."

"How old? The children, how old?"

"Up to seventeen years."

"But Charlotte's nineteen."

"I see. Well, that might be a problem. Are you sure she's nineteen?"

"Am I sure? What do you mean, am I sure?"

"If you tell me she's seventeen, then I'll have no choice but to pass on that same information."

Franzi may have been nervous and clearly on edge after all she'd been through but she was far from stupid. "Yes, that's right, how silly of me. She's seventeen, what was I thinking?"

"Then it would appear that she meets the criteria. Do you wish to proceed with the application?"

Franzi tried to think it though in the exceedingly brief time she'd been allowed. If she said no, that would be the end of it, but if she said yes, she could no doubt change her mind at any time. "Yes," she said definitively. Then as if to confirm: "Yes, I certainly do wish to proceed. Thank you, Herr Werner, thank you so much."

"Don't thank me yet. If we're successful, you'll be receiving a package of documents from a Dr. Rudolf Neumann. He's a member of the International Red Cross network and it will be on his recommendation that the application will be approved. Once you receive those documents, you'll have to take them to the headquarters of the *Geheime Staatspolizei* on Morzinplatz to have them validated. Do you understand?"

Franzi knew perfectly well that the authority he'd mentioned was the official name of the much feared Gestapo, the secret police division under the direct control of the SS. For a second or two, she felt the pulse in her temples just like that night in the closet and took several deep breaths to steady herself.

"I ask you again," said Werner, addressing her as if she were a witness in a courtroom, "do you understand?"

"Yes, I understand."

"Then we're done. Good day, *meine Frau.*"

The man didn't offer to shake her hand. In fact, there were no niceties at all as he turned to leave. At the last moment, just before he stepped out the door, Franzi called out to him.

"Wait, wait . . . When? I mean, when can I expect to hear?"

"If all goes well, you'll receive notification within a few days."

"And if not?"

"Then you won't hear at all."

"Do you have a business card? Can I reach you somewhere?"

"I'm afraid not, Frau Goldberger. I hope you can appreciate that this is a sensitive matter."

"Yes . . ."

"And please, don't talk about this to anyone, for your daughter's sake. Not even your daughter for now."

"No, I won't say a word, of course not. Thank you again."

"Good day to you."

Franzi closed the door behind him, then went over to sit down with her head resting in her hands. This was almost too much for her and she didn't know what to think. If this lawyer, Werner, worked for the Rothschilds, then it could only have been Paula, but then again, he'd said it was all being organized by the British, so maybe Jakob had somehow been involved, too.

She just couldn't seem to piece it together. All she knew was that a heaven-sent chance for her daughter had dropped in out of the gray, wintry skies, and for that alone, she was grateful.

It took a long time for Charlotte to reveal the epic saga that was her life story, and it only began after I'd confessed some of my own difficult issues. This happened fairly early in our friendship not long after my cousin had first introduced us.

At that time, I needed someone of experience with whom I could talk, someone who knew the ways of the world, and Charlotte was there for me, more than willing to listen. Back then, I didn't really know her well at all but she was one of those people who just seemed to understand.

Was it my own problems that initially encouraged her to divulge her own? It's possible, but hers were far deeper, and I'm inclined to think it was more a question of timing; that she'd reached the stage in life when she just needed to unburden herself.

When she first began, it was just a general outline of her long history, but the more she told me, the more I interest I took. Even so, it was years before the trust developed to the stage at which the details became intimate, until finally, towards the end of her days, she felt the need to open up completely.

I must say, it happened unexpectedly.

One Friday I arrived for lunch, as usual, but no sooner had we sat down than I suspected the day might be different. She wasn't depressed, but she was anxious and a little impatient, as if she'd already made up her mind to tell me everything while she was still in the mood.

When she started to speak it was almost as if I weren't there. She became transfixed by her own words, reliving the moments all over again in her mind as she confided every facet, every nuance.

Strangely enough, there was no weeping, not while she was speaking, and only when she finished did she break down. By that time, it was all just too much for her. She was inconsolable and there was little I could do to bring her around.

No fresh coffee or cheery humor would do it, so I just sat there and held her hand. Minutes ticked by as the afternoon wore on. I was late for a downtown appointment but I didn't care about that. Then, at last, she told me with the most sincere apologies that she would have to go and lie down, and that's when I left.

The same evening I called her to see if she was all right but all I got was the answering machine. Naturally, I was worried, thinking that I might have to go over there. However, the second time I dialed, she picked up, and when I asked how she was doing, she gave me the simplest of replies.

"I'll survive," she said quietly.

It was all I needed to hear. For Charlotte, I knew, the distress would only be temporary, and by the following day she'd be back to her usual self with the familiar mask of dignity and grace intact.

She was made of strong stuff, and if the events themselves hadn't finished her off, there was little chance that just the retelling would cause any serious damage.

8

The most crucial episode of Charlotte's life happened around the time of Hanukah, the Festival of Lights which, by the Hebrew lunar calendar, often coincides with Christmas, and is just as eagerly celebrated by exchanging presents.

What occurred in that December of 1938, however, was no gift.

At the time, Charlotte was still going to college each day, working as best she could towards her end-of-term exams. She'd thought that the situation there couldn't get any worse, but she was wrong. It had become intolerable, yet what else could she do but try to cope?

She continued to attend class, as punctual and diligent as she'd always been, except now she felt like an open and obvious target for the ever increasing indignities and verbal abuse.

Many blamed the Jewish students for Herr Beck's arrest, because he'd defied his own board of governors to keep them enrolled. Even the faithful Magda had become more wary. She was reluctant to be seen talking to Charlotte in public, so they met in secret behind the building while Magda smoked her cigarettes.

Worse, though, was Charlotte's feeling of guilt on the increasingly rare occasions that she called in to see Hugo.

She knew well enough that because his little store was in this district, he must have many Jewish customers, but nevertheless, she felt bad because she knew it wouldn't look good for him to be seen associating with her on a friendly basis.

Being a customer was one thing but sipping tea and exchanging confidences was something else entirely. It was all completely innocent and had been since that one evening at the dance, but it was a matter of appearances, and Charlotte wasn't worried for herself but for Hugo. He was well-meaning, as good-hearted as they come, and she didn't want to be the cause of any hardship for him. In her nightmares, she could see him being dragged away to be questioned by the Gestapo about why he was fraternizing with female *Untermenschen*.

As a result, she didn't call in to see him as often, and when she did, she lurked around the corner until there was nobody around before entering. Sometimes, she even cursed that tiny bell for tinkling, giving her away. The best time was obviously at dusk when there were deep shadows to hide her, making her feel even more like a criminal in her own neighborhood.

The oppression was forcing many in the community to conduct their affairs in a more clandestine manner and Charlotte wasn't the only one skulking around for surreptitious meetings. Her mother, too, had her secrets, but that liaison was far more illicit.

At the apartment, Franzi opened the front door to find her secret lover standing there. It happened sometimes in the middle of the day, when he knew Charlotte would be at school, but that's exactly what she adored about him. He was spontaneous. Whenever it happened, he claimed to be burning for her, unable to wait a moment longer to be with her, to feel her in his arms.

This was more than the fantasy of dancing for Franzi. This was real, and it was beyond anything she'd ever known within the sheltered context of her life. With him, there was no society pretension, no moral code that they were required to obey. None of the normal rules applied. In private like this, they could abandon all logic, all common sense.

They could remain quiet and gentle if they so wished, or they could allow themselves to slide into a state of intimate rapture, the freedom of mind and body that she believed could only have happened in the heyday of her Parisian fantasies.

Such escapades were totally new to her, but in a surprisingly short amount of time, she'd become so addicted to them that she couldn't wait for those fevered moments when she could escape this place of drudgery and fear in favor of the illusion they'd created together, a blissful fragment of euphoria.

It was as if she'd been waiting for this all her life, a culmination of all her years of virtue and rectitude. She felt she not only deserved it, she was actually entitled; a reward for having sacrificed her youth, finally granted by the heavens.

When he showed up like this, she took but a minute to change into the flimsy cotton camisole that she'd found at a second-hand stall for just these occasions, the very frivolity of the purchase having delighted her. Now he was standing behind her, their bodies touching, his arms wrapped tightly around her and his cool fingers reaching towards the delicate fabric that covered her small breasts. He kissed her neck very softly, and she began to take shorter breaths, silently longing for him.

In response, he slipped one of the loose shoulder straps from her shoulder, causing her to tremble with the sudden chill of exposure and expectation. She could feel him unfastening those loose American slacks he liked to wear and shuddered as she felt his hardness pressing against her. The other strap slid down her arms to reveal her breasts, freely displaying the tiny pink tips which protruded so far that they ached.

All inhibitions were gone, banished, as she stood there luxuriating in his attentions. One of his hands was now entwined in her loose hair while the other was moving across the plane of her stomach, slowly, slowly, ever lower, until she slightly eased her thighs open, an unspoken permission that urged him to continue.

With her eyes closed, she felt radiant, a feeling both glorious and subtle at the same time, as if she'd stepped into the very essence of Renoir.

In the passion of her mind, she was in some garret on the *Rive Gauche*, like a scene from *La Bohème,* and he was the great and celebrated artist, searching her, exploring every curve, every nuance and angle, in order to render the most exquisite justice to her beauty.

It was on one of these same days, while Franzi was so preoccupied at home, that Charlotte and the other Jews in her class were called out by name.

They were sent along to the large machine shop, which also doubled as an assembly hall, where they were lined up with the rest of Jewish student body, together representing approximately half the school's enrollment. In front of them stood the deputy principal, the stern-faced Frau Krüger, who'd taken over from Herr Beck. She fiddled with her steel-framed glasses as she announced in a clear voice that, by government decree, she was obliged to expel everyone in front of her.

She was very sorry, she told them, but she had no choice in the matter. They must collect their belongings and vacate the premises immediately. When a loud hubbub ensued, Frau Krüger called for both silence and obedience.

Like her peers, Charlotte was extremely upset, but no protestation was possible. She wasn't even permitted to speak, so she sullenly gathered her things and packed them all into her bag: her boxes of needles, spools of thread, thimbles, and fabric samples, plus all her notebooks and pencils.

When she was done, she looked around at this place where she'd spent the past few years of her life. Despite all the recent difficulties, she was heartbroken to be leaving. She had no notion of what she would do from now on and her future seemed to open up before her like a wide, empty chasm.

Charlotte descended the school steps for the last time and began the walk home. Around her, there were still signs of the destruction caused by the *Kristallnacht* rampage, unrepaired doors and windows, the shell of the burned out synagogue, even some unwashed blood stains on the pavement.

Much of the debris was still lying in the streets, from splinters of glass and wood to smashed store merchandise and shattered household furniture.

Brigittenau looked like a war zone but Charlotte had seen such things every day since it happened and was heedless to it all, full of her personal woes.

All she wanted was to hide herself, to be with her mother, to take comfort in those slender arms as she had as an infant. She had her own key to the apartment, and for a moment, she fiddled with it in the lock.

From inside she thought she heard voices but assumed it was the radio. It was only when she entered and looked across towards the open door of her parents' room that she came to a standstill, her large bag still on her shoulder, unable to believe her eyes. She felt her lungs incapable of breathing, searching for oxygen. She was in a state of shock, her face expressionless as she gaped at them.

"*Mutti*? Karl?"

These were the only words that would emerge, a combination of question and exclamation, and they both turned towards her, looking like animals in the wild caught unawares.

It was her mother who attempted to speak first, her voice little more than a stutter.

"*Liebste*? What are you doing here?"

Charlotte wasn't interested in explaining about school, or anything else. All she could see was the handsome man with whom she'd danced, the charming man with whom she'd fallen in love, the pig of a man who hadn't once bothered to call her.

Now here he was, Karl Schneid, naked with her mother. It was shocking, disgusting. To see her like this, as just a frail woman caught in the throes of a sordid affair with a younger man was appalling enough, but the fact that he was a man about whom Charlotte, herself, had been thinking ever since that one afternoon they'd spent together made it infinitely worse. It was sickening and Charlotte struggled to swallow the bile in her throat.

To fill what had become a lengthy void, Karl thought he should say something.

"Please, I know how this looks but—"

His words were only half-complete when he was interrupted by Franzi, who was already covering her embarrassment by wrapping her pale body in her robe.

"*Liebste*, I meant to tell you, I promise. It's just that Karl and I . . . We love each other. You know what that means, don't you? Remember, when you were in love with Hugo? Only this is more so. You understand, don't you? Please tell me you understand."

For a second or two, Charlotte just stared at her, unblinking. She didn't understand, nor did she wish to do so. She still couldn't move. Her school bag was now on the floor, its contents scattered, and she just stood there, mouth open, unable to speak or to listen.

In an instant, nineteen years of childhood trust had been severed, cleanly decapitated, and while it was true that the mother-daughter relationship had never perhaps been as close as it might have been, the last few months of struggle and survival had brought them together like never before. Now, suddenly, it was no more. The ever-emotional girl had been expelled from her life at school and arrived back to discover this abomination in her own home, in the same room where her father had slept.

After all she'd been through, this was the *coup de grâce*, the final blow that traumatized her nervous system and shut it down the way damp fingers can snuff out a flame.

Finally, instead of responding to her mother's pathetic appeals to reason, Charlotte forced herself to move, to turn, to leave: through the door, down the stairs, out of the building, and headlong into the streets, propelled by the depths of a confusion she'd never known before, running, not seeing anything until she didn't know where she was or even which neighborhood. She didn't care. She couldn't think, she couldn't breathe.

She just didn't know how her mother could betray her like that after they'd suffered the taunts and the jeers together, after they'd scrubbed these same streets, after hiding in that tiny closet on the night their community was destroyed.

The recollections flashed through her mind, one after the other: the time her mother baked a special dessert for her, or bandaged a scrape, or played the cello softly while she did her homework. She remembered all the birthdays and her beautiful Bat Mitzvah dress . . . and then she remembered her father.

What about her father? The poor man was out there alone, away from his family, trying hard to obtain papers for them to leave. He'd warned them what would happen. He knew what he was talking about, knew what he was doing, and he'd been right, as he was always right about everything. What did he do to deserve this? He was such a good man. It wasn't so easy to make a living, Charlotte knew that, but he'd always cared for them, always made sure they had enough to eat and to live. He was kind and gentle and she wished she was with him now. She wished she was anywhere but here.

For a few moments, Charlotte paused with a pain in her abdomen at having run so hard. In front of her, cars drove by and pedestrians passed, but she didn't see any of them, still blinded by the after-image that had been branded into her retinas: the two of them together, naked in front of her, flaunting their bodies and their love and their sex.

Charlotte felt like she was on the outside now, alone with nowhere to go, adrift in these streets filled with terror. She'd been banished from school so she couldn't lose herself in her lessons, and even if she were there, she wouldn't be able to talk to the other students, because she'd been increasingly ostracized.

She had no youth club for swimming, or skating, or hiking, because as a socialist institution, it had been disbanded. She had no father because he was away, and no mother, either, not after this. Her Aunt Berthe had returned to Krakow, and if she went to her grandparents, she'd have too much to explain.

There was simply nowhere to go. She felt like an orphan, a waif, an outcast from all of society. Her family members were like strangers and everyone else in the city loathed her. She couldn't see any way forward, no direction in which to turn, and felt that her life, as she'd known it up to this point, was over.

After a while, she found herself at the Augarten, which she only vaguely recognized, and wandered in through the iron gates just get away from the streets and the sidewalks. She wanted to hide in the bushes, to hibernate like an animal, to fall asleep and not wake up for months, maybe years, sometime in the future when all this was over and her memory had been purged.

She walked, she meandered, she looked up at the trees, then down at her feet as they trod the soft grass. How long did she stay in the park? Was it minutes or hours? She didn't even know. She'd always tried to be good, never hurting others. She'd tried to share whatever she had, to enjoy life, to have fun despite everything, to always see the best side of things, but it was all broken now. Her world had been crushed, and she didn't know if it could ever be rebuilt—and that's when she thought again of the one person, the only individual on whom she could still count.

The light was already beginning to fade, which meant it would soon be curfew for Jews, so once again she began to run. She had to get there, before it got dark and before he closed, but once she left the park, she came to a halt. She couldn't recall which direction to take, left or right.

She tried to concentrate, forcing her brain to work. She looked around, trying to find something familiar. That's when she spotted the old Rosenthal porcelain factory and it all came back to her. Using the landmark as her compass point, she framed the necessary route in her head—and then she was off again, straining her thighs and calves to move ever faster.

She didn't have much time. Her lungs were burning, but she didn't pause until she reached the small repair shop that she'd once loved to visit on the way home from school. Thankfully, it was open, and this time, she didn't hide or sneak around, she just burst uncaring through the door.

"Hugo? Hugo?" She was winded and couldn't prevent herself from panting. "Are you there?"

As often was the case, he was working in the back under the illumination of his single lamp but he came out immediately at her call. As soon as he emerged, Charlotte hurled herself into his arms and that's when the sobbing began, so much that within a short time, the front of his work shirt was completely wet.

For a long time, she wouldn't let him ago, afraid even to look up, trying to pretend that the universe hadn't gone insane, that it was all just as it was before.

At last, he eased her away from him, sat her gently down on a stool, and went behind the counter to make her some tea in a tin cup.

She accepted it gratefully and sipped at it, the steaming liquid mingling with the salt from her tears, which were still streaming down her cheeks, but when he asked her what had happened, why she was like this, she couldn't reply. His first thought was to suspect that she'd had some kind of altercation with the SA, but when he suggested it, she just shook her head, unable to tell him that it was far worse than anything the Brownshirts could have done.

For the rest of the evening, she just sat there and wept, watching him work through her blurred vision. Eventually, she began to focus on what he was doing and, for a few precious moments, she was distracted from her own distress, marveling at his brilliance and intricacy.

These days, he told her, much of his work was involved with hiding gemstones inside common objects, so they could be smuggled out by emigrating Jews. Some were heading to America, some to France, some to Palestine and some even to China, but wherever their final destination, they would need funds, so they were converting whatever savings they'd managed to amass into precious stones.

These they brought to Hugo to tuck away in tea caddies, in walking sticks, in leather belts and, Hugo's own specialty, inside pairs of horn-rimmed glasses. Very carefully, he sawed the long ear-pieces in two, then hollowed out the interior so there would be enough room for several small diamonds on each side.

It was ingenious and Charlotte congratulated him, but not for long, because then she remembered who she was and what had happened, and she was shaking all over again, as if her entire being was breaking apart from the earthquake that was inside her.

She felt like her existence was collapsing in on itself, leaving only a vacuum of emptiness, a vortex that was devoid of all sentiment.

When Hugo was finally ready to close for the night, he couldn't let her face the curfew alone, so once he'd locked and barred the store, he bravely walked her all the way back to her building, ready to defend her against anything that might happen.

It wasn't where she wanted to go, but she could think of no alternative. She might have asked if she could go with him back to his own residence, and under the circumstances, that might have been forgivable, but she didn't want to subject him to any further risk.

She cared for him too much, so she simply accepted his offer to accompany her home and was glad of his sturdy presence alongside her.

When they arrived at Staudingergasse, they didn't kiss or even stand chatting. It just wasn't safe, so they shook hands, and Hugo quickly walked back the way he came, leaving Charlotte on her own.

Slowly, she trod the stairs, but the place didn't seem the same. This was where she'd grown up, where she'd lived all her life, but it was not her home anymore. In her mind, she had no home left. The earthquake had crumbled all the foundations of her life and there was nothing worthwhile remaining. She was still alive, her heart was still beating, but her soul seemed to have dissolved.

That night, Charlotte went to bed without a word but dreaded the arrival of the morning. She slept hardly at all and awoke from tumultuous dreams just as the rays of pale light penetrated the apartment.

Her mother was already up preparing breakfast and, as expected, the atmosphere was intense, strained to the limits of endurance for both of them.

When Franzi tried to speak, to tell her daughter to hurry up for school, Charlotte refused to answer, even to explain that there would be no more school, not today and not ever. Instead, she just turned to face the other direction. For a while, they ate at the small table in silence, then they each did their chores in silence, and when Franzi turned on the radio in order to break the pall, Charlotte walked over, unplugged it from the socket and carried it to her room.

In theory, she had every right to do so, since it was hers in the first place, but this was a childish reaction and she knew it. She didn't care. She didn't want any music to brighten up the place, nor any news to depress her. All she wanted was the deathly silence, because that's how she felt.

Halfway through the morning, Franzi attempted yet again to communicate with her daughter. Once, twice, then a third time, she tapped on the bedroom door, but on each occasion all she heard was her daughter's muffled sobbing.

There seemed to be no end and she could stand to hear it no longer. She fixed up her hair and applied a little make-up, then put on her one good coat and grabbed up her large purse.

"I'm going out," she called.

There was no response, so Franzi simply left, shutting the front door firmly behind her. However, she wasn't on her way to see Karl. Today, it was back to a most precarious reality, and tucked inside her bag, alongside her wallet and identity papers, was the stout envelope she'd recently received in the mail, the one with the Red Cross trademark at the top corner.

At first, she couldn't decide whether to act on it, but she'd now come to a decision, thinking that if her daughter left, it might be better for everybody.

Outside the building, she looked carefully around her. The streets were menacing enough for a normal outing, but this was something she'd never faced before, and she wasn't at all sure whether her courage was up to the task she'd set herself.

Perhaps on another day, her daughter would have accompanied her—she was always so strong in these situations—but that was obviously awkward right now. Her mother, too, might have been a possibility, but Frau Gutmann had enough to worry about, with her husband descending all too rapidly into a state of dementia.

As a final option, Franzi's mind automatically switched back to her dearest Karl but she could hardly involve him in this. How would it have looked to the authorities? If someone had asked about their relationship, how could they have answered?

The matter was difficult enough without such unnecessary complications. She'd therefore reached the conclusion that there was nobody on whom she could rely but herself. It was nobody's responsibility but her own and she tried her best to pull herself together, but as she walked alone towards the Stadtbahn, the apprehension was already having its effect, dissolving what was left of her resolution like acid on tarnished metal.

Her destination was a large, neo-classical building overlooking the Donaukanal on the south bank. Everyone knew the structure because it had been the Hotel Metropole until the very first day of the *Anschluss*, when the head of the SS, Heinrich Himmler, had arrived from Berlin and commandeered it as the new Gestapo headquarters.

It was from here that all their Ostmark operations were directed, and it was here, too, that prisoners were brought for interrogation. They were led in through the back entrance on Salztorgasse and then dragged down to the basement cells where, behind thick foundation walls, they were tortured and mutilated until a confession could be coerced. On a quiet night, their screams could be heard from across the canal.

It was to this fearsome place that Franzi came for the express purpose of validating the exit documents for her daughter, but she knew that if it had been for any other reason, she could never have been so intrepid.

The best place now for Charlotte was with her father, away from all that had happened. It was true that Jakob wasn't romantic or dashing, none of the things that Franzi had ever desired in a man, but he would take care of their daughter, she was certain of that, and all she had to do was find the fortitude to make it happen.

Even so, as she approached the columned portico and looked up at the swastika banners, she almost had a change of heart, pausing for several long seconds in order to breathe deeply. She knew that if she walked in with any kind of hesitation, she might just collapse, and if that were to happen, she couldn't conceive the consequences. A chill passed through her entire body just thinking about it.

She wasn't sure if she was doing this out of love or guilt, she just knew she had to pull herself together and do it. Closing her eyes for a moment, she took another breath and then, against her own better judgment, she entered.

Where the hotel's reception desk had once been, there was now a counter for general inquiries. Above it hung a gold-painted plaster eagle of the Reich, and on a wall to the side was the requisite portrait of the Führer, chin set firm and eyes aglow.

Manning the counter were three SS bureaucrats going about their job with a sense of well-practiced boredom. There were already several dozen people in a line that snaked around the large lobby, so Franzi simply took her place and waited. Contrary to her fears, nobody looked at her or questioned her.

Nobody yelled at her, or demanded how she dare be here in this place. They all just walked past her, getting on with the business at hand, and it made her wonder if this was simply the normal process, or if they were ignoring her because she really didn't look Jewish at all.

For almost three-quarters of an hour, she waited her turn. Few spoke, except for a mother who held a baby in her arms and was trying to comfort the infant. It took Franzi back to when Charlotte was that age and for those few minutes, she allowed her mind to wander, taking refuge within her own nostalgia.

When she finally arrived at the counter, she fumbled with the envelope before handing the papers across. The clerk was a narrow, sallow-faced man with bony hands who scanned the documents with some disdain, then looked at her as if he had better things to do.

"What's this about?" he demanded.

"It's a train," replied Franzi, "a special train."

"What? Speak up. A train, is that what you said?"

"Yes, a special train for children."

"I've never heard of any train. So what do you want me to do?"

"It's for my daughter. The paper needs your authorization, your stamp, otherwise . . ."

"What?"

"Otherwise she can't go."

"And you think I care?" The clerk tossed the papers back across the counter. "Get out of here."

Franzi was about to take the papers and leave, but the baby began to cry and, once again, the sound reminded Franzi of everything she'd been through, from the pain of birth all the way through to the previous afternoon with Karl and somehow it broke the chains of her fear.

"Please," she said far too loudly. "It's for my daughter, you have to stamp it otherwise she can't leave. Please . . ."

At first the clerk was startled by her outburst, then he just glared at her, as other people began to take notice, including the senior officer, a bigger, more august man.

"What's all the noise?" he asked his underling. "What does she want?"

"I don't know. Some train for her daughter, or something."

"She's Jewish?" When the first clerk shrugged, the second repeated it directly to Franzi. "Are you Jewish?"

"Yes," said Franzi firmly, surprising herself with the display of bravery.

"You want to send your daughter on the children's train, is that what this is about?" He used the specific word *Kindertransport* as if he'd heard of it. "Well, is it?"

"Yes, yes, that's right."

The senior officer had heard enough and turned to his colleague with a dismissive air. "God in heaven, what do you care? Just stamp the damn thing, and we'll have one less Jew to worry about."

The man did as he was told, but he was hardly gracious about it, and pushed the completed papers back across to Franzi.

For a moment, she stood examining them and only when she was satisfied did she offer a simple, "Thank you." Then she walked away hurriedly, across the lobby and through the main doors, with many pairs of eyes watching her.

Outside, the colder air made her feel dizzy, and she had to hold herself up against one of the pillars. A woman asked her if she was all right and she nodded, before forcing herself to continue. It was as if all her energy had been drained, and she knew she had to get away from there as quickly as possible, or she might not make it at all.

Only once she was back in the apartment, with the door closed behind her, could Franzi breathe deeply enough to steady herself.

"I'm back," she called out, but like before, there was no answer. Nevertheless, she felt she had to do this now, right away, so she tapped gently on Charlotte's door. "*Liebste*, come out, I have some important news."

A minute later, she saw her daughter emerge, still holding a handkerchief to her face. "Come, sit," said Franzi encouragingly. "I have some news for you."

Charlotte came over and sat on the edge of the armchair, not wanting to make herself too comfortable. Then she waited in silence.

Franzi was still stressed from her odyssey but she tried her best to smile triumphantly as she took the authorized document from her bag. "You know what this is?"

Charlotte shook her head. "This is your train ticket. You're going to England."

"England?"

"There's a special train leaving Vienna. It will take you all the way. Your father will meet you in London. That's what I was doing just now. I had to go to the Gestapo to get it stamped."

Franzi said it as though she thought her daughter would be impressed at the feat of bravery but that wasn't the reaction at all. There was no congratulations, not even any gratitude. "So . . . what do you think?"asked Franzi. "Aren't you proud of your *mutti*?" There was no response, nothing. "*Liebste*?"

It took a few more moments, then suddenly it all came bursting out of Charlotte's mouth, a torrent of words.

"You want me to think you did it for me? Don't lie to me, you did it for yourself. You only want me to go England so you can have him for yourself. Why don't you admit it? Why can't you be truthful, just for once?"

"Please, *liebste* . . ."

Franzi reached over to touch her daughter's hand but Charlotte pulled it away.

By this time, the tears were flowing again, and the words were stifled by the handkerchief. "I'm not your *liebste*, don't call me that." She looked up with her tear-streaked face, and her mood changed instantly from deep resentment to outright anger.

"How could you do that?" She'd raised her voice, almost to screaming pitch. "Why did it have to be him? Why?"

Then she thought of something else, a new line of attack. "How long?" she asked. "Was it right after the dance?"

Franzi looked disconsolate and gave a long sigh. She was still holding the papers, and for want of something to do, she made herself busy by folding them neatly. "What difference does it make?"

"It makes a difference to me."

Franzi just shook her head slowly, the moisture forming in her eyes, too. "You don't know . . ." she began softly. "All these years, I've been so alone. You don't know."

"And what about my father? Are you still married to him? Well? Are you?"

"Yes . . . I'm still married to him."

"So maybe I should tell him, what do you think?"

"If that's what you want to do, I can't stop you, but I wish you wouldn't. Your father's a good man. I didn't do this to hurt him."

"No, just to hurt me."

"No, I swear to you, *liebste*. I swear, as God is my witness."

"God? What does God have to do with it?" Charlotte was becoming frustrated with her own arguments, so she came back to her original question. She just couldn't seem to shake it. "But why Karl? That's what I don't understand. Why did it have to be Karl, of all people?"

"I don't know, *liebste*, I don't know. It just happened."

There was not much else to say, and they both fell back into the same pervasive silence as before. A mother is supposed to know her daughter, but it was at that moment that Franzi realized she hardly knew Charlotte at all.

It was several days later when Charlotte took the tea that Hugo offered her, scalding hot as always. They were in their usual places in the cramped store, she on the stool while he stood behind the counter continuing his work.

"Hugo," she said. "I'm here to say goodbye." She spoke in a flat monotone, with no expression in her voice, or on her face. Her attitude, her entire being, was different now. She felt like she was living in a void.

The more she'd wept, the more she felt raw and exposed, so she'd shut down to protect herself, to prevent any further damage to her system. Her natural emotions had been frozen, turning the instinctive warmth that had always defined her personality into a core of hardened ice.

Hugo looked up at her. "Where are you going?"

"You don't seem surprised."

"Why would I be surprised? Jews are leaving all the time. They pay me good money to do this." He indicated the implements in front of him and the work he was doing. Today he was fitting some tiny gems inside a tie-clip.

Charlotte gave a minimal nod, almost imperceptible. "I'm going to England."

"Good," he said simply.

"That's where my father is now. You remember my father?"

"Yes, of course I remember him."

That's right, thought Charlotte, *of course he does*. On the one occasion Hugo met him, her father had struck her. That was the only time in Charlotte's life it had ever happened, and it was for lying to her mother.

How things had reversed, Charlotte mused. What a twist of irony. Now it was her mother who was lying, and it was so much worse.

What would her father say now? Would he strike Franzi, too? It was Hugo's voice that brought her back to reality.

"When do you leave?" he was asking.

"Soon."

"I'll miss you."

She gave him another nod, this time allowing herself the slightest of smiles. "I'll miss you, too."

"What will you do? In England?"

"I don't know," she said. Strangely, she hadn't even thought of that yet. "Get a job, I suppose. I don't really know what it's like. I've never been out of Austria before."

"Me, either."

"First I'll have to improve my English. Do you speak English?"

"*A . . . little . . . bit,*" said Hugo, trying in his own halting way to speak the language.

"What do you think's going to happen? People say there'll be another war."

"People like to talk."

"I suppose so."

"Is your mother leaving, too?"

At this, Charlotte just took another sip of her tea. It was a way to avoid answering, but the silence stretched out, and she didn't want to treat Hugo like that. "No," she replied eventually. "No, she's staying here."

"She can't get a visa for England?"

Charlotte didn't want to lie but couldn't bring herself to tell the truth either.

"It's difficult," she replied, avoiding the issue, and she was grateful that he didn't pursue the subject. She looked at him, at his face, open and honest. There was so much she wanted to tell him. He'd been a good friend, in every sense of the word, and perhaps in some other life they might even have made it work together.

"I should go," she said softly.

She put down her cup, stepped around the counter, and gave her gentle Hugo a soft kiss on the cheek, a dry replica of the first one she had given him all that time ago.

"Thank you for everything," she said. Before he had a chance to reply, she turned and left, hearing only the tiny, tinkling doorbell on her way out.

As a coping mechanism during the final weeks before her departure, Charlotte's soul had completely stultified.

In her mind, the best analogy was from the Book of Genesis, in which Lot's wife was turned into a pillar of salt by the angels after she turned to look at the heavenly fire raining down on the evil city of Sodom.

A pillar of salt, a block of ice, a slab of stone . . . However she thought of herself, these were merely the mental images that enabled her soul to subdue all feeling, right through to that final morning in late December when she was due to leave.

She hadn't shed a single tear since the afternoon her mother returned from Gestapo headquarters with the embarkation papers, and by the morning of her departure, the emotional girl was no more.

The spontaneity was gone. That was another Charlotte, a previous Charlotte, a happy-go-lucky Charlotte who no longer existed.

Once the taxi had arrived, and the driver had hauled her baggage downstairs, she just stood in the center of the small apartment and gazed around blankly: at the kitchen, at the old furniture, at the closet where they'd hidden themselves on that frightening night, and finally, through the open door to her own tiny cubicle of a room.

That was where she'd spent her entire childhood, where she'd grown up. Before the *Anschluss*, it seemed like that life would go on forever, but afterwards, in just a few short months, her world of school and youth clubs and fun had vanished, replaced by public loathing and private heartbreak.

For a moment, her gaze came to rest on the radio, the same appliance her father had brought back from Nuremberg all those years ago.

She couldn't pack it, and anyway, it probably wouldn't work where she was going, so it became her parting gift to her mother. How many times would Karl now come over and listen to it, she wondered? How many times would they dance or make love to its music?

"*Liebste*, we have to go." Franzi was standing by the front door, all wrapped up in her coat, scarf, and gloves against the winter chill.

Charlotte took one last, sweeping look around then tried to shut it all out of her mind as she followed her mother downstairs and into the aging vehicle. It was noisy and smelly, but that was of no account.

As the driver steered his slow way through the streets of Brigittenau, all Charlotte could think about were the places she'd known so well: her primary and secondary schools, with all her friends and teachers; also her technical college, which seemed like history to her now.

Then there was the Augarten, with its flowers in summer and skating rink in winter; and Hugo's little shop, too, which she would perhaps miss most of all. Silently and without any outward expression, she bid her farewells to all of them. She didn't know when, or even if, she'd ever see any of them again.

After traversing the entire city center, the taxi arrived at Felberstrasse, turned into a broad entrance, and puttered to a stop right in front of the busy Westbahnhof terminus. Franzi fished in her purse to pay the driver, then hired a porter with a small wagon to follow them inside with the bags.

She could hardly afford it, but today was special, and anyway, none of the labor was very expensive because these gruff, downcast men needed the work so badly.

Although the Nazis had gained power with bombastic promises of economic as well as military renewal, none of it had yet trickled down to their meager level.

Inside, the station's cavernous concourse was crowded with families, the noise intense with the hubbub of anxious conversation and the sounds of children running, shouting, giggling, or bawling in their apprehension. In the background, repetitious announcements echoed from inadequate loudspeakers while, every so often, the hissing steam and grinding wheels of an arriving or departing locomotive rendered everything else inaudible as it permeated the air with smoke and soot.

Franzi had arranged to meet her parents here under the enormous clock, but many people had decided to do the same thing and it was difficult to navigate the throng that was milling around.

She told Charlotte to wait and not to move from the spot while she went to search for them and eventually emerged from the turmoil with her parents behind her. Franzi held her mother's hand who, in turn, gripped tightly on to her father.

He was a sad sight to see as he staggered along behind, not really knowing who or where he was, his expression vacant and lost.

"All the children," he kept saying as he gazed around. "All the children."

As Charlotte dutifully kissed her grandmother, she felt those thin arms wrap around her tightly, almost desperately. Although they'd never been all that close, Charlotte quite liked her grandparents and was genuinely sorry about what had happened to their lives, especially her grandfather's dementia.

He had, perhaps, been a little overly pretentious in his younger days, but he'd possessed a capable brain, and that was the pity of it. Nobody deserved to lose their most essential faculties in that way.

Once they'd expressed their greetings, the four of them made their way towards a hand-written sign that Franzi had spotted with the single, scrawled word: *Kindertransport.* Next to it was a crude arrow pointing the way towards the distant platform where a long train was standing. First, however, they had to wait in line for the guard to inspect their papers, and it was an effort just to keep Herr Gutmann from wandering off on his own.

When they finally reached the front, they were all required to show their papers before they could proceed any farther; however, the man took particular interest in Charlotte, looking back and forth from her documents to her face.

"You, you're seventeen?" he asked her dubiously.

"Yes," she replied.

She added nothing else, so it was up to Franzi to rekindle some of the bravery she'd so recently discovered within herself. "It's been stamped by the Gestapo," she told him pointedly. "I took it there myself."

"I can see that."

"So what's the problem?" she demanded.

Her unusual attitude even managed to surprise her own mother. Nobody had ever heard Franzi talk like that.

The guard, too, was confused about how to respond to such confidence. Most people in line were only too willing to acquiesce to his authority. "There's no problem," he replied warily, before handing back the papers and permitting them to pass.

As Franzi knew well enough, the guard's change of heart had nothing to do with generosity or even tolerance, but was merely a response to the word Gestapo.

Like anyone else, this simple security official really didn't need to risk any trouble from the dreaded secret police. It just wasn't worth it, far easier just to let these people through.

As more families pushed onto the platform, it was becoming congested with people, baggage, and all those children, but each grouping was self-involved, ignoring all others, fully preoccupied with last minute fussing while huddled against the bitter winds that whipped through the open-ended structure.

Some stomped their feet on the concrete, others tried to blow warm breath on gloveless hands. Noses ran and eyes watered but this was not merely due to the chill. Unlike Charlotte, most of these youngsters had nobody to meet them in that far-away land and would officially become orphans the moment they arrived.

They would either be taken in by volunteer British families from city or farm, or consigned to some state institution where they would be housed and fed, but little else. Their parents here in Vienna knew the risks, knew that it would be something of a lottery for their children to find a good home, but there was nothing they could do.

They'd been given this chance to get at least one member of the family away from the nightmare and they were only too glad to take it.

"Excuse me," said a woman, tugging on Franzi's arm. She sounded weary. "Is that your daughter?" The woman indicated Charlotte, who was standing just a couple of paces away.

"That's right," said Franzi.

"How beautiful she looks. Is she going on the train?"

"Yes, I am," said Charlotte, interjecting. She didn't care for being discussed in the third person while she was within earshot.

"This is my son," said the woman. She put her hand on the shoulder of a shy boy with dark, scruffy hair and eased him forward so they could see him. "He's only seven and . . . Well, I was wondering if you wouldn't mind looking after him."

Franzi glanced questioningly at her daughter, who just shrugged her response. "Yes, of course she will," Franzi told the woman.

"Thank you, thank you so much. That's such a weight off my mind. Thank you. Did you hear that, Yossi? This nice young lady will look after you. Now you'll do exactly like she says, all right? You understand?"

Yossi nodded his assent.

"Only to London," said Franzi. "After that . . ." She didn't finish the sentence because it wasn't necessary.

"No, I understand, of course," replied the woman, a little less enthusiastic. Still, for her it was better than nothing. "Can they sit anywhere on the train, the children?"

"I believe so."

"Good, so they can sit together."

The woman began to tidy the boy in preparation, patting down his hair and licking a handkerchief to wipe his face. That's when Franzi began to realize that she, too, would have to start saying her goodbyes.

"All the children!" said her father again, from out of nowhere. This time, it was more of an exclamation, as if he'd just realized where he was, on a crowded railway platform. "Where are they taking all the children?"

"It's all right," said his wife. "They'll all be safe, don't worry."

Charlotte stepped forward obligingly to let them hug her and kiss her one more time—first her grandmother, then her mother, whose tears were just beginning to form—but she, herself, still felt nothing. It was as if it were happening to someone else and she was outside her own body, watching from afar.

Meanwhile, the words began to gush out of Franzi in free-flow. "Will you write to me, *liebste*? Please promise me you'll write. And give my love to your father. And your Uncle Hershel, all right? And his wife, too, although I've never met either of them. Will you write? Please say you'll write."

"Yes, I'll write," said Charlotte, her voice flat.

"You promise?"

"I promise."

"Oh my God, *meineliebe* Liesl, what am I going to do without you? You're my life, you know that? Please be careful. Will you be careful?"

"Of course."

"Good, good. Now, in your bag there's some lunch, you can share it with the boy, but eat most of it yourself, all right? Who knows when you'll get another good meal? You had no breakfast, you must be hungry."

"I'm fine."

There was a guard's whistle from the far end of the platform and before it was even complete, a blast of steam bellowed from the locomotive.

"My God, my God . . ." repeated Franzi, her hand to her mouth, her face now streaming uncontrollably. "I'll never see you again, I'll never see you." She pulled Charlotte towards her for another hug, bringing her daughter's head down so she could whisper in her ear. "Please say you forgive me, *liebste*, please."

"I forgive you," said Charlotte, but again, the words that emerged were lifeless.

Franzi wasn't entirely satisfied but she tried her best to paste a smile onto her colorless face. Then she unfastened the thin mauve scarf she was wearing and gave it to

Charlotte. "Take this," she said, before giving her another hug.

All this time, the porter who'd followed them through with his cart had been waiting patiently, but as soon as Charlotte moved to board the train, he lumbered after her, inadvertently pushing people aside as he manhandled the baggage. Yossi's mother, too, uttered a few last words of encouragement to her son, then pushed him gently forward with his own bag, gesturing for him to go with Charlotte.

In a minute or two, they both appeared at the window of the nearest compartment, with Charlotte's height dominating the other children. She slid open the panes at the top and peered down at her mother and her grandparents. Franzi was blowing kisses and wiping her eyes, doing neither very successfully, so Charlotte politely blew a kiss back.

She knew she should also be in tears, that she should be showing some kind of emotion, but it wouldn't come. No matter how she tried, she couldn't force it, and she just stood there, staring down at them.

There was another whistle and that's when all the extended families on the platform began to panic, some waving, others weeping, with many mothers almost fainting in their hysteria. Next to Charlotte was the small boy, Yossi, who had no clue what was happening, and he, too, shed no tears, spoke no word. He just accepted everything blankly, but only because his infant mind was paralyzed by the frenetic activity.

All along the train, adults were reaching across to touch the window glass, grasping at their offspring, missing that one last kiss, that one final hug, before sending them off on their own to . . . what? Everyone was so worried because nobody really knew. They had no idea what would happen to their children in England, or to themselves if they remained here in Vienna. All seemed to recognize, if only subconsciously, that this morning at the Westbahnhof was like a small break in the passage of time, a last moment when they would all be together before the tension and the oppression bore down again; before the ordeal was made even more hopeless by the lack of any future that their children represented.

Charlotte just stood there leaning her head out as far as it would go. She could feel the blast of steam as the engine fired up and the acrid smell penetrated her throat and caused her to cough. Her mother was choking a little, too, as was her grandfather. This couldn't be good for his lungs.

Then came the final train whistle, this time longer and somehow more permanent. To Charlotte, it was just like in high school when they were doing exercises in the yard. The gym teacher used to blow a whistle when she wanted the class to change into another routine, and that's how this train whistle sounded, too, as if somebody was blowing for everything to change.

She felt the train shudder and heard the screech as the heavy-gauge wheels spun, trying to gain traction. Then, at last they began to chug away slowly and Charlotte had to strain just to see her retreating family. Her mother was now running along the platform, dodging people while trying to keep pace as the momentum gradually increased.

It was difficult for her to move quickly in the clothes she was wearing, and once or twice, she almost tripped. She reached her hand out to try to touch her daughter one last time, her face twisting with the contortion, but to no avail.

Charlotte leaned out of the window as far as she could for a final glimpse of her mother's auburn hair until the diminutive figure was just a wisp—and then the train emerged from the station into the pale light, and Franzi was visible no more.

Charlotte stood watching for a while, then collapsed into the seat, suddenly alone and overwhelmed. In her hand was the mauve scarf that she'd been given, and subconsciously, she allowed her fingers to caress the thin fabric.

Yet, as she stared out at the walls and roofs of western Vienna, all she could see was an endless replay of her mother and Karl, a mental picture she just couldn't seem to expunge. She was underway, her escape complete, but she still didn't know what to think or how she should be feeling.

She just watched the monochrome landscape drift by as the Viennese suburbs gave way to a winter countryside. Around her, the five children in her compartment also tried to settle themselves, exhausted from their drained energy and separated from their parents for the first time in their young lives.

By international agreement, the *Kindertransport* was obligated to take a lengthy route across the continent from Vienna all the way to the Hook of Holland, but to make that journey, it first had to pass through the heart of Hitler's Reich, via Nuremberg and Frankfurt.

For most of the way, the train continued without disturbance, stopping only briefly to take on fuel and water. There were adequate toilet facilities on board for the children and, twice a day, the Flemish conductor, a stooped man with amiable eyes and a thick black mustache wheeled a squeaky cart which contained small boxes of sandwiches. They were always the same: stale bread with a thin filling of paste which tasted vaguely of fish.

There was nothing to drink, so the children scooped what they could from the washroom faucet, even though it was murky and tasted foul. Charlotte warned everyone in her compartment not to drink too much, but inevitably there was one who ignored her, another boy about the same age as Yossi, and he began to suffer from diarrhea. At night, she tried to close her eyes just to shut it all out, but the children were restless, and she was rarely able to snatch more than an hour's sleep at a time.

Eventually, the train slowed to a crawl and then lurched to a standstill in the northwestern German city of Köln. Here, everybody on board, every last child, was ordered to disembark by a loud SA official on the platform. On his arm he wore a swastika armband, on his hip a holstered pistol. In Vienna, the Brownshirts didn't usually carry such weapons: wooden clubs or other crude implements, but rarely any kind of firearm.

"Come on," Charlotte said to Yossi. "We all have to get off the train."

The other children in the compartment, ranging from six to fourteen, followed them silently. It seemed that Charlotte had become the *de facto* group leader but she wasn't sure she wanted that responsibility. It wasn't that she was especially afraid of the situation. In fact, she was beyond feeling very much of anything. It was more that she just couldn't be bothered with it all. She was tired: of the children, of the train, and of life itself.

More orders were yelled, telling them to line up—"*Schnell! Schnell!*" quickly, quickly—and before long, there were several hundred Jewish children standing at attention along the entire length of the platform.

Many had forgotten to put on their coats and were now shivering. As for Charlotte, she stood there impassively, a statue, with little Yossi by her side, clinging to her hand while a pair of junior SA men, no more than Charlotte's age themselves, began counting. Once, twice, then a third time, the children were counted, a process which took over two hours.

Was it bureaucratic mania, or sheer vindictiveness? Charlotte wasn't able to work it out. According to the original letter from the Red Cross, the transport agreement stipulated that no children would be harmed along the way, but that reassurance wasn't enough to reduce the levels of anxiety.

For them, it was just more of the same harassment they'd experienced back home, except this time, they didn't have their parents to shield them. Some were fighting to hold back their tears. Some were straining not to soil their underwear, not always successfully.

One girl of fifteen or sixteen had blood from her cycle clearly dribbling down her legs and Charlotte wished she could have gone along to comfort her, the same way the blonde youth leader once did when they were hiking in the mountains.

Fortunately for Charlotte, nobody came to question her, about her age or anything else, because in her uncaring mood, she might have said something to place her in very real peril: an overly assertive response, perhaps, or even a harsh word or two. If so, she'd never have been allowed back on the train, and once it left, she'd have been beyond even the questionable protection of her Red Cross credentials.

In Hitler's Reich, a young Jewish woman alone had no rights whatsoever. Rape, beatings, the camps: all had become commonplace, yet Charlotte seemed strangely oblivious to the dangers. Even when the youngest of the Brownshirts paused to look her up and down, her eyes remained frigid and glassy, staring straight ahead into the middle distance as if he weren't even there—and that might well have been what saved her, because after waiting a few seconds in vain for some kind of response, the game grew tedious, and he strolled on, feigning arrogance and disinterest.

After the senior SA official was satisfied that all his figures tallied, the children were ordered back on to the train
on the double. Some of them were kicked if they weren't
fast enough, but as far as Charlotte could see, all made it
back on board, cold and afraid but otherwise unhurt. From
Köln, it took just an hour more to get to the Netherlands
frontier, and once again, the train came to a lurching halt.
At this point, customs inspectors mounted the train to inspect each child's papers, but these men were Dutch.

They presented a far more pleasant demeanor and the
procedure was merely symbolic. No child was about to be
seized and thrown off, so it wasn't long before the train
was able to rattle its way across the border, from Germany
into the Netherlands. Within minutes, the Flemish conductor came along the train in a far more buoyant mood, passing from car to car to make the announcement.

"It's all right," he told them in his basic German. "You're
safe now, you can say what you want."

In Charlotte's compartment, none of the children really understood this geographical change until she, herself,
started to talk, asking them how they were doing, if they
were all right, anything to drive out the fear which seemed
to have impregnated their young souls.

The journey, however, was still far from over, and
it wasn't until the following morning that they finally
reached the end of the line: the ferry port at the Hook of
Holland. Here, for the first time in her life, Charlotte caught
a glimpse of the sea. It wasn't blue or green as she'd seen
in pictures but a monotonous shade of charcoal, stretching
all the way to the horizon where it merged seamlessly into
the heavy nimbus clouds.

The children were told to leave their baggage on the
platform, that everything would be organized, and then

they followed the officials across the tracks, on to the quayside, up the gangplank, and at last, onto the boat. This caused great excitement, and when they all converged on the main deck, it set loose a boisterous mass of noise and enthusiasm. Some began to push each other and run, their small muscles having been confined for too long, and it was a major task for the adults just to round them up and keep them from disappearing over the side.

The exception, however, was little Yossi, who refused to let go Charlotte's hand and remained in his tremulous state, dazed by all that was happening. As the boat eased away from the dockside, the children were herded into the cafeteria lounge where they were served strong tea in tin mugs, just like the ones in Hugo's shop, but no food in case of seasickness.

As it turned out, the precaution was unnecessary because it was a fairly mild crossing. Despite the winter swells, the winds behaved themselves, as did most of the children, although one boy of ten did cause some minor disruption when he managed to sneak his way into the bowels of the ship and had to be brought back by a greasy-faced engineer.

The vessel didn't take the normal ferry route across to Dover, making its way instead to the ancient coastal town of Harwich in the county of Essex, north of the Thames Estuary.

Here, the junior refugees were led into the large shed where they were required to wait in line yet again while they were questioned by officials, asked about their state of health, and examined carefully for lice and other diseases. For Charlotte, this was especially embarrassing, and she refused to allow anyone to touch her until they replaced the male doctor with a more acceptable female nurse.

The children were also handed any number of leaflets and brochures, even though many couldn't read a word of English, and the only notice in their own German language was to explain how foreigners must behave on these shores.

The headline read "You are a guest of Great Britain," and the text which followed spelled out what was required of them in the most patronizing detail, stating that aliens were required to respect local English decorum. This meant talking quietly, using discretion, and acting at all times in what was deemed "a civilized manner."

The full process took several long hours, after which the weary children were escorted onto yet another train, this one bound for London's Liverpool Street terminus, the designated reception point for all the *Kindertransport* trains originating in both Vienna and Berlin.

The journey through the bland English countryside was slow and uneventful, with the cows and horses they passed hardly even bothering to raise their heads. Then there was a long stretch through the endless outskirts of London, which seemed full of illegible signs and strange-looking vehicles driving on the wrong side of the road, until the thunderous commotion of their arrival.

The crowds and noise were dizzying, and some of the children, suddenly afraid and fearful of being split up from each other, began to sob all over again.

So far, Charlotte had accepted the journey with equanimity, a calming, if somewhat cool, adult presence, but as the train jerked to a stop, she felt the involuntary emotions of excitement and apprehension beginning to creep up on her, which she just couldn't allow.

She refused to give in to such sentimentality. As yet, she still hadn't decided whether to tell her father about his wife's infidelity, or whether to respect her mother's wishes and remain silent about the whole affair. It was this, more than any thoughts of a new life, which occupied her mind.

As she alighted, she was thankful that a smiling woman of the Royal Auxiliary stepped forward, offering to relieve Charlotte of the responsibility for Yossi. At last unburdened, she was able to proceed along the platform, back and forth, searching each and every face until finally she saw him, standing high on a flatbed cart, waving at her frantically: a stocky, balding figure comically bouncing around like a chubby chimpanzee.

Charlotte moved towards him as rapidly as she could, pushing and shoving her way through to reach him. She helped him clamber down, then grabbed hold of him with both arms. After days of arduous travel, the tension had given way to, if not joy, then certainly relief.

She was still in tight control, still dry-eyed and impassive, but nevertheless, for a long time the two of them just stood together in the cavernous station, clutching at this miracle of salvation, deafened by the roar, yet oblivious to everything but each other.

It took Charlotte twenty-five years before she entrusted me with the truth about her mother's relationship with Karl and her reaction to discovering them together. In trying to describe these feelings, she had trouble finding the right words until I suggested the idea of numb.

"Yes, that's it," she said, "that's what I felt . . . I just felt numb, like at the dentist when you get the injection, your mouth goes numb. You know that feeling? That's what it felt like to me, like I'd had one of those injections in my brain."

This was by far the most difficult chapter of her long story, and it was like the culmination to everything I'd heard and seen. Suddenly, all those private moments when she became upset over trivialities or broke down in tears made more sense, and I began to understand why she'd developed such deep volatility.

It wasn't just the nefarious stealing of a handsome young man that had affected her so profoundly, although that was hard enough. It was the act of betrayal by her own mother and the reaction of an innocent, impulsive, loving girl—especially after they'd become so close, after they'd survived so much together.

Charlotte, with her reserves of strength, had tried to help and protect her mother from the most rabid abuse, even using her own body as a shield, only to be repaid by the most outrageous deceit. Yet, even after all of that, she still couldn't bring herself to loathe her mother because she wasn't built that way. That's why, when it happened, she just willed herself to shut down, not from anger, but from confusion.

However, there had to be a corollary to all of this, and the one thing she hadn't yet told me about was the other half of the parental equation. I therefore waited until the time was right and then asked her the obvious question.

"Do you think your father ever suspected anything?"

"Suspected? You mean about my mother and Karl? How? Only if she told him herself in a letter, and I'm sure she didn't. Am I a hundred percent sure? No, who can be so sure of anything? But I hope he didn't know. I hope not. Enough that I was hurt like that, I wouldn't have wished it on him."

9

London was not at all the way Charlotte had imagined.

She knew it was still a monarchy, and she'd read all about the pageantry of the guards who wore the red coats and the high fur hats, but the brief ride from Liverpool Street Station to Whitechapel Road in the working-class East End was disappointingly boring.

It was just narrow, rain-soaked streets, crowded with ordinary people scurrying about their business under black umbrellas. It didn't really matter though, because all she wanted to do was sleep.

She was more exhausted than she'd ever been in her entire nineteen years, and she snuggled up to her father in the back of the large cab, holding on to his arm, secure in the knowledge that he was there to take care of things.

Even though he'd been absent for most of her childhood, she'd always felt that he knew how to take care of things. From her youngest days, he'd been her protector.

They would be staying at her Uncle Herschel's place, the second floor apartment where he lived with his wife, Leah, and his son, Frank, who was just a couple of years older than Charlotte, but was now in the army, just like his father had been. Her father informed her of all this as they rode in the taxi, but what he didn't say was that there would be a surprise party for her when she arrived.

When they finally stepped through the door into the apartment, it seemed as if it were bursting with family. Most of them were on Leah's side, plus some friends and a few neighbors, all there to greet Charlotte: to shake her hand, pat her on the back, and make her feel welcome.

None of them could possibly imagine how it must have been for her back in Vienna, yet all were full of sympathies. Some spoke English, others tried their best in Yiddish, but both languages were difficult for her to comprehend.

They were trying to be nice, but they just didn't realize that back home in Vienna, the Goldbergers and the Gutmanns had spoken only High German in front of her. At school, she'd learned basic French, plus some rudimentary English, but the teaching was poor, and although she'd obviously inherited some of her parents' instinctive ability with languages, her understanding was still fairly limited.

It was the reason, everyone assumed, that Charlotte seemed somehow cold and distant as she greeted them— that, plus the journey, the fatigue, and heaven-only-knew what horrors she'd witnessed—so they all did their best to be reassuringly jovial around her, while quietly telling her father not to worry, that she'd be fine once she settled in.

The introductions seemed endless, so many strange faces, but the one she liked most was her Uncle Herschel, or Uncle Harry as he preferred to be called. To Charlotte, he appeared to be a near-duplicate of her father, slightly bigger and a bit more roly-poly, but with very similar characteristics. He was businesslike and worldly but, at the same time, easy-going and full of good humor.

It was just as well because his wife, Leah, was something of a busybody and given to feeling victimized. On this day, she'd laid on a fine show with plenty of food and local beer, but she'd been a lot less happy at the prospect of Charlotte's arrival, due to the extra work it would mean.

As she now muttered to her husband, she was glad to see that the girl was robust, and hopefully, she'd pull her weight around the place.

The one person Charlotte hadn't yet met was Frank, her first cousin, who was late coming in from his base at Aldershot, southwest of London. With such a crowd in the room, she didn't see him when he first walked through the door, and by the time he found his way over to say hello, he was already in his shirtsleeves.

It was only when Charlotte turned around to greet him that her face registered the shock. Her legs suddenly felt weak, and her father had to grab her arm to prevent her from collapsing. Frank was clean-shaven and sandy-blond, a bit like Hugo, but he was wearing a brown shirt. It was standard British Army issue, but to Charlotte, for that one instant, it was enough to remind her of the dreaded SA.

"Whoa, it's only me," he said with his friendly Cockney accent. "Long time since I had that sort of effect on a girl."

Everyone laughed, and Charlotte, too, tried to smile politely, but she was still overcome and had to sit down on the chair that Frank hauled over for her. Yet even though she felt faint, she refused to let go of her rigid self-control, remaining insular and totally detached from her ever-fussing relatives.

That evening, after everyone had gone, she made her excuses and retired to the room they'd given her, which turned out to be Frank's room. Since Frank was now home on leave, he would be sharing it with her. She could hardly believe it, but there it was: a bed for her, plus a small temporary cot for him, separated by a large old blanket that had been hung over a laundry line.

It had to be this way, her father explained, because they had very little room. He, himself, would be sleeping on the sofa in the living room. By going to bed early, she was under the covers by the time Frank came in.

"Sorry about scaring you like that earlier," he told her, as chatty as if he were still in his army barracks, bunking with his platoon. "Silly of me, never realized. Must have been something awful what you went through over there. 'Course, you know we have those Nazi bastards over here, too, don't you?"

His English was rapid and not easy for Charlotte to follow, especially from the other side of the blanket, but she was able to catch the gist. "The SA?" she asked, surprised.

"Yeah, whatever you call 'em, we got 'em, too. All the bloody same. Don't get me wrong, nothing to worry about though, not like over there. Here, it's just a few of 'em and they got no power, not really. Just like to cause a nuisance sometimes, that's all. Did you hear what happened? Must have been, oh, couple of years ago now. Not far from here, actually, was all over the news."

"What? Sorry . . ."

"Am I talking too fast? That's my problem, I know. I'll try to slow it down a bit. All right, so what happened . . . there's this bloke, this man, called Mosley, Oswald bloody Mosley, right here in England. And anyway, he likes Hitler, likes Mussolini, you following me?"

"Yes . . ." she replied hesitantly.

"All right, even slower. So, anyway, he's got all these supporters, Blackshirts, they call 'em. Not Brownshirts, but Blackshirts. So he arranges a march, wants to have a big Nazi rally, like what they have over there in Nuremberg, you know?"

"Yes, I know."

"Only he wants to do it here, in the East End. Well, he made a big bloody mistake with that, I can tell you. What happened, we find out when he's coming. So we all go out and line up in the street, wait for him. You with me?"

"Yes. You wait for the Blackshirts."

"Right, right, that's very good. Fantastic, your English."

"Thank you."

"Anyway, so we're there, waiting for him down on Cable Street. That's not far from here. There was Jews like us, and the Irish from down the docks, and all kinds of people, thousands of us . . . and then there's them, marching along with Mosley at the front, bunch of bloody idiots. They had all the police around them, too, protecting 'em, but we didn't care. I don't know who started it, but before you know it, we was all piling in, knocking 'em around like I don't know what. You should have seen it, we gave 'em what for, I can tell you that."

"You fight?" asked Charlotte, not able to distinguish between tenses.

"Yeah, with the Blackshirts. Gave 'em a right rollicking."

"Rollick . . ."

"Rollicking—bashing—We knocked hell out of 'em."

"So, you . . . win?"

"Are you kidding? Yes, we bloody won, drove 'em all away, the Nazis and the bloody coppers, too. Absolutely, we bloody won. They never came back here again, that's for sure. Bunch of bloody idiots." Frank chuckled to himself as he remembered the epic street fight that the newspapers had taken to calling *"The Battle of Cable Street."*

Charlotte, however, was trying hard to imagine such a thing. Here, instead of Jews scrubbing the roadway, they fought back against the Nazis, but she didn't take much satisfaction that she was now living in a place like this, because all she could think about was her mother, still back there in Vienna, still facing the same dangers each day when she went out—and that, in turn, made her wonder about the nights. Was her mother also frightened then, or was Karl there to keep her company?

It was all Charlotte had been able to think about since it happened: that one mental image she'd retained of the two of them naked together, like a photographic plate permanently etched into her memory.

Did they really love each other, as her mother had claimed, or was it simply sex for its own sake? Was she just a whore, lusting after an attractive young man in his prime? Or was Karl nothing but a common gigolo, finding easy prey with a slightly older woman?

Who was the predator, and who was the quarry, or were they equally guilty? Charlotte still hadn't settled on any kind of answer, and despite her weariness, she lay awake for some time, listening to Frank's gentle snoring, and attempting yet again to work it out in her mind.

The following morning, the family all had breakfast together, five adults squeezing around a creaky wooden table. The apartment wasn't much larger than the one in Brigittenau, but here the inhabitants could at least take pride in the luxury of indoor faucets, a built-in bathtub, and a toilet that flushed.

It was crude but the water flowed with reasonable pressure and was even drinkable to the extent that it wouldn't necessarily cause sickness if someone were to swallow down half a glass.

The food was different, too. Here they drank tea with milk, not lemon, and ate toast for breakfast because, as Aunt Leah said, "What else can you do with bread once it goes stale?"

They weren't poor though, merely average for the area, which consisted mainly of tradespeople and stallholders from the local Petticoat Lane Market, orderlies from the nearby London Hospital, plus an assortment of bus conductors, motor mechanics, construction workers, and kitchen staff.

The district was also home to various small-time criminals and prostitutes, whose money was nonetheless just as valuable in helping to keep the pubs in business and the economy functioning.

All told, it was exactly the kind of place where immigrants settled, and in addition to the East European Jews who'd arrived during the great influx at the turn of the century, there were Jamaicans, Africans, Indians, and several other small communities who had somehow made it over from those far-flung empire outposts.

After they'd finished eating, Jakob and Charlotte accompanied Frank as far as the Underground, known universally as "the Tube," which was the first stage of his journey back to camp. Charlotte was sorry to say goodbye, even though she'd now have the bedroom to herself, but he promised to finagle another pass in time for her twentieth birthday, which was just a few weeks away.

From there, father and daughter continued walking, all the way along the busy streets of the East End as far as Aldgate. It was their first chance to be alone together since before the *Anschluss,* and although she remained in her somewhat reserved state, Charlotte found it pleasant just to stroll and take it all in, open and unafraid, with her protector right by her side. They passed the time conversing in German about their experiences; what Jakob had done since he'd come to London, how he'd learned about the *Kindertransport* and arranged it all through Aunt Paula and the Red Cross.

From Charlotte, the talk was of life under the Nazi regime, especially the details of what had happened on *Kristallnacht*, which both astonished and appalled her father. In answer to his probing questions, she also provided some vague generalities about how her mother was coping, mostly in terms of money, food, getting around, that sort of thing; all the fundamentals but none of the reality.

There was so much to talk about that they didn't pause until they entered a local workers' café for a lunch of bacon and egg sandwiches, a new delight that Charlotte found delicious.

It was just as they were settling down with their strong, milky tea that Jakob made the comment, "You know, *liebste*, you've changed."

Immediately, she flushed with embarrassment. She was perfectly aware that she'd changed, also how and why it had happened, but she really didn't want to get into that topic—not now and maybe not ever. "How?" she asked, feigning innocence to cover her reaction. "How have I changed?"

"I don't know. Your attitude. It's as if . . ."

"As if what?"

"I don't know. Somehow, you've lost your sense of fun. You used to be so cheerful, so enthusiastic about everything, and now . . . Well, that's all right. I understand. It's no wonder, with what you went through, but it'll come back, I know it will. You just need some rest, a little peace and quiet, a little time to yourself. How does that sound?"

She nodded. "It sounds good."

"I'm taking a week so we can be together, you know, to *schmooze* a little, as your Aunt Berthe used to say, but then I've got to go back to work."

"You're working? I didn't know."

"Of course, I'm working. What, you think I can live on *bupkis*? I'm still wiring money to your mother. Who do you think pays her rent?"

That was something else for Charlotte to think about while she was sipping her tea. While her mother was taking Karl into her bedroom, it was her father who was footing the bill. Yet, still, she didn't say anything. She just let him continue talking.

"Anyway, your Uncle Harry gave me a job for now. Not much but what else can I do? I'm still on a tourist visa. I can't work, I can't start a business, nothing. But I'm grateful to him, I really am. He had to fire one of his managers to give me the work, which he didn't like doing, but, well, that's life I suppose."

He gave a sigh and there was a lengthy silence. Around them, the customers talked and smoked, sturdy types with bad skin and patched clothes who jostled past the tables as they arrived and left. Again, it was up to Jakob to break the wordless barrier between them.

"So, what would you like to do for the week? See the sights? I haven't seen them myself yet. Reminds me of when I took your mother around Vienna for the first time. Did I tell you we got in to see the horses without paying? Did I ever tell you that story?"

"Yes, *vati*, you did."

"Yes, yes . . . of course I did. So, where? What do you want to see? Do you have any idea? Want to meet the king? They say he's a nice fellow. I'll see what I can do to arrange it."

Charlotte appreciated the attempt to lighten things up, but she was wondering if their conversations would ever be the same again, or would they always—would *she* always—be so restricted that their time together felt awkward. Yet how could she tell him the truth?

She longed for the chance just to blurt it all out, but what would that achieve, she kept asking herself. How would it help? It might even make things worse between them. So she held back and continued to suffer her lonely anguish, uncertain and unresolved, but too afraid of the revelation to give voice to it.

For the rest of that week, they walked around half of London, and as long as the talk was centered on her favorite subject of British royalty—who had been imprisoned in the Tower, who was beheaded at Smithfield, who was interred at Westminster Abbey—their discussions were pleasant enough.

At Charlotte's request, they also went to see the glamorous store windows of Regent Street and Oxford Street, where she was able to gaze longingly at the latest fashions from Paris and New York. It was all so different here, so free and adventurous, but these feelings of liberty turned against her each night, casting their ominous spell of guilt and accusation before she fell asleep.

That was when the SA stomped back into her brain and spat on her clothes and forced her to hide in that dank, smelly closet. The pulse in her temple felt like the beat of her mother's heart, and if she lay perfectly still, she could still feel that frail body next to hers, trembling with the fear of being discovered.

Sadly for Charlotte, the weeks' vacation with her father was over soon enough. The days of playing tourist came to an end and her new life in London soon settled into its own monotonous rhythm.

During the day, Jakob would go off with Uncle Harry to spend his time calling up distributors and repairmen and loan officers at the bank. In the meantime, Charlotte stayed at the apartment, doing exactly as her Aunt Leah commanded. This meant several solid hours of cleaning, dusting, cooking, shopping and laundry—especially laundry of which there seemed to be an endless amount.

Uncle Harry was a fussy dresser, and her father had become that way, too: every morning a clean shirt, along with clean socks, underwear and handkerchief. It was the professional way to be, they said, which might have been true, but it meant an endless mountain of washing and ironing for Charlotte.

In truth, she didn't mind the hard work. What she disliked far more was Leah's attitude, which was not only demanding but also totally humorless. Unlike her mother, Aunt Leah didn't even allow the radio to be played, at least, not until Jakob made a special plea, asking how Charlotte would ever learn English if she didn't hear it spoken.

Harry, too, thought that sounded reasonable, so Leah was outvoted and had no choice but to relent, but she only turned it on in the afternoon, and even then, only if satisfactory progress had been made during the morning.

For Charlotte, the radio was neither entertainment, nor teacher, but a joyless reward for which she was expected to be suitably grateful, and this was how the time passed until her birthday came around, when Frank came home for the weekend as he'd promised.

Thanks to his engaging personality, life for Charlotte was immediately more cheerful than it had been for a while, and on the very first evening, after supper was finished and the dishes washed, he suggested to Charlotte that they go along to the local pub. He had some friends there he'd like her to meet. When she looked questioningly at her father, he just waved her away.

"Go already," said Jakob in his comic version of Yiddish. "You're twenty years old now, you want I should tell you what to do?" Then, because she didn't understand Yiddish very well, he had to spell it all out in German, but it somehow lost its humor in translation.

Charlotte's English, however, had improved dramatically in such a short time, and despite the noise of a Whitechapel pub on a Saturday night, she was reasonably capable of keeping up with Frank and his friends. They seemed like a good bunch who knew each other from way back.

None were in the forces like Frank, so the fact that he was still in uniform made him the constant focus of their teasing. He didn't seem to mind, though, and he laughed graciously at their jokes, no matter how crude and tasteless.

At one point, when Charlotte accompanied Frank to the bar to help him bring back a round of beers, she found herself alone with him. Maybe it was the beer, or maybe just the spirited atmosphere—more fun than she'd had since she could remember—but before she could stop herself, she asked, "Do you have a girlfriend?"

He looked at her. "Excuse me?"

"This is the word? Girlfriend?"

"It's certainly the word if you're asking what I think you're asking."

"Sorry?"

He smiled as he took the large tray of drinks from the barmaid. "No," he said simply. "I don't have a girlfriend."

"Why?"

"Why?"He smiled. "I don't know why. I just don't, that's all. Not everything makes sense, you know."

At that, she nodded her agreement. She might have argued that nothing at all made sense, but she wasn't at the pub for a philosophical discussion, she was here to enjoy herself, which she was trying to do.

It was close to midnight when they returned to the apartment and had to tiptoe past the sofa where Jakob was already asleep in order to reach their shared room. They weren't drunk, nor were they entirely sober, and the most difficult thing was to prevent their mutual fits of giggling.

Since they couldn't turn on the light, they had to feel their way in, with Charlotte leaning on Frank's shoulder for support. When she tripped over a pair of shoes in the dark, she grabbed on to his arm, but her momentum was too advanced, and all she succeeded in doing was pulling him down on top of her, as they fell onto the bed.

There were more hushed giggles, but their faces were now very close to each other, and all Charlotte could think about was Hugo. Without too much mental debate, she raised her head the slightest amount and found her lips directly on his.

For a moment, he didn't react but then he broke away. "We shouldn't," he said.

She didn't respond, mainly because she hadn't fully understood that negative form of the verb, but it didn't matter. He was still very close, so she kissed him again. This time, he didn't pull back.

He took it more seriously, and before either of them knew what they were doing, they were writhing together, smothering each other, their hands chasing each other across their bodies.

Charlotte felt his erection grow, but she didn't care, and neither did he. They were first cousins sharing a room with their parents right next door, but there was no way they could bring themselves to stop, or even slow down. The only requirement was to remain quiet.

Charlotte had never before had such close contact with anybody but she needed it now more than ever. She'd lost Hugo due to her father, and she'd lost Karl due to her mother, but she refused to lose Frank, no matter what the circumstances.

After just a minute or two, Frank had her sweater open and then her blouse. She was helping him, undoing buttons here and there, pulling at sleeves, and unclasping tiny hooks. It was feverish and thoughtless and exceedingly stupid.

They didn't even have any protection but that was of no concern to Charlotte. She needed to be close to someone, to trust and be intimate with someone. She'd held her emotions in check for so long that she was desperate for some kind of release.

It was her twentieth birthday, and it seemed like losing her virginity to Frank was as good a present to herself as any.

After Frank returned to base, Charlotte was shattered by loneliness, and the spring of 1939 became a season of slowly descending misery. True, she no longer had the Brownshirts to fear, but that just took away the visible danger. The real enemy was within herself.

During daylight hours, the only people with whom she could speak was the obdurate Aunt Leah or, when she went shopping, the curt counter staff. In theory, the men of the house were meant to come home in time for dinner, but in practice, they were often late and always exhausted.

Business was hard, and neither arrived in much mood to talk. All they wanted was to eat and then sleep. She could have perhaps found some kind of friendship amongst Frank's crowd, the people she met at the pub, but without his presence, they didn't mean much to her, and anyway, there was still too much of a language barrier for it to feel natural.

In many ways, she missed Vienna—missed her activities and her youth club and her day trips to the mountains—but that was an old Vienna which didn't exist anymore. Somewhere within the depths of her soul, there was also a longing to get back to that optimistic spirit she'd once enjoyed, but it was beyond reach, and she just couldn't figure out how to reawaken it.

Most of all, she missed being able to stop by Hugo's little repair shop to talk things over, and the more she thought about him, the more she realized that he was the one with whom she'd wanted to be intimate, not Frank at all.

At best, Frank had been a momentary surrogate, and the instant she realized that, things with him were never the same. Whenever he came home on leave, they were friendly enough and still went to the pub occasionally, but there was never any repeat of that first night.

It was as if they both knew, without even speaking the words, that their brief tryst, their *one-night stand,* as it was known in English, had been merely an anomaly, a distraction, no different from adding the sweetness of white sugar to improve the bitter taste of English tea.

The ever-worsening political news didn't help either, not that she completely understood it, but she sometimes listened to her father and his brother discussing it in their late-night weariness, and they appeared to be getting more and more depressed.

By their estimation, another war seemed inevitable and probably sooner rather than later. It was already raging in North Africa, where the Italians were pushing to control Abyssinia, Ethiopia, and Suez; also in the far east, where the Japanese were invading large swathes of China.

Even in Europe, the Fascists in Spain, supported by German legions, had recently won a victory in the bloody Civil War. Now, it seemed, it was just a matter of time before the rest of Europe would erupt in the same way.

On this, both Jakob and Harry were in total agreement, and the fact that two such wise heads had come to the same conclusion was enough to convince Charlotte that some great and unknown disaster wouldn't be long in coming.

The way they saw it, Hitler was the driving force, the ambitious aggressor right in the very center of Europe, and the rest of the countries, both large and small, were busy making treaties with each other to try and counter him. Yet these weren't real alliances.

As Harry said, they were more like dance partners, with the participants making all kinds of rapidly constructed pacts, then reneging almost as soon as they'd been signed whenever a newer and scarier scenario was in the offing. All had been frightened by Germany's takeover of Austria and Czechoslovakia.

Within a matter of months the Nazis were in control of both great capitals, Vienna and Prague, and everyone was wondering which might be next. Budapest? Warsaw? Maybe even Paris? Like Jakob, many had read *Mein Kampf* and knew that Hitler had designs on expansion, but nobody really knew where.

That was why the so-called major powers, France, Russia, and Britain, appeared to be in such a panic. In each case, they were worried about being out-maneuvered, or worse, encircled by the others. Events came to a head during that long, warm summer. One morning, during the third week of August, the world woke up to the unthinkable: a treaty of convenience between Nazi Germany and the Soviet Union, whose ideologies had been assumed to be diametrically opposed.

Hitler and Stalin had always mistrusted each other, yet here they were, with this one agreement, tilting the global balance of power toward their own spheres of influence. Through their respective foreign ministers, Ribbentrop and Molotov, they'd somehow managed to forge an agreement and, as every intelligent observer knew, the prime target of this new alliance would be Poland, which lay between them.

Despite a flurry of diplomatic activity, neither France nor Britain could do anything about the situation—in Paris, Prime Minister Daladier called it a *fair accompli"*—and it placed both governments in an impossible position.

After the takeover of Czechoslovakia, they had both guaranteed Poland's security, hoping that the threat alone would act as a discouragement. Yet Hitler, with Stalin's explicit public support, and together with his Axis partners, Mussolini in Italy and Hirohito in Japan, now had the necessary momentum to continue his planned march forward.

On the first day of September, Germany invaded Poland with fifty-two divisions, consisting of a million and a half men at arms. To thrust their way through home defenses, they employed a strategy they'd tested in Spain which came to be known as *Blitzkrieg,* or "lightning war." While the Panzer tank brigades pounded every obstacle in their path, the Stuka dive-bomber squadrons caused chaos behind Polish lines, scattering troop columns and fleeing refugees alike.

Hitler had sworn never to repeat the grinding trench battles of the Great War and this devastating new method of wide open warfare allowed him to move with a speed that even his own generals had not thought possible. According to legend, a Polish regiment of mounted cavalry actually raised their sabers and charged, magnificent and foolhardy as in the days of old, only to be crushed mercilessly by the iron-clad tanks, an anecdotal report that came to symbolize the mismatched confrontation.

The only response France and Britain could legitimately make to this all-out invasion was to fulfill their security obligations by issuing a clear ultimatum: "Pull back your forces from Poland or a state of hostilities will exist between us". Believing they had neither the means nor the will to act, Hitler chose to ignore their demands, and World War II had begun.

For the Goldbergers of Whitechapel, it meant they now had even more family worries. In the city of Krakow in southern Poland, there was Berthe, Adolfo, and their aging father. In London, mass conscription was now in effect, which meant that Frank couldn't hope to be discharged any time soon.

On the contrary, as a ready-trained infantrymen, he would be one of the first sent across the Channel with the Expeditionary Force. In the meantime, general civilian evacuation from major cities was also underway, and Harry came up with the concept of moving before they were sent to a place they didn't want to go.

His reasoning was that if it were his own choice, they'd be able to transfer to Southend, the working-class seaside resort to the east of London where Harry now had more business than in the city. His wife, Leah, happened to agree with his thinking, as did Jakob, and they began to make detailed plans, but before they could complete their move, the government acted first. It happened one morning as Harry, Leah, Jakob, and Charlotte were having breakfast together. There was a knock on the door, and Charlotte went to answer it, only to find a uniformed constable, with his high helmet and his bright silver buttons.

"Morning, madam," said the officer in his most official tone. "Does a Mr. Jakob Goldberger reside on these premises?"

"Yes . . ."

"Might I have a word with him?"

"Please, just a minute," she replied and went back to get her father.

Jakob may have already suspected what was about to happen, because he gave a knowing glance to his brother before saying to Charlotte, "That's fine, *liebste*, stay here, I'll go deal with it."

Then, in just a few minutes, he returned with a sigh in his voice. His Majesty's Government had determined that male German-speaking aliens were to be interned.

"*Liebste*, listen to me. I have to go away for a while."

Charlotte got to her feet, a sudden wild look in her eyes. "With the police? They're taking you away?"

"I'm sorry, *liebste*, but there's not much I can do about it. It'll be all right. It's not a Nazi, it's just a bobby on a bicycle. You'll stay here with your aunt and uncle and help them to move, all right?"

"No, no . . ." Charlotte rushed to hold him, as if by doing so, he wouldn't be able to leave.

He wrapped his arms around her, as he'd done that first day at Liverpool Street Station, and patted her shoulder. "Come on, now."

"No, you can't go."

"Before you know it, I'll be back. I promise you."

"How long?"

"I don't know, *liebste*. I don't know. Remember what I told you in Vienna? Strong, smart, and careful? That's how you must be." Gently, he eased her away from him.

"No," she kept saying, like a child. "No . . . no . . ." Then she turned to her Uncle Harry. "Why does he have to go? Please, you can't let him go." It was the most emotion she'd displayed to either of them since she'd arrived. Harry looked at Jakob, who replied with a shrug. There was nothing that either of them could do and it left Charlotte wishing that her cousin, Frank, would return to give the policeman a rollicking, a bashing, like he had the Blackshirts.

She couldn't understand why her protectors were never there when she needed them, and she just sat there in her own morose silence long after her father had disappeared with his suitcase, accompanied along Whitechapel Road by the constable wheeling his bicycle.

Several weeks later, Charlotte sat at the table and began writing a long letter. Uncle Harry had yet to come home from work and Aunt Leah was trying to get her to move out of the way so she could set the places for supper.

"What's that you're so busy writing, anyway?" Leah asked her.

"Letter," Charlotte replied brusquely. She'd learned that the best kind of rebellion was to give the most minimal answers.

"And who is it to, this letter?"

"My mother."

"Your mother? Really? Don't you know there's a war going on?"

"Yes, I know."

"And what are you going to tell your mother in this letter? About how you do so little around here? About how ungrateful you are for a roof over your head?"

"No, I tell her about my father."

"Your father? That's a joke for a start."

Charlotte could ignore much of what Leah said but not this, not about her father. "What you mean?" she demanded in her limited English.

"What do I mean?" Leah was about to answer but then changed her mind. "No, I don't think you don't want to hear it."

"What? *What*?"

"All right, you want to know, I'll tell you. Your mother doesn't want to know about your father, so don't waste your time. She doesn't love him, she never did, not even when they first got married."

Charlotte looked at her aunt, trying to work out what the woman knew and what she didn't. For one brief moment, Charlotte was startled into thinking that Leah must know about Karl, but then she realized her aunt was just talking in general. "I don't understand."

"Never mind, it doesn't matter now. She's there, and he's here. Maybe it's just as well."

Charlotte became resentful. "You know nothing."

"Don't you speak to me in that tone."

Charlotte stood up from the table, ready to defend her parents the way she'd once defended her mother against the boy from the *Hitlerjugend*, but she didn't have to follow through because her Uncle Harry walked through the door.

Immediately, he sensed the atmosphere. "What's going on?"

"I write to my mother," Charlotte said to him. "Then, tomorrow, I go see my father."

This was an idea she'd been contemplating for a few days, but before her aunt could register a protest, Harry held up his hand, a signal that the remark had been addressed to him, and that he would take care of it.

"He's far away from here. I don't think you realize . . ."

"Yes, I realize. I see the map. It's called the Isle of Man. I know also how to get there."

"How do you know that?"

"I ask people. The woman at the shop, she told me. She has her husband there also, at the Isle of Man. She tells me how to go there. I take the train to Liverpool. I take the boat to Douglas. You see? I know. Tomorrow, I will go."

Again, Leah was about to say something, her expression dismissive as if Charlotte were just a silly girl, but again, Harry held up his hand.

"You know, *liebste*, it's not so easy."

He called her *liebste* like her parents, but from him, Charlotte didn't mind so much. "Train to Netherlands, boat to England," she replied in her halting English, reminding him of the journey she'd already survived. "This time, not so hard."

At this, she saw him smile, and for an instant, he looked exactly like her father.

"You're right," he said gently. "But what I meant was that here in England, you're an alien. You know what this means, to be an alien?"

"Sure I know. The woman tell me. When I go to Douglas, first I must go see the police and they give me . . ." She came to a stop, having forgotten the word.

"Permission, is that what you mean?"

"Yes, permission."

Harry nodded. It appeared to be a more knowledgeable answer than he was expecting, but he had another point to make. "It's also expensive, to go to the Isle of Man." Before she could question the word, he chose to explain it. "What I mean is, it's a lot of money."

"I have money."

She was thinking of the funds her father had given her so that she could buy her own things, like clothes, underwear, and makeup without having to be embarrassed to ask each time. She didn't have much, but based on what the woman in the store had told her, she'd figured it might be sufficient if she were prudent.

Harry considered the issue while she watched him, making him self-conscious. Finally he gave up and offered a major shrug. "All right, all right. You're twenty years old, you want to go, so go. I can't stop you."

His wife was immediately outraged, but he simply shook his head in her direction, and she held back from any comment. Instead, she just threw up her hands as if wanting nothing more to do with such nonsense and turned towards the stove in order to get busy with supper.

It sounded so simple: train to Liverpool, boat to Douglas. However, working out the details proved to be highly complex, and Charlotte was secretly glad that her Uncle Harry volunteered to take time off in order to go with her from Whitechapel to Euston, the rail terminus for the northwest.

In the booking hall, the clerk who served them was an elderly man close to retirement, with tufts of gray hair poking out from under his peaked cap, yet he seemed to have the entire timetable memorized.

He was also very patient, which was just as well, because it took a great number of questions and calculations to buy the tickets: third class from Euston to Liverpool's Lime Street, traveling on the London, Midland & Scottish Railway via Rugby and Crewe.

From there, a twenty-minute walk to Prince's Landing Stage at Pier Head in order to make the afternoon sailing on the ferry *Tynwald* operated by the Isle of Man Steam Packet Company. This would take her to the island's main town of Douglas, a crossing of about four hours, weather permitting.

There she would proceed directly to the nearest police station in order to obtain authorization to see her father. Then she'd have to find herself either a rooming house or bed-and-breakfast hotel for two nights. Finally, after all that, she'd have to accomplish the whole journey again in reverse.

To Harry, it was a daunting challenge but not to Charlotte. Every time he asked her if she understood, she gave him a confident "yes," and he wasn't entirely certain if she really did comprehend the difficulties involved, or was just putting on a show of youthful bravado.

After they'd purchased the tickets, they still had an hour before the morning train was due to depart, so Harry took her for tea in the cafeteria, now crowded with servicemen in uniform. The nation simply wasn't ready for war and there was considerable confusion surrounding every aspect of the draft. It wasn't just the immense organization needed to move men and materiel around the nation, it was also the effect of removing people from the workforce while maintaining essential services, as well as industrial production.

Young men by the thousand were being hauled out of factories, offices, and universities to be sent far from home—and in the middle of all this disruption, a single young woman with faulty English intended to travel half the length of the country to go see her father, an alien who'd been judged a danger to the state and was now interned behind barbed wire. According to Harry, it was madness, but he felt a responsibility towards his brother, so the least he could do was write down all the instructions clearly on a scrap of paper and give her a little more money, as much as he could afford, just in case she ran into something unexpected.

Then, as he was racking his brain trying to think of how else he could prevent any possible trouble before it happened, he came up with an inspiration, a flash of an idea, proving once again how the Galician Goldberger family could be ever more resourceful when they put their mind to it. The concept was simplicity itself. The government was nervous about German sympathizers and spies. Fine, so why did Charlotte have to be German?

"You know what to do?"asked Harry suddenly. "Tell them you're Polish."

"Tell who?"

"Anyone who asks. Just tell them you're Polish."

"But I speak German."

"Yes, but they won't know that if you only speak English. They can't tell one accent from another. As long as you tell them you're Polish, they'll have sympathy because of what Poland's going through right now."

"What if they see my papers, my passport? It says I am born in Austria."

Harry thought about it, but only for a moment, because he had an answer for this, too. "Doesn't matter. Tell them your family's from Poland, tell them your father's from Poland, but you just happen to be born in Austria, *versteh*? And you know the beauty of that? It's the truth."

"And my mother?"

"They won't ask. Just make sure you keep saying your family is Polish. Keep saying it over and over and all they'll think about is Nazi tanks and bombs, trust me."

Even in her youthful naiveté, Charlotte could see how that made sense; and as he'd pointed out, it was no more than the truth. She nodded her agreement and, at last, Harry sat back on the wooden chair of this hectic station cafeteria with a satisfied expression. He'd done all he could.

Finally, he remembered something else and, from his inside pocket, he pulled out a slightly crumpled white envelope, already sealed. "Here," he said, "I want you to give this to your father, all right?"

She took the envelope and looked at it curiously. "What is it?"

"Never mind. It's private, that's why I sealed it. Please don't open it, just give it to him. Will you do that?"

Charlotte nodded again and placed it in her bag. For her, it was of no consequence; probably something about business they didn't want anybody to know.

Then she sat back, too, and looked across at this man who so closely resembled her father in every possible way.

"Thank you for all this," she said quietly and saw him return a gentle smile.

Charlotte was fortunate to be accompanied on the journey to Liverpool by a chatty soldier, a lanky man with a lopsided face and untidy brown hair, who took the seat next to her and immediately shook hands, informing her that his name was Trevor. As he proudly told her, that strange accent she detected was what they called "Merseyside," which took its name from the river, or if you really wanted to sound local, you called it "Scouse".

What really interested Charlotte, though, was when he told her that he'd spent his childhood summers on the Isle of Man. His Auntie Margaret still lived there, he said, but she was alone now because his Uncle Patrick, or Paddy as they knew him, had died a year or so back.

"Does she have a room I can stay in?" asked Charlotte.

"You mean like a bed-and-breakfast? I don't know. Maybe. Would that help? Is that what you're looking for?"

"Yes. For two nights."

"You know what? When we get to Liverpool, I'll phone if you want, you know, to ask her. She might be glad of that. Not just the money, but the company. Always liked a bit of company, did our Auntie Margaret. Likes to chitchat."

"Chitchat?"

"Natter, gossip, talk. Where you from, anyways? You got a bit of an accent yourself."

"My family is from Poland," she replied.

"Oh, bloody hell. You got my sympathies, luv."

Charlotte smiled her acknowledgment, even as she mentally thanked her Uncle Harry for the suggestion. It seemed to work. Trevor had been nice enough already, but with this piece of knowledge, it was almost like they'd become comrades-in-arms, with all the mutual respect the designation conferred.

Indeed, there was nothing untoward about his congeniality at all as far as she could tell: no romantic motives, no improper moves. He was just an affable young man, perhaps a little homesick, who seemed content merely to talk, and the fact that she was foreign was, for him, all the more interesting.

During the long hours that followed, she told him a little of her life back home, but she did it carefully without actually using the word Vienna, so for all he knew, she could have been speaking about Warsaw or Krakow. She revealed no personal information, just a little about how they lived: about her family's apartment, about her trips into the mountains, about her favorite sports.

In return, he spun endless stories about her island destination, starting with its precise location half-way across the Irish Sea and its first inhabitants who were Vikings. It was famous for its cats without tails, he said, which fascinated Charlotte because she'd never heard of such a thing, and also for motorcycle racing, which he used to watch as a kid.

Then there was the unique native language that a few of the older residents still spoke, as well as the many fine beaches where he used to play, and the horse-drawn trams along the promenade, which he loved to ride whenever he could afford it. By the time the train ground its slow way into the Liverpool terminus, she felt like she, too, had spent her summers in Douglas.

As promised, he called his Auntie Margaret long distance from a public phone in the station but couldn't seem to get through, so he gave Charlotte the address and said she could use his name as a reference.

In addition, he was kind enough to walk her partway to Pier Head and give her directions for the rest, so she was able to arrive at the landing stage in a good frame of mind.

She was well pleased at this new acquaintance she'd managed to make, and content, too, that she'd made the decision to get away from that stultifying Whitechapel apartment.

Does a positive attitude breed better luck? she wondered. She thought that perhaps it might, because when she arrived at the shipping office, she was informed by an official that she was extremely fortunate. In another week, the man said, half the steamers in the fleet were to be commandeered by the navy for the war effort, including the vessel she was about to take, the MS *Tynwald*.

If she'd waited, she'd have found a far more irregular service, with the sailing schedule reduced and the resulting passenger accommodation severely limited.

Often, the Irish Sea can be fairly rough, but on this day in late September, the four-hour crossing to the Isle of Man was as smooth as her first voyage from the Hook of Holland, with the weather unusually mild for the time of year.

Charlotte stood alone by the deck rail, and for the first time in a while, allowed her mind just to drift. She gazed at the dark swell ahead and at the white wake behind and enjoyed the aerobatics of the gulls which followed them a good distance from the shore, diving for the scraps that were tossed from the galley.

Watching them made her hungry, and with the extra money Harry gave her, she was able to afford a cheddar sandwich. Despite her accent, she was treated with courtesy and respect, which only confirmed what she'd already discovered: that despite the country's reputation for being somewhat aloof and patronizing towards foreigners, it could also display a civilized side, almost quaint in its amiability, which was very welcome.

Of course, none of this changed the harsh fact that they'd interned her father but this journey to see him had at least given her the chance to create some kind of balance in her mind. These were normal people with normal fears but they weren't inherently malicious—nothing at all like the Nazis—and that gave her some small cause for optimism.

Once the ferry was safely docked in Lower Douglas, she descended to the quay, walked right up to the nearest uniformed officer at the exit of the facility, and asked him where the nearest police station might be.

"Not far at all, miss," he told her, and gave her directions along with a brief tip of his helmet.

"Thank you, most kind," she said in return, a phrase she'd picked up from Frank at the pub.

The local constabulary, like the metropolitan force in London, was primarily responsible for the arrest, internment, and filing details of all internees within their jurisdiction.

In theory, any senior police official could therefore provide visitation rights, but the particular sergeant she saw, a middle-aged man with thin strands of nicotine-tarnished hair, told her very politely that it was beyond his authority.

"But I am here from London. I must see my father."

"I'm sorry, miss, you seem like a presentable young woman, but he's a citizen of Austria and so are you, and we can't allow the risk of collaboration, now can we?"

Charlotte wasn't sure about the word *collaboration* but she could guess. "We're not German," she said, attempting to remain as reserved as the British themselves. "We're also not Austrian, not really."

The sergeant looked down at the card in front of him, which he'd pulled from a large metal cabinet in an adjacent room. "Says in the file that you are."

"Yes, but just our passports. My family is from Poland."

"I see. Well, that's a shame about that, what's happening and all, but not much I can do, miss. Wish there was."

Charlotte wasn't willing to let it go. "So how can I see my father? Can you please give me some advice?"

The sergeant looked at her, then appeared to develop some empathy. First he looked both ways like one of the furtive thieves he no doubt took into custody, then he leaned his elbow on the counter so that the whole weight of his bulky shoulders was hunched over. Quietly, he said, "Look, I shouldn't be telling you this, but you're an attractive girl, and I happen to know that the sentry on early shift, he's a bit sweet on the ladies, if you know what I mean.

"So if you talk to him nicely . . . not do anything, you understand, I wouldn't want to condone nothing like that . . . but if you talk to him, he might make a phone call inside. I've known it to happen. That way, your dad can come outside, and you can maybe chat a bit through the wire, long as there's no contact. How's that sound to you?"

Charlotte was listening intently, trying to catch every nuance of what he was saying. She could hardly ask him to repeat it. By the end, she thought she understood and nodded her sincere appreciation.

"Can I use your name?" she asked him.

The sergeant smiled at her cheekiness. "No, you bloody well cannot," he replied, then picked up the file, ready to take it back to its place in the cabinet. The interview was over. Then, as an afterthought, he said, "You're Jewish, right?"

Charlotte wasn't at all sure how to answer. Just like in Vienna, he'd obviously deduced her identity from her name, but over there, it would have been not so much a question as a deliberate provocation, an order to scrub the streets, or worse. This man obviously had no such intent, so she simply responded with a cautious nod.

The sergeant looked at her for a moment. "Well, maybe it's not my place to say, but for what it's worth, miss, I don't think you Jews deserve none of what's happening, what we read about in the papers. You're just people like anybody else, am I right?"

"Yes . . . Yes, thank you," she said to him, relieved that her supposition had been confirmed. If not, it could have been awkward.

That's when she remembered the address Trevor had given her and decided to take advantage of the situation while she could. She took out the piece of paper, unfolded it and handed it across the counter. "Do you know this place?" she asked. "It's where I can stay."

He squinted at the scribble, trying to make it out. "Oh right, of course, luv, not far at all. I'd say about ten minutes' walk. Here, I'll draw you a map."

Taking a stubby pencil from his pocket, he went to the trouble of sketching out the route, along with abbreviations for the street names. As he passed it back to her, he gave her a final warning, joking in tone, but serious in its message. "No monkey business with that sentry lad, now."

Charlotte had no clue about the phrase *monkey business* but she'd become fairly adept at perceiving vocal tones in order to grasp the meaning. In response, she just smiled shyly, causing the officer to wink at her before he went back about his business, very much the father-figure of the station.

All-in-all, it had been a strange encounter as far as Charlotte was concerned, a contradiction that somehow seemed to summarize for her the entire British attitude. On the one hand, he'd refused to allow her permission like the civil servant that he was, yet on the other, he'd gone out of his way to be as personally helpful as possible.

The town of Douglas was a typically Victorian seaside resort, small and provincial, which had once again become an unlikely center of the war effort. During the last war, a remote barracks had served as the internment camp, but this time, several hotels at the northern end of the promenade had been taken over.

As Charlotte walked along the sea front, she could see them in the distance, surrounded by wire, but she didn't approach them, not that afternoon. That would be tomorrow's adventure, she decided.

Since it was already close to dusk she thought it better to use the remaining light to find a place to stay, so she did her best to follow the rough map the sergeant had drawn, which led up the incline of Buck's Road to a narrow sidestreet packed with row houses.

When she found the number she was seeking, she walked directly up to the front door and pushed the button. She could hear the high-pitched ring inside.

The thin lady who answered had smoky gray hair, pulled back and held in place by an Alice band. She was wearing a mid-blue twin-set outfit over a skirt of dark tartan, which was fastened Irish style with a large clasp. On her feet were worn carpet slippers decorated with orange pom-poms.

"Mrs. James?" This was Trevor's family name.

"Yes?"

"My name is Charlotte. I met your . . ." A little flustered, she couldn't think of the English word for nephew, so she improvised.

"I met your Trevor on the train and he said you maybe have a room for two nights. I pay, no problem."

"Oh, I see. You're not exactly English, are you dear?"

"My family is from Poland . . ." Charlotte hesitated, then thought she should probably tell the truth. It would be all too easy for the woman to guess anyway.

"My father came here by the police. But we are not German, we are Polish, so I think a big mistake. I come from London on the train to see my father. This is how I met your Trevor."

Mrs. James was still making her assessment. "I see, I see . . . Well, all right, I suppose, if Trevor sent you. You say you can pay?"

"Yes."

"You'd better come in then. Are you hungry?"

"Yes." Actually, Charlotte was famished. All she'd eaten the whole day was that one sandwich on the boat.

"All right, well, I'll see what I can do. I have a spare room upstairs, where Trevor used to stay when he was a lad. It's the war, isn't it? We all have to make an effort."

Charlotte half-expected to find two beds with a blanket between them, just like in Whitechapel when she'd first arrived, but that wasn't the case. Here, she found a pristine little room with a chest-of-drawers, a narrow mirror and a single divan, neatly made up.

Who might stay here now, Charlotte couldn't even begin to guess, but she didn't really care. She was just grateful that she'd found somewhere clean and hospitable. The meal of corned beef and potatoes that Mrs. James served her in the kitchen hardly had any taste at all, but that didn't matter.

It was edible, and Charlotte did her best to chat with Mrs. James as Trevor had recommended, but by the time she'd finished eating, she was so exhausted that all she could do was make her excuses, tramp back upstairs, and collapse on the bed.

From the moment she awoke, Charlotte was thinking about her appointed task but there was never any likelihood that she would try to sweet-talk the sentry as the police sergeant had suggested.

Even if language were no problem, she just wouldn't know how to go about it; and even if she did, she would never have compromised her integrity in that way, especially as a means for seeing her father.

Yet she still needed the man's cooperation, so as far as she could see, there was only one option left open to her. After she'd introduced herself with some pleasantries about the weather, she got right down to business. "How much to tell my father I'm here?"

The sentry was good-looking in his own boyish way, with a Romeo's dark eyes but cute, baby-like dimples around his chin. For a moment he was startled by her direct approach. "Your father's interned here?"

"Interned, yes. How much?"

The young man gazed at her, trying to assess what she was all about. He seemed to like what he saw, a good-looking girl with strength and a bold attitude, because his face opened up into a broad smirk. "We're talking about money, right?"

Charlotte well understood the implication. "Yes, money," she replied firmly.

"All right, keep your hair on. So let's see . . . I think a fiver should cover it."

"Five pounds?" For Charlotte, that sounded like a great deal of money, even with the extra from Uncle Harry. "I don't have five pounds. I can give you two."

He thought about it but not for long. "Two and a kiss. My final offer."

"No, just two. If everything is all right, maybe after I give you a kiss, maybe not."

He flashed her another grin, even broader. He had nice teeth and knew it. "Deal," he said with finality and reached out, offering to shake on the agreement.

This, she accepted. "Deal," she repeated, a word her father had taught her. Then she opened her purse and handed over the money.

The sentry nodded his thanks and lifted his phone. "What's his name?"

"Jakob Goldberger."

Thirty minutes later, there he was. Like an apparition, her father was standing in his shirtsleeves on the opposite side of the fence. They were nowhere near the sentry post but farther along the hotel facade, because the reunion was unofficial, and the soldier had told them not to make it obvious. When Jakob saw who it was, his jaw dropped and his eyes widened.

In response, Charlotte waved to him and returned his disbelieving gaze through the fence. He'd lost a little weight and looked pale in the morning light—and that's when she at last broke down. To see him standing there like that, a forlorn figure behind the wire, like a criminal, was just too much, and for the very first time since she'd clamped down on her emotions, the dribbles of moisture began to roll down her cheeks. She couldn't help it.

She'd held it all back for so long, against all the terror and the upheaval, but now her face was streaming to the point that she could hardly breathe. Her legs couldn't hold her and seemed to give way as she collapsed at the foot of the wire, her hands gripping it tightly, her knuckles white. Jakob, too, wept to see her, especially like this, but there was little he could do, either to help her, or to comfort her. Instead, he just leaned over as far as he could to touch her fingers with the tips of his own.

"Stand up, *liebste*," he urged her softly. "Please, stand up."

She couldn't stand up, and she couldn't even answer. She was far too choked up, and the words refused to emerge from her throat.

Eventually, she found her voice. "Don't speak German," she managed to say through her tears. Eventually, as requested, she climbed slowly to her feet, her hands still holding on for support. "You must speak English and tell them you're Polish, that's what Uncle Harry says."

Jakob thought about it for a moment, then switched to English. "Good advice," he agreed. "But what are you doing here?"

"I came to see you."

"I can see that. But how? With who?"

"Just me, with nobody."

"On your own?"

"Why not?"

"Where are you staying?"

"The aunt of my friend."

"*Mein Gott, meineliebe,* Liesl . . . Sorry, English . . . My God, my dear Charlotte."

His literal translation sounded so silly that she laughed out loud, but the sound had to force its way through the sobbing and came out as a gurgle.

Her father laughed, too. "That's better," he said.

"So, maybe I must call you Dad," she said, continuing the same humor.

"Dad . . ." he replied, testing it out. "Yes, I like that. Very simple . . . Dad, dad, dad."

There was more laughter, this time mixed with a bout of coughing. Then she remembered something. "I have a letter, from Uncle Harry."

"Good, so pass it through. Wait, wait, don't let anyone see you. Roll it up first."

They looked in all directions, but there was nobody around this morning. The entire northern stretch of promenade seemed clear of both traffic and pedestrians. Even so, she hurriedly rolled the envelope into a tight tube and poked it though as if it were a secret plan for the nation's downfall. Jakob took it surreptitiously, then tore it open and scanned the short note.

His reaction came as a grin. "You want to know what it says?" he asked her. "It says I have a very brave daughter and that I should be very proud of her."

"It says that?"

"Yes . . . and he's right."

"I don't feel brave. My face is wet."

"So stop crying."

She smiled, sniffed, and tried to comply. "How long must you be here?"

"How long? They won't tell me. Maybe a few weeks, I don't know."

"Only a few weeks?"

"Maybe. They have what they call 'tribunals,' the government, where they have people judging each case. They say a few weeks, but who knows?"

"Do you eat? Do you sleep?"

"Don't worry about me, I'm fine."

"*Natürlich* . . . Naturally . . . I worry."

"Well, don't."

She put her hands to the wire again. She needed to touch his fingers, to feel his warmth and to let him feel hers. He was all she had now, and she just couldn't face the thought of losing him, too, so she began to talk about plans for the future. It was a way of coping.

"When you come home . . ." she said very quietly, hesitating before she completed the question she was about to ask. She wasn't sure what his response would be, but this was something she'd been thinking about for a while.

"When you come home," she began again, "do we have to live with them? With Leah and Harry?"

"You don't like Leah and Harry?"

She looked at him, unsure of herself. She didn't want to insult him by criticizing his family. "I like Harry," she replied. It was only half a reply, but it was the truth.

Jakob nodded, as if he knew perfectly well what Leah could be like. "We cannot live with them anyway," he told her.

"No?"

"They're going to Southend for the business, but even if they let me out of here, I can't go where I like. I must stay in London. Those are the rules."

"Good," she said simply. "We can find a place?"

"Maybe. I hope. There's not much money. All my savings, everything . . . it's all gone."

"We can do it."

"*Liebste,*" he said, slipping back into whispered German, "I cannot even send money to your mother anymore." She gazed at him and could feel his discomfort. She knew how hard it was for him to admit something like that, how proud he'd always been of his ability to make a living for his family. How could she now tell him that her mother was no doubt being supported by Karl, that she might not even need her father's money?

"*Vati* . . ." she said, also reverting to her native language against her own advice. It was just so much easier. "Leah said that *Mutti* never loved you. Is that true?"

Jakob looked at her, as glistening droplets seeped through the corners of his eyes. He couldn't bring himself to answer, but for Charlotte, that in itself was enough.

"So why did she marry you?" she asked him.

He shrugged. These were impossible questions. "I don't know, *liebste,* I wish I did." Then he sighed, as if there was no reason to hide anything anymore. "I'll tell you the truth. It's time you knew. Your mother's parents . . . your grandparents . . . They really wanted me to marry Paula."

"Aunt Paula?" This was the first time Charlotte had ever heard this. "Aunt Paula?" she said again, disbelieving.

"She was the eldest. That was the *shidach*, or that's what they thought. But when I saw your mother, it was what the English say . . . *love at first sight*."

"So she accepted, just like that?"

"No, not just like that. Of course not. It took a long time, but finally, yes, she accepted. What I mean is, nobody forced her."

"And she never loved you? Never?"

Another sigh emerged. "I don't know. The day we got married, that's when she told me she didn't love me. And you know what I said, what I answered? I said you'll learn to love me . . . but I don't know if she ever did. It's possible, I just don't know. Who can ever really see into another person's heart?"

Charlotte didn't know how to respond but just thinking about it brought more tears. To her, it was now all so simple, so obvious—and so tragic. Her mother had never loved her father, and to make it worse, he'd left her alone all those years to go traveling on business. Eventually, when Karl came along, it all just happened, just as her mother said. In a way, it was almost inevitable, and Charlotte couldn't understand why she hadn't seen all this for herself. It didn't make her feel any better, or any more forgiving, but at least she was beginning to comprehend the motives involved.

As a daughter, she'd only ever seen Franzi in terms of motherhood, but in this brief moment of clarity, she saw her for the first time as just a woman: confused, lonely, and afraid; a woman who had found herself tied to a marriage she never really wanted. It all made so much sense.

She also saw her father as something else, too: a man overburdened by his own sense of guilt at leaving his wife behind. Here he was in an internment camp, an independent spirit with his freedom denied, yet still so responsible that he couldn't stop thinking about the situation half a continent away. Jakob shook his head with the weight of despair. "I just don't know what she's going to do," he said. "Your mother over there, with no money."

"Perhaps she can go to my grandparents. I think they get money from Zurich."

That seemed to calm him a little. "I hope so," he said. However, a moment later, it all came pouring out. "I felt so bad, you have no idea how bad I felt, leaving you and your mother there like that. You have no idea. I tried to get the papers, I tried, I tried. Then I received a letter from your mother to say she wants to be with her family. Not her husband, her family. She says she cannot leave them."

Charlotte listened and was on the brink of interjecting, of revealing the lie for what it was, but she forced herself to hold back, asking herself yet again what good the truth would do at this stage. It would wound him and might even kill him, or at least kill his spirit, and he needed every last bit of his strength just to survive here.

"So then . . ." he was saying, "then I heard about the train, the *Kindertransport*, and I thought to myself, maybe I can bring my daughter out. If not Franzi, then at least *meineliebe* Liesl."

At this, he raised his hands to his face, trying to hide his streaming cheeks, and that was how the two of them remained for a long time: on either side of the fence, separated by wire, but connected as one by their mutual tears.

Charlotte was in a highly depressed state after this particular anecdote, so I did my best to try to bring her out of it.

"Did you kiss him?" I asked her.

She looked across the table at me, her eyes still reddened. "Kiss who? My father?"

"No, the sentry . . . with the nice teeth and the cute dimples."

That's when a smile found its way through, like a stray beam piercing a rain cloud. "No, I forgot," she admitted.

"You forgot?"

"I never went back." Then a small laugh. "That's the first time I thought of that."

"And Trevor? How about Trevor? Did you keep in touch?"

"I didn't have his address. All that time on the train, I didn't get his address. I sent a Christmas card one year to his aunt in Douglas and asked her to give him my regards, but he didn't write back. Nor did she. Maybe he died in the war, I don't know."

"And Frank?"

"My cousin, Frank. He was a good boy. Oh, a funny thing about Frank. You know, he was rescued from the beach . . ."

"The beach?"

"You know, where the army was. On the beach, when they were all rescued and brought back."

"You mean Dunkirk?"

"Yes, yes . . . I couldn't think of the name for a minute."

She was referring to the coastal town in northern France where the British Expeditionary Force and several French divisions were encircled by the advancing German Wehrmacht and trapped on the beaches. Over three hundred thousand might have been annihilated, but Prime Minister Churchill asked anyone with a sturdy boat to set sail across the English Channel and help the Royal Navy ferry them home. Hundreds answered the call, and the successful operation came to be regarded as one of the miracles of the war.

Of course, technically, it was a military defeat, but it was heralded in England as a major psychological victory and keeping up the Dunkirk spirit went on to become a rallying cry.

"So what happened?" I asked her. "With Frank?"

"What happened, he was rescued from there. You know how? By the boat from the Isle of Man."

"Really? That's some coincidence. The same one you took?"

"I don't know if it was the same one. But the same type."

"Small world."

"You're telling me."

By this time, Charlotte's mind was well away from her father and his heartbreak, so we were able to continue with our lunch. Outside, the day was bright and her tiny blue budgie, Ricky, was chirping happily, so the mood changed.

Then, from all her carefully saved scraps of paper, she managed to find a joke that she'd torn from a magazine, so the story of her life was held in abeyance for yet another week.

10

Of the seventy thousand Germans and Austrians interned by the British government during those first few weeks of the war, over fifty thousand were Jews like Jakob Goldberger, who had arrived on their shores seeking refuge.

As Jakob told Charlotte, cases were being heard on an individual basis before tribunals all across the country, and each was categorized in one of three ways: an *A* classification meant a danger to the state and included Fascists like Oswald Mosley and other Nazi sympathizers; *B* was exempt from internment but subject to certain restrictions; and *C* was fully exempt.

Jakob only received a *B* classification, but it meant release within four months of his arrest, and he was suitably thankful. By just after the New Year, he was back hugging his daughter, but to his mild embarrassment, she wouldn't let him go, holding on with her arms around him for what felt like several minutes.

That day, and in the weeks that followed, she went with him everywhere: into the kitchen to help him make tea; outside when he needed a cigarette, a habit he'd picked up during internment; to the grocery store, or the post office, or anywhere else.

"I'll come with you" was her most frequent expression.

Even when he just needed some time to be alone, she was always there, and it was only because he found it so hard to refuse her.

During this period, they were still living with Harry and Leah, but that would only be temporary. The process of packing to move to Southend was almost complete and the Whitechapel apartment's rental would terminate at the end of the month. After that, Jakob and Charlotte would need somewhere else to live, so their main preoccupation together was scouring the classifieds in the *Evening Standard*, calling up landlords, and taking any number of buses and trains to go inspect potential places to live.

The business arrangement between Harry and Jakob was that the former would leave town to ensure the revenue stream on the Essex coast, while the latter would remain and try to pick up the pieces of the enterprise here in the city. In that way, they would be like partners, senior and junior to be sure, but with a joint personal interest in the health of the small company.

For Jakob, it suited his character far better than remaining an employee and gave him the necessary incentive to put everything he had into the endeavor. The only problem was that, for the time being, income from the London side remained negligible, so for the price Jakob was able to pay, there were very few apartments available. Anything they found adequate proved far too expensive.

He felt terrible saying no each time Charlotte found something she liked, and even though she was understanding and never complained, he spent a lot of time apologizing; yet more guilt to add to his existing stockpile. "I'm sorry, *liebste*" became his own well-worn expression, and he grew weary of saying it.

Eventually, just before Harry and Leah moved away from Whitechapel, Charlotte found a possible basement flat on Stamford Hill, a segment of the main A10 north-south artery in the borough of Hackney. Jakob went with her to see it but neither of them were too impressed.

In a previous existence, it had been nothing more than a coal cellar and was still impregnated with black dust. There was grease on the floor, too, where somebody had stored motor oil. The only light entered by a high, narrow window which was cracked and thick with grime.

In terms of facilities, there was a small, two-ringed stove and a tank for generating hot water, but both were powered by gas and had to be used sparingly along with the single radiator, because there was a coin meter and the rate was excessive. Washing facilities were in the form of a scratched sink and there was also a narrow bathtub tucked behind a partition but, like the rest of the place, both were filthy. Charlotte had the impression that it was this or nothing and tried to remain positive. "It's all right, *Vati*," she said with as much cheerfulness as she could muster. "I'll clean it up." They still spoke German when they were assured of privacy.

"This mess? You can't clean this up."

"Sure I can. I'm not afraid of hard work, you know that."

"*Liebste*, please . . ."

"No, *Vati*. You'll work to earn a living, and I'll work so we can live." It was a neat turn of phrase and she nodded to herself at her own sagacity. Then she added, "What else can we do? Sleep under a bridge?" That was the issue for Jakob. He didn't like what was being proposed but he had no alternative to suggest. After all his efforts over all those years, it had come down to this.

His wife was still stuck in Vienna, his family, including his wonderful sister, Berthe, was now equally trapped in Poland, and his only child, his beautiful daughter, a refugee who'd once scrubbed the streets for the Nazis, was now about to spend her days here in London cleaning out a coal cellar because he'd run out of money and couldn't afford anything better.

He still had a useful brain, but after the Isle of Man, his reserves of energy were low and if it weren't for Charlotte and her tenacity, he might well have given up, just surrendered himself to his fate—which, in his case, would probably have meant black market profiteering or some other criminality, no doubt resulting in further internment or perhaps even a prison cell.

Reluctantly, he decided to take the apartment, and that's when Charlotte got to work. Her state of mind hadn't changed—it was still fixated on her mother and all that had happened—but at least she was now alone with her father, the two of them working hard and supporting each other, and that fact alone kept her going through the strenuous days of toil.

In that same year of 1940, summer arrived early in Vienna, the fine weather merely serving to mock those, like Franzi and Karl, who were most affected by the ever-increasing restrictions. Their lives, too, had become a paradox, an alternating existence between reverie and reality. When they were together with the door closed, they could enclose themselves in the wrappings of their own sensual trance, their afflictions forgotten and their hunger only for each other.

Outside, however, they were subject to same desperate privations as everyone else in their community, an ongoing siege of their will and their energy that threatened to engulf them.

To manage the situation, even just to exist, they lived on hope. In their case, this came in the form of their daily wait at the embassy, not of Britain or America, but of France: an elegant, rococo-style edifice in white and gold situated just off Prinzeugenstrasse, not far from the broad greenery of the Palais Schwarzenberg.

Since the curfew prevented them from staying out evenings, to keep their place in line, they had to return each morning afresh, but as long as they made the effort there was the chance, however slim, that they would somehow manage to obtain the treasured visa and that everything would be as they'd so often imagined. It was a secret world they'd created just between themselves and they kept the flame alive while they waited by discussing the life they would lead in Paris: what their occupations might be; which boulevards they would stroll and which museums they would visit during weekends.

On the streets outside the embassy, people still taunted them, jeered at them, but Franzi had ceased to be afraid. She no longer felt alone and responsible but blithe and carefree, as symbolized by the smile on her face and the way she wore her hair, her beautifully lustrous hair, which now hung long and loose on her shoulders, forever tousled as if she'd just woken from another night of intimacy.

By her side was Karl, an attentive presence, his charm augmented by his tolerance, never complaining, and always ready to embrace and enclose her. As the weeks passed, they became used to this ritual of self-indulgence, but then it all came to a crashing end, along with their private vision of a future together.

It happened on one day in the middle of June when the doors of the embassy closed permanently. They were turned away and told not to return. Germany had invaded France and the politics of barbarity had taken precedence yet again.

After bypassing the supposedly impregnable French defense line, the Wehrmacht had entered Paris with almost no opposition. With events moving rapidly, what was left of the government under Marshal Pétain was pleading for an armistice, and within days, Nazi troops were goose-stepping their way through the Arc de Triomphe. As a final gesture of humiliation, Hitler then made Pétain sign terms of surrender in the very same rail car as the Germans had been forced to use after the last war, back in 1918.

For Franzi, word of this new occupation came as a fatal blow to her very being. If the Wehrmacht had already arrived, then the Gestapo would soon follow, the Brownshirts would own the boulevards, and life would be the same for the Jews of Paris as it was in Prague, Warsaw, or here in Vienna.

Wherever they went, the Nazis turned every dream to *dreck,* and Franzi was beside herself with sorrow, sinking into a lasting depression. Her one aspiration had been demolished, reduced to ruins by the march of jackboots. Although she and Karl were still together, their mutual desire undiminished, things could no longer be as they were.

With this news, the physical world had brutally imposed itself on their fantasy existence, and life became the intense, everyday struggle they'd tried so hard to avoid. They'd survived on hope alone, and now, even that hope was dead.

The fall of France and the Low Countries had a brutal effect in England, too. The country was isolated without the support of any major power. They still had their old empire, all those far-flung colonies and dominions, but none were prepared for war, and anyway, they were all too distant to be of much practical help In the meantime, the European nations were falling like skittles. After Poland, there was Belgium and Holland, as well as France; and after that came Denmark, Norway, and Greece; all occupied with embarrassing speed and all now firmly under the swastika flag.

In London, Prime Minister Churchill's only remaining ally of consequence was U. S. President Roosevelt, good ol' FDR, but White House policies were stymied by an isolationist Congress who wanted no part of any new European war. If it weren't for the Royal Navy guarding the English Channel and a badly-stretched Royal Air Force performing daily heroics above the home counties, Britain, too, might have succumbed to the early onslaught—and the danger wasn't yet over.

The government was still fearful of an invasion, either by landing craft or parachute, and defensive preparations were hurriedly set in motion. In cities and towns, air raid shelters were excavated, sirens tested, and drills ordered.

The most critical facilities were sandbagged and guarded around the clock. Humble urban backyards were cultivated to grow vegetables and park railings were torn down for their value as scrap metal. Everywhere, the nation was switching over to a war footing, and even the young Elizabeth, heir to the throne, chose to set an example by training as a common motor mechanic so she might be of some real use.

Amidst all of this, basic commerce had to continue, including the innocuous and highly trivial business of slot machines. That was why, on one Friday in early October, Jakob met his brother, Harry, who was just in town for the day, and took him for lunch at Bloom's delicatessen, a Jewish-owned landmark on Old Montague Street.

Ostensibly, they were there to discuss several client contracts that Jakob was in the process of renegotiating but talk had so far centered on the war and its likely scenarios. When that discussion was exhausted, they continued eating their matzo ball soup in silence until Harry switched to another topic, even further from business.

"How's Charlotte doing?" he asked, mopping up the last drops from his bowl with a thick slice of black bread.

Around them were other denizens of the Jewish East End and the two brothers fitted seamlessly into the crowded atmosphere.

Jakob sighed before answering. It was difficult for him to talk about his daughter. "Working herself to an early grave."

"That bad?"

"Worse," replied Jakob. "You have no idea how she works, that girl. I get home, she's still got her sleeves rolled up, scrubbing walls, washing clothes, sewing, cooking supper . . . and I don't know what else."

"You're a lucky man to have such a daughter."

"You think so? To be honest, I'd prefer if she had a husband and a couple of children to take care of."

"Does she go out at all, meet people her own age?"

"Not that I can see."

"So how's she supposed to find a husband?"

Jakob still had his mouth full, so he made a gesture as if to say that was exactly the problem. Yet he was full of his own guilt and, eventually, he felt he had no choice but to give in to Harry's unasked question: "All right, all right . . . You're going to tell me it's unhealthy for a girl her age to be cooking and cleaning for her father. Believe me, I know."

"Did I say anything?"

"I just don't know what to do about it."

"Push her out."

"I can't do that."

"You have to. It's for her own good."

"I get home late, she always wants to have something ready for me."

"Listen to me. You start slowly, one evening a week. You say you're eating out with a client. You say, Charlotte, here's a few shillings, go have some fun."

"What few shillings?"

"Jakob, stop worrying. I'll give you the money."

"I don't want your money."

"What, now you're so proud? You don't want the job, either?"

"That's different."

"Why? Why is it different?"

"Look, she's my daughter, my responsibility."

"Fine, I'll *loan* you the money, will that make you feel better? But Jakob, for heaven's sake, once in a while, get her out of there."

Whether Jakob liked it or not, he had to acknowledge the wisdom of the advice. He was fully aware that Charlotte had been acting more like his wife than his daughter, organizing their accommodations and arranging their life around the chores and the budget. Even on Sunday afternoons, the only time they ever took any time off, it was to go for a stroll together arm-in-arm around the Stamford Hill area.

As he left the small restaurant and walked his brother to the station, Jakob made up his mind to force the issue. Charlotte's welfare had to become another primary duty, right up there with rebuilding Harry's business, otherwise it would never happen.

Perhaps, he thought, *he should have taken more of an interest in her private life back in Vienna, instead of slapping her the first time he ever met one of her boyfriends, but all that was in a very different past, and it was far too late for such regrets.*

In the Stamford Hill area, there were two parallel streets known as East Bank and West Bank, but they had nothing whatsoever to do with the river. They were simply narrow residential lanes overlooking a railway cutting and the banks in question were nothing more than descending borders of thick, weed-like shrubs that grew untended each side of the track. It was for this reason, the chance to see a little greenery amidst the urban sprawl, that Jakob and Charlotte often made this area the destination for their weekend walks.

On the Sunday following Jakob's lunch with Harry, they happened to be on West Bank when a short, sturdy young woman, about Charlotte's age, came down the stone steps of a row building in overly high heels before toppling right into their arms. She had a high, curved forehead, expressive eyes, and a droll sense of Jewish sarcasm in her Cockney voice.

"If they'd made the pavement correctly," she said to them, "that wouldn't have happened." It was such a ludicrous comment and she said it in such a dry, deadpan way that Jakob just laughed out loud.

"Are you always this funny?" he asked her.

"Yes, sometimes I fall down laughing."

More laughter erupted, this time from both of them, and Jakob decided to introduce himself. "Jakob Goldberger," he said, reaching forward to shake her hand. "And this is my daughter, Charlotte."

"My name's Sadie Blay, pleased to meet you."

"Pleased to meet you, too, Sadie Blay."

"Sorry, but I've got to run," said the young woman. "Hopefully, not too fast. It's been nice talking to you."

"Take care," said Jakob, still amused, as he watched her hurry off. Then to Charlotte, "What a funny girl."

They continued their walk with their random encounter apparently forgotten, but the following Sunday afternoon, as they were taking shelter from a downpour at a small café, who should walk in but the same Sadie Blay.

It was Jakob who spotted her and called her over to join them. He bought both girls tea and then made some excuse about having to go to the tobacconist. He'd recently taken to smoking a pipe. As a result, the two girls were left alone together, and it might have been awkward, except that nothing was ever awkward for Sadie, because she'd developed the habit of coming directly out with the truth.

"Your dad arranged this, you know," she said, to Charlotte's surprise.

"Really?"

"He wants us to get to know each other."

"He thinks you're very funny."

"I know, a lot of people do . . . but it's not my fault."

Charlotte laughed. "How did he arrange it?"

"He came to our flat and asked me to meet you here. He said you haven't been in England very long and didn't have any friends yet. Where are you from, if you don't mind my asking?"

Charlotte was about to say Poland, simply because she'd got into the habit, but somehow, with Sadie, she also had the urge to be honest. "I'm from Vienna."

"Vienna . . . Do you know how to waltz?"

"Yes, of course."

"And is the Danube really blue?" It was a silly play on the title of a famous piece by Strauss.

Charlotte laughed even louder, as her father had done. "No, it's gray."

"You know, I thought so. Have you seen the Thames? It's gray, too. Do you think they're connected?"

For ten full minutes, Sadie led the conversation like this, most of it nonsense, while Charlotte just answered simply and smiled along, thoroughly entertained on this rainy Sunday afternoon. It was hard to imagine that, in the world beyond, there was a vast war being fought, with shells and shrapnel and the screaming of innocents caught in the crossfire.

"There's a dance next week," Sadie was saying. "Would you like to come?"

"A dance? What kind of dance?"

"At the club. Some of the boys will be home on leave."

Charlotte flushed for an instant, unable to prevent herself thinking back, first to Hugo at the youth club dance and then to Frank who was home on leave when they engaged in that irresponsible night in Whitechapel.

She also thought of Karl but tried to put that out of her mind. To divert attention, she said, "I have nothing to wear."

"So come in the nude. The boys won't mind."

"I'm serious."

"I can lend you something."

"No, I'm too big."

"You're not too big, just too tall," replied Sadie. Then she thought for a moment. "Here's an idea," she said. "I've got a full-length evening gown, but on you, it'll be mid-calf."

"What color is it?"

"Blue . . . unlike the Danube."

"Or the Thames." The humor was contagious, and Charlotte's English had improved sufficiently that she could enjoy it. She was still chuckling when her father returned to join them.

His trilby hat was wet from the rain, but his lit pipe had been sheltered by the brim, and he was puffing on it contentedly, pleased to see that his daughter and her new friend were getting along well.

Afterwards, as Charlotte and her father walked in lockstep, sharing their tattered umbrella, she leaned over and said, "Thank you."

"Thank you for what?"

"For what you did."

"I did nothing."

"So thank you for nothing."

At that, Jakob smiled, instantly recognizing Sadie's style of humor. This was the first time in months that Charlotte had sounded so light-hearted and it was good to hear.

In the great and ugly scheme of things, it was just a minor triumph, but with so few of them these days, even the smallest had become meaningful.

It was around this time, in the autumn of 1940, that Hitler's air force, the Luftwaffe, changed tactics, from raiding military installations to the unprecedented mass bombing of British cities, starting with London.

Every night, hundreds of black-crossed aircraft armed with both explosive and incendiary bombs targeted the capital. German propaganda called this new campaign Total War but the English gave it their own name. They called it the Blitz, a shortened form of the German term *Blitzkrieg.*

The first operations were against the docklands area, but over the course of the next twelve months, the attacks broadened to include major infrastructure across much of the country. At the ominous wail of the sirens, people ran to designated shelters, either basements or Tube stations, while above, entire neighborhoods were bombarded until all that remained were piles of rubble. While people hid underground in relative safety, they had no way of knowing if their homes were still standing, or worse, whether relatives and friends were alive or dead.

The Führer's general staff had convinced themselves that bombing on such a scale would not only destroy the means of waging war, but also the morale of the populace, thereby obligating the obstinate British government to bow to public opinion and forge some type of peace, but they miscalculated and failed on both counts. Citizens of every class and background not only withstood the attacks, but responded with a more determined morale and a greater loyalty towards the leadership.

Their valor in resisting this nightly devastation was even cheered across the Atlantic, with dramatic broadcasts by early radio luminaries like Ed Murrow and Bill Shirer helping to reshape American perception.

In between air-raids, the pubs and cafés and theaters defiantly stayed open for business, even as repair crews worked all night to restore power lines or patch up water mains.

It was in this hazardous environment that Charlotte and Sadie became such good friends that they were more like sisters, sharing everything they had and laughing their way through the chaos.

People were being killed and injured all around them, either blown apart or buried under bricks and concrete but, like much of the population, the two girls found that a sense of humor was a healthy antidote and they became popular figures in the places they frequented, lifting people out of their misery: Sadie with her Cockney wit and Charlotte, the spirited refugee, showing them how to be brave.

Each Wednesday afternoon, Sadie's half-day off, Charlotte traveled to the West End, where they met for coffee and a sandwich, then went to a matinee movie. Both agreed that Betty Davis and Humphrey Bogart were their favorite stars but any feature would do. Whatever was playing, they watched and enjoyed.

One time, they saw a scene in which the women painted the backs of each other's legs with eyeliner to make it look like they were wearing rare and expensive silk stockings, so Charlotte and Sadie decided to try it for themselves. It didn't really work, not like in the film, because their legs were too pale to fool anyone, but they had enormous fun in Sadie's bedroom, taking turns to try to get the lines straight. At one stage, Charlotte just collapsed on the floor, she was laughing so much.

"What on earth are you doing down there?" Sadie asked her, at which Charlotte just doubled over, almost unable to breathe.

Their attitude helped prove the theory that Charlotte had developed on her journey to the Isle of Man: a good spirit helps generate good fortune.

Despite all the day-to-day difficulties and hardships, the close of 1941 saw their world rewarded with the best possible news—the Americans were now in the war to join the British, as well as the Russians, who had themselves been invaded by the Nazis.

Although everyone naturally commiserated with the terrible loss of life at Pearl Harbor, it was heartening, and also a huge relief, that this most powerful friend and ally was now fully on their side.

It was a moment to celebrate. As it happened, Uncle Harry was in town when the first bulletins came through, and with his characteristic largesse, insisted they all go out to drink a toast.

That same evening, a boisterous crowd of Jews invaded the Shakespeare pub in Stoke Newington and ordered pints of beer all round: Harry, Jakob, Charlotte, Sadie, and a small gang of their friends.

It was Harry himself who began to sing *The Star Spangled Banner*, but he couldn't get past the first line because he didn't really know the words, so each one of them tried in turn to continue. It was all in vain but it didn't matter. They gamely hummed and dah-dah'd in grand voice through to the end, some even rising in harmony.

Then Harry yelled out, as if to the entire USA, "Welcome to the war!"—and they drank long and hard along with the rest of the bar, even though there were no Americans present, or anyone who'd actually been there.

Glimmers of optimism had returned, not just for Winston Churchill and his government, but also for the transplanted Goldbergers of Vienna, whose circumstances were also beginning to improve.

For Jakob, it came about through business. The new trickle of well-paid American troops into the capital, he believed, would eventually grow into a stream and soldiers on leave. All had one thing in common. They would need sources of amusement: beer and dancing and also the penny arcades he supplied with their cheap but harmless diversions.

As far as Charlotte was concerned, it was a matter of building on this new life she'd worked so hard to create. She had a parent she could respect and a friend she could trust, both of whom were willing to reciprocate by satisfying the fundamental needs that her soul had been missing all this time.

While her father had begun to restore her sense of devotion, Sadie was the one who had reinstituted the aspect of fun, helping to restore some of that natural enthusiasm Charlotte once possessed. Despite the endless toil and the falling bombs, Charlotte was starting to feel some semblance of rejuvenation—until a different kind of explosion threatened to undermine all the progress she'd made.

It happened one Tuesday morning when an unusually cool wind blew through Stamford Hill and brought with it the delivery she wasn't expecting.

Her father had already left, and she was busy tidying up after their breakfast of toasted sandwiches with ersatz butter and the rare treat she'd come to enjoy, fat-laden bacon rashers. Such food was not exactly according to the tenets of their faith, but Jakob still had very little religious inclination, and, besides there was a war going on. Bacon was nourishing and, just as important, reasonably affordable.

The only problem was that the smell of the frying continued to permeate the cellar long after they'd eaten, and on this particular day, Charlotte thought that if she opened the door, the strong breeze might help propel it away. It was just as she reached for the knob that she was surprised by a thick blue envelope dropping through the narrow letter-box.

It fell at her feet with a soft thud, and even before she bent to pick it up, there was something about it that caused a stir within her. Possibly it was the image of Hitler on the stamps, but more likely, it was the writing which, even from a distance, she recognized all too well. For several seconds, she just stood there looking at the letter, almost afraid to touch it. She just didn't want all those feelings to return; didn't want to be haunted any longer by those old ghosts of fear and guilt and betrayal and anger.

How did it even get here, she wondered? By what means could a letter journey across a ravaged continent and hostile waters to plop down in north London as if it had come from just around the corner? She couldn't seem to work it out and only when it occurred to her that it might be some kind of trick did curiosity compel her to reach down to pick it up.

This was no trick. Yes, it was her mother's handwriting. Yes, it was addressed to her as *Fräulein Liselotte Goldberger*, and yes, the return address was *Staudingergasse 11, Bezirk 20, Wien, Ostmark.*

From the tape at the back, it appeared to have already been slashed and inspected by the GPO censors. However, before she opened it, she first carried it over to the old wooden chair by the small table on which she and her father had so recently eaten breakfast together while chatting amiably about trivialities: things to do today, items that needed laundering or mending, how much budget was left for groceries, and so forth.

After she sat down, she stared at the envelope in her hands for several more seconds as if she were holding a grenade. Then, all at once, in a fit of defiance, she ripped off the tape and unfolded the wad of flimsy notepaper. Each page had been thoroughly filled on both sides, with added thoughts written sideways along the margins. As ever, the German was beautifully phrased, with each educated sentence well-constructed, and as Charlotte began to read, she could hear her mother's voice, as if whispering just over her shoulder.

Once, twice, she went through it, devouring every word, but by the third time, she was already feeling nauseous, distraught by the memories and sickened by the meaning. After all that, the letter was nothing more than a rationale, a carefully composed argument that attempted to explain why it happened, why her mother had to resort to such tactics.

I know you would have never left Vienna if you'd fallen in love with Karl. I had to get you away, so I did what I had to do in order for you to be safe. Believe me, liebste, that was the only reason I took him from you, so you would be free to go.

Charlotte read it all through yet again, before throwing it down on the table in disappointment and disgust. She might have been a child when she left, but she was an adult now, so why could her mother possibly think she'd be prepared to swallow any of this bilge?

Every part of Charlotte's being knew these were lies and excuses for what had been no more than a selfish act, nothing but narcissism. It was pathetic, and she couldn't understand why her mother would waste this rare and precious opportunity, when it would have been so much more effective if she'd been honest and perhaps even a little humble. A simple confession coupled with a sincere apology in just a few lines would have been acceptable— but this? This letter was nothing but an abomination and she resented its very presence.

Hurriedly, she folded up the sheets of paper, replaced them in the envelope and then hid the package amongst her private things where she knew her father would never go. Right next to it in the drawer was the mauve scarf that her mother had given her as the train departed the Westbahnhof on that terrible final day, but now the folded fabric seemed to have become tainted, as had Charlotte herself.

The rest of that day, she went about completing her chores like a zombie: in the small flat; in the street; even at the butcher's shop where she discussed the various cuts of meat in a state of trance. Everything seemed to have come unraveled, and for those hours, her mind was taken back to Brigittenau, to dancing with Karl, to waiting for his call which never came, to having fallen into such an impossibly deep and naive love that when she saw the reality of her mother's behavior, she'd been shocked to her very core.

She saw all this now—and yet she didn't. She couldn't extricate herself from the hurt of that final moment when she was expelled from school and returned home to catch the two of them in the very act.

After cleaning the streets together, after surviving the jeers and the threats and the abuse, after emerging petrified but miraculously unscathed from the terrors of *Kristallnacht*—that her own mother, her flesh and blood, could betray her like that. The awakening and recurrence of the pain brought forth by her mother's letter was too much for her to bear, and by the end of that Tuesday afternoon, she'd slipped back into her former mental paralysis, tearless and devoid of feeling.

The happy-go-lucky Charlotte had submerged yet again, only to have its place reclaimed by the morbid Charlotte, as if this were now her natural state of being.

Then, at about six o' clock, a strange thing happened. She was peeling potatoes, her hands chapped and raw, when the telephone rang. It was her father, calling to say he'd be an hour or so late. This was nothing unusual, it occurred frequently. What was unlikely, however, was the way in which she replied: as cheery and bright as if nothing at all had happened, glad to hear his voice and pleased that he'd had a good day.

Her response had been so instinctive that it was only once she put down the receiver that she realized what she'd just done. Throughout the day, she'd been wondering whether to show her father the letter, maybe even to tell him everything, the unadorned truth, but she realized now that she didn't need to do that.

Why destroy his life, too, when she could use her own powers of pretense to get by? Was this a new maturity, she wondered? She didn't know, but as she put the vegetables on to boil, threw away the peelings, and began work on salting the chicken parts she'd purchased, the wings and the neck and the feet, she began to see that nothing had to change.

Like a revelation, she suddenly understood that for her father, as well as for her friend, Sadie, today was the same as yesterday, and tomorrow would be the same as today. In other words, if Charlotte didn't alter her attitude in any way, then it would be as if none of it was real: neither the original episode, nor the letter which had reminded her of it so vividly.

At that moment, she resolved to bury all knowledge beneath the veneer of normality. If the light of optimism could not penetrate the darkness of her soul, she reasoned, it could at least reflect from a shiny surface; and this was the strange metaphorical image that she determined she would carry with her. This was the birth of the great enigma, the opaque, protective persona that would last until the end of her days.

It would be difficult to overestimate the positive effect that Charlotte's beloved friend, Sadie, had on her attempts at emotional recovery. More than her childhood pal, Trudi, and her adolescent colleague, Magda, Sadie willingly took on the role of sister-companion; not to share secrets and passions but to add fun and laughter. As a result, she was there when Charlotte needed her, neither demanding nor expecting anything but the simple pleasure of friendship.

While their original meeting was by chance, and their first conversation engineered by a concerned father, the fact that the relationship grew into something real and permanent was due almost entirely to Sadie's irrepressible character, especially that always dry, but often silly, sense of humor.

I say this unreservedly even though Sadie was actually a relative of mine, a second cousin on my mother's side. It was through her introduction that Charlotte and I got to know each other.

Both during and after the war, Sadie worked for an importer at the Covent Garden wholesale market, shipping in fresh vegetables from places like the Azores, South Africa and elsewhere. While others were conscripted—like my mother, for example, who was trained by the RAF as a Morse

operator and sent to serve in Egypt—Sadie's job was officially deemed essential to the war effort, so she was spared from
the military.

I recall that when I first arrived in London from the north
of England, my office was only about ten minutes' walk from
the market where Sadie worked. Often, I'd wander up there
for lunch and bump into Sadie at the old Bonbonnière café,
where her short frame would be squeezed in between fellow
market workers, and I'd have to lean over plates of sausage-
and-mash just to give her a peck on the cheek. By that time,
she'd become feisty as well as funny, in a senior position with
her food import company and well capable of issuing sharp
orders to truckers and porters twice her size.

Some years later, when my own organization transferred
me from London to Montreal, it was only as an afterthought
that cousin Sadie happened to mention her good friend,
Charlotte, who was residing in the same city. I was duly given
a contact number but I didn't bother calling immediately.

I was far too busy taking on my new career responsibilities
and settling into the North American way of life. Eventually,
at Sadie's continual urging, I got around to introducing myself, but even when I finally did get to meet Charlotte, it was
merely on a semi-formal basis: invitations to family gather-
ings and so forth. Only later did we become fully acquainted.
Even to this day, I'm not entirely sure why Charlotte didn't
confide in Sadie the way she eventually did to me. My cousin
was someone who both spoke and appreciated the truth, so
I'm sure she would have been ideal in that respect.

All I can suppose is that the timing wasn't yet right, that
Charlotte was perhaps still too brittle and vulnerable for such
revelations. Still, it was good that Sadie was there for her. In
many ways, she acted like an antidote to such poisoned emotions, someone who came along at exactly the right time in
Charlotte's life; if not to heal, then certainly to distract her
from the symptoms.

11

In one of history's most unfortunate ironies, the steadily increasing strength of the Allied forces was inversely proportional to the obliteration of those whom the Nazis had designated *Untermenschen*: sub-humans.

By 1942, these victims of Hitler's ideology had expanded to include the physically and mentally disabled, the homeless and other vagrants, plus anyone they chose to label *deviant*, such as homosexuals.

However, far more numerous than any of these groups were the officially targeted ethnic populations, including several hundred thousand Romany, plus the eleven million Jews, whether of "full" or "mixed" blood, who in-habited every corner of the continent.

In this last case, the stated policy was not merely to consign them to slave labor, or even ethnic cleansing by physical removal, but a deliberate and systematic genocide. The details of the policy were expounded at a small gathering of officials from leading Reich ministries and agencies, held at a former Jewish villa on the shores of the Wannsee, just outside Berlin.

The brief meeting was held under the auspices of the SS—namely Obergruppenführer Reinhard Heydrich, Head of the Reich Central Security Office, assisted by Oberstleutnant Adolf Eichmann, from the Gestapo's Office of Jewish Affairs. Heydrich revealed to the attendees that advanced human experiments with carbon monoxide were now ready to be applied full scale at Belzec, Sobibor, and Treblinka, as well as at a massive new facility called Auschwitz-Birkenau in southern Poland, using a more efficient cyanide compound called Zyklon B.

The planned procedure would begin with evacuation from main population centers to transit ghettoes and, from there, transportation by cattle train to the extermination camps. At the end of the process, bodies would be burned to ashes by industrial, gas-fed crematoria so that there would be no identifiable remains. However, before the new plan could be carried out, Heydrich was assassinated by Czech agents in a British-planned operation. Supervision of the genocide was thereby consolidated under the leadership of the more bureaucratic Oberstleutnant Adolf Eichmann, who was obsessive about the need for secrecy.

Despite the vast nature of this undertaking, word of the atrocities filtered out very slowly, and there were many amongst the Allied authorities who just refused to believe the sheer scale of the operation, because there was simply no historical precedent on which to base such a conclusion.

Even when a few of the victims managed to escape from the camps or the trains, risking re-capture in order to provide eyewitness accounts, their testimony was discarded as overblown rhetoric. The notion that anyone, anywhere, could even devise, never mind execute, such a monstrous scheme was beyond human conception.

Even Jakob himself, the world-weary cynic, could not appreciate how far and how fast the situation had deteriorated for the Jews of central Europe. He continued to seek visa approval from whoever would listen and kept writing letters to his wife in Vienna, and to his family in Krakow.

Did any of his mail get through? While he remained personally unaware of any such success, at least one of his communications must have been received, because it was the only way Franzi could have learned of her family's Stamford Hill address. It's even possible she wrote separately to each of them, her husband and her daughter, but only the communication to Charlotte actually reached its destination, and because of its specific content, Charlotte couldn't even tell her father about it. She just couldn't risk him discovering the truth.

Yet even if she'd disclosed its arrival, there would have still been few clues as to her mother's circumstance. In addition to explaining about Karl, the letter mentioned their ambition to see Paris and how, for a while, they'd lined up at the French embassy until it shut down, but that was all in the past. As for the future, there was nothing at all, because even Franzi herself couldn't have guessed that within just three months, her life would be over.

It would have been sometime in October that Francesca Goldberger née Gutmann, also known as Franzi, Fannie, or Faegel depending on documentation, stepped off the train with hundreds of others at Theresienstadt in the occupied territory of Czechoslovakia.

This was the ghetto which, for the sake of internal and external propaganda, had been designated a model of progressive confinement, reserved for the Jewish intellectual, artistic, and social elite, as well as for other exceptions such as holders of civil office and honored war veterans. In fact, Franzi might even have volunteered to be transferred.

Many German, Austrian, and Czech Jews actually went there willingly, visualizing it as a potential escape from the stifling and abusive persecution of their home cities. They were told—and needed to believe—that this would be merely a retreat, more like a summer camp than a concentration camp.

In such a location, they were advised, they would have the benefit of living amongst their own people, of running their own affairs free of the constant fear, and of enjoying full cultural independence. Compared to the heavy restrictions and daily violence to which they'd become accustomed, it must have sounded like a relative paradise.

This was the promise, the alternative that was presented not only by the Nazi administration but by many of the Jews' own civic leaders who were also deceived. Of course, the reality turned out to be very different.

Whatever she was expecting, Franzi would have been met on her arrival at Theresienstadt with enormous contradictions. It's true that, at first glance, she would have seen a ghetto life that tried its best to flourish, to live up to the mirage. There were art shows, music concerts, drama productions, school lessons, sports activities, news-sheets, and even a special camp currency, all supervised by a structured Jewish council.

Yet, in stark contrast, there were also tightly cramped accommodations in infested barracks, no medicines or toilet facilities, no safe drinking water, rampant typhus and cholera, malnutrition verging on starvation, and crippling injuries from hard labor and severe punishments for minor infractions, all of which led to thousands of deaths even before deportation to the extermination camps.

However, perhaps the most poignant tragedy of Theresienstadt was the denial. No matter how the prisoners suffered, many simply refused to acknowledge that they'd been duped and maintained the optimistic lie that if only they tried harder, all would be well.

Like elsewhere in the camp system, the motto on the gate read *Arbeitmachtfrei*—work brings freedom—but there was never any freedom to be gained, either physically, culturally, or spiritually, because those who survived were bound for the gas chambers of Auschwitz.

In the unlikely event that Franzi had the strength to stay alive that long, she would have been transported in a cattle train, then herded in line through the selection process where the handsome camp doctor, Josef Mengele, stood on a box and with a simple wave of his hand, decided on temporary life or instant death.

The few who were selected were primarily young males of sound physique, so Franzi would have been directed along with the rest towards the shower bunker, where she would have undressed on command. This final pretense, the concept of calling the gas chambers "shower rooms" in order to facilitate a peaceful entry, was the last assault on logic and hope. Once the allotted number had crowded inside, the heavy doors would have been slammed shut, then the lights extinguished. That's when the panic would have begun, the terrified cries and the frenzied prayers.

The next sound Franzi heard would have been the hiss, not of water, but of gas, followed by several long minutes of retching and writhing agony as her lungs absorbed the toxin: the painful termination of a most desolate life, laden with mistakes and burdened by regrets. In those very last moments, would Franzi's thoughts have been with her distant husband, with her abandoned daughter, or with the lover for whom she was willing to sacrifice everything?

Finally, just before her corpse was cremated, her mouth would have been examined for gold teeth, and her hair, that beautiful auburn hair, would have been shaved to use as pillow stuffing back in the Reich.

At the time, neither Charlotte nor her father knew anything of Franzi's fate, although both were only too aware that the crucial time for her to have left was at the moment of the *Anschluss*, while the German troops were still marching in.

If she'd picked up and departed for Prague that very same morning when the borders were still open, she might have made it to England on a tourist visa the way her husband had done, and she would now be with them, sharing in their new life as their situation slowly began to improve.

The Goldberger brothers had been right about the business. Soldiers required amusement in their off-duty hours, and the streets were now full of them. They were primarily British but with increasing numbers of American, Canadian, and Australian troops; also free French, Dutch and Poles. With Harry expanding in Southend and Jakob working minor miracles to rebuild in the city, their revenue was improving, as was their disposable income.

At long last, Charlotte and her father were able to move from that dismal coal cellar and rent the entire ground floor of a house. It was still in Stamford Hill, not far away, but the difference was immense.

It was cleaner, drier, with more light, and for Charlotte, the great convenience of a full kitchen with a real stove and a nice table at which to eat. There was still a meter for hot water but at least they now had more money with which to feed it.

As a reward for all the hard work, Jakob, ever the animal-lover, bought them a dog. It wasn't one of the large breeds but a small, friendly terrier, black and white with floppy ears, his tongue always ready to lick Charlotte's hand. He was already six months old, but they gave him a new name anyway, Bobby, which sounded so English, and to which he soon began to answer.

Bobby accompanied them everywhere. During the day, he walked the errands with Charlotte, and in the evenings, he slept peacefully by Jakob's slippered feet. Weekends, he went walking with them, too, and quickly became recognized around the neighborhood. Eventually, two more creatures also joined the household.

First, a stray cat showed up at their back door and stayed with them because they didn't have the heart to stop feeding it, closely followed by ownership of a talking parrot which they took in because one of Jakob's friends was leaving town and couldn't take it along. So now they had three animals to look after but Charlotte didn't mind. It meant she always had company during the day and could give voice to her thoughts without sounding like she was talking to herself.

One night she arrived home after an evening out with Sadie to find the dog by her father's feet, the cat dozing on his lap, and the parrot sitting on his bald head, all of them quite comfortable. It was like something out of *Dr. Doolittle*, and she reacted with a fit of giggles that she could hardly control.

"You know what we should do?" she said to her father, once she'd calmed down. "I mean, if we ever have the money."

"What's that?"

"Get a camera. All we have is photos of the old life. We have a new life now. I think it's about time we had some new photos."

Her father nodded his agreement, which was a difficult thing to do with the parrot up top and this gave rise to yet more hysteria.

In general, this could be counted as a good time in Charlotte's life. There were still shortages, and the rationing system that was in effect made shopping an obstacle course of empty shelves and missed opportunities, but she learned to cope and found that, much to her own surprise, this charade she'd invented for herself, this inside-outside recipe for happiness, appeared to be working.

Only occasionally did the tears spill out and only when she'd made sure she was alone, preferably in the dark; like the evening her father was delayed and the air raid sirens began their dreadful wail. She wasn't too worried, because she knew how cautious he was, how quickly he went to the nearest shelter, and she'd promised him she would always do the same.

The most important thing to do on these occasions was to remain calm; to turn off the stove and the lights according to the official blackout protocol, then head along to the assigned shelter at Stamford Hill Underground station.

There was usually an hour or more between the time the south coast radar installations picked up the approaching aircraft and the moment the first bombs began to fall: more than sufficient for her to descend the long staircase and settle on the dimly lit platform. With her, she usually brought an old cushion to alleviate the stark cold of the concrete and sat there with her back propped against the tiled wall.

Often she tucked a book in her bag for something to do in the shelter, or sometimes a pack of cards to play solitaire, but on this occasion she hauled out some darning and got busy mending a pair of her father's socks. Around her, as always, were hundreds of ordinary people: local families; night shift workers; a few soldiers; plus the passengers from any bus or train which happened to be in the area.

On this night, Charlotte was sitting next to a young mother, possibly in her late twenties, who already had two children and, clearly, a third well on the way. The oldest was a scruffy boy, aged five or six, with smudges of dirt on his face, while his curly-haired sister was still just a toddler, her voice a constant bawl and her nose running.

She must have still been teething, because she put her grubby fingers back in her mouth no matter how many times her mother pulled them out. Charlotte couldn't help but take pity on the mother, trying so hard to manage, and offered to help by looking after the little girl.

There wasn't really much she could do to quiet the child, so she just took her in her arms and rocked her gently, whispering a few words of encouragement. Then, without even realizing it, she began softly humming a tune from her childhood, a Brahms lullaby that her mother used to play to her on the cello. The melody came so easily to her that the memories came flooding back: her mother's deep love for music, as well as the instrument itself which had been her prized possession.

It was with this strange infant wrapped in her arms that Charlotte at last began to appreciate how her mother might have felt so out of place in the drab, domestic world in which she found herself. With such a natural tendency towards learning and culture and philosophy, Franzi's life should surely have been filled with libraries and lecture halls, researched essays and earnest debates.

This should have been her existence and might well have been, had her parents been more enlightened; or had Jakob not fallen in love with her; or had the Nazis not invaded; or had her husband and daughter not left her behind . . .

Charlotte sat there with the child as the bombs fell, both above her and inside her, exploding her grief and devastating her carefully constructed equilibrium.

Later, she would try to restore the balance, but for the moment, in that unlikely refuge, she could afford to let go of the discipline and give way to the underlying emotions she knew would always remain a major part of who she was.

The next morning, she was having breakfast with her father, both of them bleary-eyed after the long night. It was something to which Londoners had become accustomed after two years of the Blitz. The only consolation was that, by this time, the Allied air forces were starting to give it right back with heavy raids on German cities: the Americans by day, the British by night.

Cheering them on to inflict rampant destruction was hardly a noble sentiment, but nevertheless, there was the strong feeling in the streets and in the shelters that the Nazis had started this concept of Total War, so let's now see how they liked it. As Charlotte sipped her tea, she glanced over at her father, who was busy reading a first edition of the *Daily Telegraph* that he'd picked up on his way back from walking the dog.

"*Vati* . . ." she said in her native language. "Do you think *Mutti* is still alive?"

He lowered the newspaper to look at her, his mind obviously still full of the day's news. "You mean with all the bombing? I don't think our planes can reach Vienna yet."

"I don't mean the bombing."

"What then?"

"Last night, I was looking after a little girl in the shelter . . ."

"Good for you."

"No, what I'm trying to say is that near us were some Hasidim who were talking. I could hear them."

"You understand Yiddish now?"

"Only the gist," she admitted.

"And what were they saying, these Hasidim?"

"They said there are no more Jews left in Vienna, that they've all been taken away. Is that true?"

Jakob took off his reading glasses and sighed. "I don't know, *liebste*."

"Where would they take them?"

Jakob had heard the stories, too, but wasn't sure how much to tell his daughter. "They have special places."

"You mean the Kz?" This was how the concentration camps were known in German: *Konzentrationslager*, or Kz for short.

"You know about that?"

"Is that where they've taken *Mutti*?"

"I told you, *liebste*, I don't know."

Charlotte could hear the impatience in her father's voice, or was it just the same element of remorse that she, too, felt during every waking moment. "Do you ever pray for her?" she asked him.

"Pray? Pray to whom? To the Germans to let her out? To the British to let her in?"

"I meant to God."

"Ah, God." He smiled, but without any humor, and went back to reading his paper, turning the pages hurriedly as a way to distract himself from the conversation.

Charlotte, however, still wanted an answer. "Do you?"

"Do I what?"

"Do you pray to God?"

Once again, he looked at her, this time more intently. "Do *you*?"

"No," she confessed, "that's why I was wondering . . ."

"You want to pray, is that what you want? Fine, so go ahead, pray. Let me know if it works."

"Do you think it might?"

"What do I know? I suppose it can't hurt."

"So why don't you do it?"

"I didn't say I don't."

"But you didn't say you do, either."

Jakob took a long breath. This was beginning to sound like a Talmudic discussion. "Listen, *liebste*, what I do and what you do are two different things. This God we Jews are supposed to believe in . . . He answers to individuals. Each of us can talk to Him directly. We don't have to go through a rabbi, or a pope, or a parent, either. What it means is that if you feel like praying, you do. If not, you don't, understand?"

"I think so."

Charlotte sat there and considered it as she finished her breakfast. He still hadn't told her definitively if he prayed or not. She was inclined to believe that he didn't, but for some reason, he couldn't bring himself to say it. Was he ashamed of not praying? She didn't want to ask him such a brazen question, so she let the matter drop.

In the district of Stamford Hill, where Jakob and Charlotte resided, there were, in fact, several thousand members of the Hasidic community, whose traditional male garb of long black coats and broad-brimmed hats made them highly visible around the neighborhood.

Gregarious by nature, they could often be seen walking in pairs, deep in discussion, or strolling majestically with families of five or six in tow. They usually gathered around the same locations: near their synagogues, yeshivas, and other institutions, of course, but also the many kosher stores and restaurants where they would congregate, either inside or just outside on the pavement. Like the rest of the population, they went to the public shelters during air raids, as Charlotte had observed.

It also happened that one of their number worked as a mechanic for Jakob, a burly man whose name in English was Solomon, but who preferred to be called by his Jewish nickname, Shlomo. There wasn't much finesse to his skills, but give him clunky equipment like a slot machine, put a heavy spanner or screwdriver into his broad hands, and he could work wonders in a short period of time.

Jakob valued Shlomo's services, but couldn't really afford to pay him the market rate, so he allowed him to take

Friday afternoons before the start of *shabbos*, the Sabbath, as well as the *yomtovim*, the Jewish holidays and festivals, of which there were many.

For Shlomo, these considerations were worth more than money, and the two of them, employer and employee, got along as well as could be expected. There was never any critique about Jakob's own religious practice, which had always been lackadaisical, but one day he received an informal, hand-written note in English from Shlomo's *tsadik*, the leading *rebbe* of his particular sect, asking Jakob if he could come to the synagogue office for a meeting. The note implied there was some urgency to the request.

It was therefore on the following Thursday that Jakob found himself sitting in the man's dusty office waiting for him to appear. The small space was cluttered and lined with crowded bookcases, as might be expected, but when the *rebbe* himself showed up, he was totally contrary to the aging stereotype.

Sometimes, on the death of an aging patriarch, a respected scholar of unusual ability might be deemed worthy of succession, and in this case, he was relatively young for such a position of honor. Still in his fifties, he had clear skin, neatly trimmed facial hair, and steel-rimmed glasses, as opposed to the sallow face, shaggy beard, and heavy black frames of yesteryear.

Instead of a hat, he wore on the back of his head a large white yarmulke with a Star of David embroidered in gold thread, an emblem which reminded Jakob a little too readily of the yellow stars that Jews were now being forced to wear all across occupied Europe.

"Good morning, *Rebbe*."

"Good morning, Mr. Goldberger," replied the *rebbe* in well-educated English. "I'd like to thank you for coming in today."

Jakob gave him a courteous nod. "Your note sounded urgent."

"Well, yes, I believe that might be a fair description." The *rebbe* polished his glasses on a clean white handkerchief, as if filling time while he decided where to begin. He seemed to be in no hurry. "Our mutual friend, Shlomo, tells me you have a daughter, am I right?"

"I thought he was already married," replied Jakob.

The *rebbe* laughed good-naturedly. "No, no, it's nothing like that, I promise you. No, I was simply mentioning it because . . . Well, because as a father bringing up a daughter alone . . ."

Immediately, Jakob objected to the implication. Since he'd not yet received any practical evidence of Franzi's death, he preferred to remain optimistic.

"Excuse me, *Rebbe*," he interrupted, "but just to set the record straight, I'm not bringing up my daughter alone. I have a wife who's currently trapped by that gang of *mamzahs* over there in Austria. Maybe you heard about it?"

The *rebbe* was a little shocked by the use of the provocative word *mamzahs*—bastards—while at the same time polite enough to be embarrassed by his own faux pas.

"I'm sorry, Mr. Goldberger, please forgive me. Yes, of course, I fully understand. I didn't mean to imply otherwise. But it's true nonetheless that, for the time being, there's just the two of you and . . . Well, not to beat about the bush, we have your daughter's education to consider."

"Her education?"

"Don't you want her to be educated?"

"She's twenty-four years old."

"Ah, I see. Yes, I'm aware of her age, but I was thinking more of her religious education."

"Why? You don't think she's religious enough?"

"Mr. Goldberger, sorry to put it bluntly, but you eat bacon sandwiches for breakfast."

Jakob tried to control himself. He could feel the anger welling up inside him like a geyser about to erupt, but instead of becoming irate, he just sat back and did the opposite. He smiled. "We like bacon sandwiches," he said impishly. "Very nourishing."

The *rebbe* understood that Jakob was teasing him but wasn't especially amused by it. "Mr. Goldberger, please."

"I'm sorry, *Rebbe*, but we're both busy people, so tell me, what's all this about?"

The man sat forward, elbows on the desk, hands clasped neatly. "Of course, what you do is up to you . . ."

"Of course."

"But I think a first step might be to join a synagogue. You're not a member of any right now, are you?"

"Did Shlomo tell you that, too? Maybe I'll have a word with him."

"He's just doing what he thinks is right."

"What's right is for him to mind his own business."

"Well, that's as maybe. But let's get back on track, shall we, Mr. Goldberger? How do you feel about joining a synagogue?"

Jakob willed himself to calm down. "Listen, *Rebbe*, I appreciate what you're trying to do. I know you mean well. But I don't think it's such a good idea, not for me."

"May I ask why not?"

"Why not? Do we really want to get into theology here?"

"Theology? Is that what you think this is about?"

"What else?"

"Judaism, Mr. Goldberger. *Yiddishkeit*. Call it what you will. It's not about what we believe, but about who we are. You, of all people . . ."

"Me, of all people, what?" He knew very well that the rabbi was talking about escaping Vienna but he challenged the man to say it out loud.

The *rebbe* hesitated. "What I mean is that you should know how precious this is, what we have. For five thousand years . . ."

"Please, *Rebbe*, do me a favor. Don't give me the 'five thousand year' speech. I know all about the five thousand years. What you're telling me is that if I don't join a synagogue, I'll personally be responsible for bringing down the entire temple."

"Well, yes, in a way," replied the *rebbe* quietly. "If everybody did as you do, we wouldn't even have a temple."

Jakob was prepared to acknowledge there might be some truth to that, even if he wasn't yet ready to concede his position. "Let me ask you something, *Rebbe* . . . Isn't it true that, as a Jew, I can speak to God directly if I want?"

"I thought we weren't getting into theology."

"It's what I told my daughter. I just want to know if it's true."

"Of course, it's true."

"Good, so now tell me. Why should I join a synagogue if I can talk to him in my kitchen if I want? Maybe while I'm eating my bacon sandwich."

There was a deep and somewhat exasperated sigh from behind the desk. "With all due respect, Mr. Goldberger, that's hardly the point. It's the synagogues and the yeshivas which maintain the faith, which keep us together as a community."

"No, *Rebbe*, with all due respect, it's the rest of the world that does that. They persecute all Jews whatever our personal beliefs and that's why we stick together. I can tell them all I want . . . I never pray, I never keep kosher . . . and you know what? They'll still send me to the damn camp."

"I must say, that's a very pessimistic attitude."

"Pessimistic? No, just realistic." Here, Jakob paused, deciding he'd said enough. He didn't come here with the intention of starting an argument, so it was perhaps time to change the tone. "Look, *Rebbe*, I'm not saying you're wrong, and I'm not denying His existence. Once, maybe, but not now."

"I'm very pleased to hear it."

"What I'm saying is, I just want to do it my way. Is that too much to ask?"

"But without the institutions, what kind of faith can we have?"

"So fine, I'm not telling *you* what to do. By all means, teach the Torah, conduct the services, no problem. Do what you like. There's always people will follow you. Just not me, that's all." Jakob got to his feet. That was all he was prepared to say, and he was ready to go. He needed to get out of this stuffy office and breathe some air. First, however, he reached across the desk to shake hands as a gesture of consolation and goodwill.

The brief meeting had been more antagonistic than he might have wished and he didn't want to leave on bad terms.

"Listen, *Rebbe* . . . I just want to say that, well, I'll be happy to make a what-you-call-it, a donation, to your synagogue. I've got nothing against what you do. Actually, I admire it. You keep the spirit alive . . . but please don't ask me to join, all right?"

"It's your choice, Mr. Goldberger."

Jakob was about to reply but held back. Instead, he offered a thoughtful smile before making his own way down the stairs, through the front doors, and into the morning sunlight. He wasn't angry or upset, but still, he couldn't help thinking that the man had some nerve, asking him to come down here like this and then telling him that his daughter wasn't religious enough—his own daughter who'd suffered the horrors of *Kristallnacht* for her faith.

That evening, Jakob arrived home at a reasonable hour, and together with Charlotte, took the dog for a walk before supper. After they'd strolled some distance in silence, just enjoying the mild evening, Jakob asked her a question. Since they were on the street, he followed their self-imposed rules by speaking English, a language with which they'd both become fairly conversant.

"The other day, you asked me, do I pray? Remember that?"

"Yes, of course, I remember."

"All right, so now I'm asking *you*. Do you think you're religious enough?"

"What do you mean?"

"I went to see a Hasid today, a *rebbe*."

"Why?"

"Good question. You know what he said? He said we eat bacon sandwiches."

"So what?"

"I know, so what? But I think he was trying to tell me you need a religious education."

"I had my Bat Mitzvah."

"That's true. Maybe I should have said that."

"What more religion does he want?"

"He wants us to join a synagogue . . . you know, become a member."

"Why? He needs the money?"

Jakob chuckled, proud of his daughter's powers of perception. "Sure, he needs the money, like everybody. He has people to pay, buildings to fix. But I don't think it's just the money. I think he means it . . . about *Yiddishkeit* and all that."

"But that's not your way."

"No, *liebste*, it's not."

The German word *liebste* caused her to look around to see who might be listening, but there was nobody within earshot. "Don't call me that in the street," she told him in a half-whisper.

"What, *liebste*? Sorry, I forgot."

"Anyway," she said, "who does he think he is? He can't tell us what to do."

"You know what I told him? I said bacon sandwiches are very nourishing."

"You said that?"

"Yes, but I'm not so sure he liked it."

At this, Charlotte smiled, and the subject was dismissed, no longer worth talking about.

However, it did make Jakob reconsider the larger question, the one she'd initially asked, the one about whether he prayed or not. He'd told her it couldn't hurt, so he was wondering now why he didn't do it himself. On the other hand, the corollary was also true: that all the prayer and devotion in the universe hadn't saved the Hasidim, who were being sent to the camps just like everyone else.

It was with the camps in mind that he thought about her yet again: Franzi, his little Franzi, his first and only love. He'd never been with any other woman since the day he first met her, and he recalled how he'd carried that hand-colored picture of her so close to his heart during the previous war when he was at the front; how just dreaming of her had helped save his life. He was sorry he didn't have that photo anymore.

Somehow, it got lost during all his years of travel, but he still had the memory imprinted on his brain. For Jakob, just thinking about Franzi was a prayer of sorts.

The war was over before they had any firm news of what happened to her. They'd followed all the turning points in all the battles, had read avidly of the military exploits at places like Monte Cassino, Normandy, and Iwo Jima.

When the end came, they celebrated the destruction of Nazi Germany and the suicide of Adolf Hitler as if it had been a personal vendetta: days of beer and whisky culminating in a headache the likes of which Charlotte had never experienced.

Then, just a few months later, they were equally moved while watching the Movietone News reports of the solitary bombs that had demolished Hiroshima and Nagasaki, instantly concluding the war in the Pacific. As Harry said on emerging from the movie theater, "It's a new world," and they all nodded sagely.

More horrifying still was the footage showing the liberation of the death camps: grainy images of survivors, no more than skin-draped skeletons with hollow eyes; mounds of bodies being bulldozed into mass graves; grim-faced American soldiers standing in the gas chambers and the crematoria, bathed in the white glare of the camera lighting as they pointed at the shower nozzles and the ovens.

They saw all this, and they tried not to think the unthinkable, yet they couldn't avoid it. As much as they'd celebrated the end of the war, they were now in the deepest of mourning: for Berthe, for Adolfo, for their father. Like millions of others, the entire Polish branch of the Goldberger family had just disappeared, leaving a great emptiness that even the rough justice of the Nuremberg war trials couldn't heal. It also didn't go unnoticed by Jakob that this was the same town where he'd once eaten dinner with Max Grundig, founder of Grundig Electronics, who first gave him the copy of Hitler's book *Mein Kampf,* written in 1924 and threatening even back then to use gas on the Jews.

They also didn't know what happened to Franzi—not until one cold morning in the February of 1947. Since the end of the conflict, Charlotte had taken it upon herself to write to every organization which might conceivably have news. Then, at last, just a few days before her twenty-eighth birthday, she received a reply from the Jewish Refugees Committee, based two hundred miles away in the city of Manchester.

When she tore it open, she found only two short paragraphs informing her that, through the offices of the Red Cross, they now knew that her mother had been sent from Vienna to Theresienstadt in October, 1942. They said they were sorry to convey such distressing news and that they would continue to search for any further information, which would be forwarded immediately.

Alone, Charlotte just stared at the note for a long time, before a sudden thought caused her to hurry into her room and pull out her mother's letter, which she'd kept hidden all this time. She needed to check the date it was written, July, which was just three months before she was deported.

Did her mother know what was about to happen? Was that why she wrote it the way she did? Instead of excuses, was it simply a means for her to clear her own conscience before the end? Charlotte had none of these answers, but once again, she began to weep uncontrollably.

Just like in the Underground station during the Blitz, her hidden emotions broke through the outer shell that she'd so carefully constructed, and she just couldn't prevent the tears from gushing out. Hour after hour, they poured down her cheeks, until her father came home and found her asleep in the chair with her handkerchief soaked and the dog whimpering by her feet.

Sometimes, while Charlotte was telling me these harrowing tales, she would pause in order to find her way over to a drawer or cupboard. It took enormous effort for her to get up from the chair and tap her way around the apartment with her steel walker, and while she did so, all talk would come to a stop.

Eventually, she would haul out some album or file and then spend another minute or so searching it until she discovered exactly what she wanted to show me: either a photograph, a document, a souvenir, or just a relevant article torn from a publication.

Only once she was sitting again, would she continue the story she was relating, and somehow, what she was saying always seemed so much more immediate when I had the visual evidence in front of me.

She didn't keep the most historical items but the most personally meaningful. These items included the scrap of cigarette paper on which the SA kommandant had scrawled his signature after Charlotte and her mother were forced to scrub the streets, the British government's greeting, printed in German, telling aliens how to behave, and the letter from her mother, folded and re-folded so much that it was difficult to decipher, explaining her reasons for stealing Karl.

Bound together with the letter was that final brief communication from the Jewish Refugees Committee saying her mother's name had been found on the manifest of those deported to Theresienstadt.

However, the one object she hauled out most often was the framed, eight-by-ten professionally taken portrait of Franzi, the only likeness of her mother that Charlotte still possessed. She didn't keep it on the wall or on the sideboard like her other important photographs but in a cupboard, and on each of the countless occasions that she lifted it out, she would ask me the same plaintive question.

"I think my mother loved me, don't you?"

She would then be transported into some kind of reverie, forever trying to rationalize Franzi's words or actions, even those that, with hindsight and perspective, seemed to be inexcusable.

These mementos, preserved for sixty or seventy years, were Charlotte's most cherished possessions, but also important to her were the dozens of other souvenirs scattered around the apartment—figurines, glassware, and the like— brought back as gifts from all over the globe, including several from my own travels.

All were valued, no matter how kitschy some of them might be, and each had its rightful place. Especially prominent was her collection of sewing thimbles, displayed proudly on the wall of her dining room as a reminder of her formal training as a seamstress.

The one thing she made me promise in regard to all these personal effects was that, after she was gone, I would sort it all out and donate whatever was appropriate to the Holocaust Museum archives.

Like so many of her generation, it was vital to her that some permanent record be kept, not only to bear witness, but perhaps more importantly, to keep the individual memories alive.

12

After six years lost to the war, people everywhere were trying to rebuild their lives, searching for some semblance of everyday normality.

Families were starting to go on holiday again, even if it was just a day trip to the seaside, and all those returning soldiers on belated honeymoons still needed something to do on a rainy afternoon: a scoop of shellfish in a paper bag, a shoot-'em-up flick, and afterwards, some laughs in a penny arcade with machines maintained by the Goldbergers.

Such amusements offered a few hours of harmless distraction, and for many, that meant a great deal.

As a result of his improved financial position, Jakob could now turn his attention to other matters. One was naturalization, for which he applied on behalf of both himself and his daughter.

It took considerable paperwork and a formal interview, but unlike the negative pre-war situation, the atmosphere was now far more open. Eventually, their new status came through, which made them eligible for passports and also, if they so wished, a change of name. The latter suggestion was Harry's, the idea being that if the whole family was now British, they should perhaps Anglicize themselves completely.

Thus, Goldberger became Goldhill, an approximate translation; Jakob became Jacob, although he didn't much care for it; and his daughter, who up to that stage was still officially Liselotte, would be permanently known as Charlotte. Unlike her father, she actually preferred her new name, because hearing it was so much less painful.

Another issue, of even greater importance, was some kind of future for the offspring of both households. Frank, recently demobbed from the army, was native to England, and therefore reasonably self-sufficient, but Charlotte was another matter.

While Jakob believed that time would take care of everything, his brother wasn't so sure. It was none of Harry's affair, he knew that, but he felt he should say something at least, even if there was the likelihood that Jakob might reject his interference out of hand.

They were both in Southend on this occasion, a nice break for Jakob, and as they strolled the promenade, he relished the cleanliness of the estuary breeze and the cry of the gulls that soared and wheeled, a symbol of this new-found freedom.

They stopped to buy fries at a small stand: "six-penneth of chips," in the lingo of the Yorkshireman who served them. Then they doused their servings in the freely available condiments of salt and vinegar and carried them along the pier to chew them down. In the distance was the silhouette of a commercial vessel, steaming its lone way across the horizon bound for who-knows-where with no need of armed protection. It was good to see.

"There's something I was going to talk to you about," said Harry, attempting to start the conversation as casually as possible. "If you don't mind."

"If I don't mind?" replied Jakob. "That means you think I'll mind."

"You might."

Jakob tossed one of his fries to a nearby gull and they both watched as the lucky bird became the object of much squabbling by the rest of the flock.

"So?" asked Jakob.

"It's not easy."

"Harry, for Pete's sake . . . Isn't that what the Americans say? For Pete's sake? Who is this Pete, anyway? Is he famous?"

"I don't know. Look, Jakob, it's about Charlotte."

"What about Charlotte?"

"You won't like what I'm going to say."

"I think I already guessed that much."

"Fine, so here it is . . . I don't think it's so good she's living with you like that."

"Like what?"

"Like . . . Well, like a wife. Jakob, it's unhealthy."

"Unhealthy? Harry, what are you saying?"

"No, no, no . . . . Not like that, heaven forbid. No, what I mean is, you know, keeping house, looking after you while you work."

"Harry, we've been through all this. You told me to push her out, and I did."

"I'm not talking about the occasional day out."

"So what are you talking about? She's not my servant, she's not my prisoner. She can do what she wants."

"No, you still don't understand."

"That's because you're not explaining it so well."

"I'm trying, believe me."

Jakob gazed out at the gray-green swell of the sea. "Tell me the truth. Has she met somebody? Did she tell you because she's afraid to tell me?"

"No, why would you think that?"

Jakob shrugged. "It's happened before." He was thinking again of that time with Hugo, when he completely overreacted. "It's more difficult with daughters, being a parent I mean. It shouldn't be, but it is. Harry, why are we talking about this? What's the real reason? Why here, why now?"

"All right, if you must know, it's ever since you got that letter, the one about Franzi. Before that, well, to be honest there was some hope, but now . . ." Harry couldn't bring himself to complete the thought.

"What are you trying to say?"

Harry took a long breath. "What I'm trying to say is that Charlotte feels sorry for you."

"What?"

"She thinks you need her. It's like she's dedicated her life to you. She's what now . . . thirty years old?"

"Almost."

"So she's been twenty years with her mother, now another ten with you. She's not a girl anymore, Jakob, she's a woman. She needs to find a life of her own."

At that, Jakob looked at his brother, mouth open, ready to protest. Then he gave up, turned back to the sea, and there was another long silence. Eventually, he gave a shrug. "Fine, fine, for the sake of argument, let's say you're right. What you want me to do about it? You want me to throw her out on the street?"

"Me, I don't want anything. What you do is up to you."

"Now you sound like the *rebbe*."

"All right, you want an answer, I'll give you an answer. I think you should talk to her, encourage her to leave."

"Find a husband, have children?"

"Maybe. Why not? Or study and become a doctor, who knows? The world's more open now, anything's possible. But whatever it is, it's got to be hers."

Jakob nodded slowly and could offer nothing further. There was no more Yiddish, no more sarcasm. Although he was reluctant to admit it, he was ready to agree that his brother might just have a point, and if so, the question would be how to approach the topic with Charlotte.

It was definitely something he would need to think about, and it made him long for the company of Berthe.

His brother, Harry, had fine instincts, but his sister would have given him practical advice: what to say, what to do, and how to go about it. He mourned Franzi, but in his own way, he missed Berthe just as much.

Jakob knew it would be hard to ask his daughter to leave but he'd also figured out that it would be just as hard for him to accept the fact. This was a major acknowledgment on his part, a conclusion he'd reached in the weeks following his chat with Harry on the promenade.

He was used to having Charlotte around, and he couldn't deny that she made things comfortable for him, but perhaps that was the problem, he reasoned. Perhaps he was just too comfortable and that was why he hadn't seen it for himself.

One Wednesday evening, she was late returning from her regular outing with Sadie, so after taking the dog for an evening walk, he sat alone in the fading light, waiting for her. It was a kind of a test, he imagined, an opportunity to see what it would be like, living there on his own without her, but all it did was confirm that he wouldn't like it very much.

All the more reason, he felt, that he had to give himself a kick in the backside in order to do something.

When she finally arrived, it was nearly dark. She was full of apologies as she removed her coat, tied on her apron, rolled up her sleeves, and got busy, hauling out the pan to heat up the stew that she'd already prepared. There was some fresh bread, she was telling him, so would he also want potatoes? How hungry was he?

As he listened to her, he realized that Harry was right. Such care was unhealthy, and that made him feel even worse, but what could he say to her?

"We saw such a good film," she was telling him as she ladled the steaming food on to the dinner plates. "*It's Magic* . . . did you hear about it?"

"No, *liebste*."

"Sadie told me what was the first title, over there in America—*Romance on the High Seas*—Much better, don't you think? So much more glamorous. That's a word they use in the papers. I like that word, glamorous . . . like Hollywood.

"Anyway, what it was about, was a big mix-up with a woman who sends another woman on a fancy boat, because what she wants to do is stay behind and watch her husband to see if he's cheating on her.

"Meanwhile, on the boat, her husband has sent a detective to check up on her, but this detective thinks she's the first woman . . . you see?"

"No, *liebste*."

Charlotte just laughed as she unfastened her apron and sat with him at the table. "Like I said, a big mix-up, but it was funny, you know? A lot of fun. She's very good, that new actress they have in it, Doris Day. Did you ever see her?"

"No, *liebste*."

His uninterested denials were a continuing source of amusement for Charlotte, and Jakob marveled at how happy she seemed, how content with her life. Yet that was exactly the problem. "Oh, I nearly forgot," she said, as they began eating, "you know what Sadie said to me? It was such a compliment, she can be so nice, that Sadie. It was as we were coming home on the Tube. We were talking about the film and I said to her how beautiful she was."

"Who, Sadie?"

"No, the actress in the movie, Doris Day. So tall and blonde. And you know what Sadie said to me? She said I was like that. She said I could be an actress, too, you know, in Hollywood."

"But you're not blonde."

"Not the blonde part. She said I was tall and beautiful. I didn't believe it, I know she was just saying that, but wasn't it nice of her?"

"She's a nice person."

"I never thought I was like that, I mean, I try to look my best . . ."

It was while Charlotte continued fussing about the grand compliment she'd received that Jakob had his idea. It just plopped into his brain, and unlike his usually cautious way of doing things, he simply came out with it.

"*Liebste*, listen a moment. Tell me something. Did you ever think of going there? To America?"

The question seemed to come at Charlotte from out of nowhere and she stopped talking in surprise. "Why? Is that where you want to go?"

"Not me, no. But I'm not talking about me, I'm talking about you."

"Me?"

"Did you ever think about it?"

"You mean to Hollywood?"

"Well, no, maybe not Hollywood. That's over on the other side. Maybe New Jersey."

"Where's New Jersey?"

"On this side. We've got cousins there, did you know?"

"Maybe you told me. I don't remember."

"So? Did you ever think of going?"

"Why? For a holiday?"

"No, to live."

"To live?"

"It was just a thought. It's just that . . . I was thinking, what do you want to do with your life?"

"With my life?"

"Don't just repeat everything. You're thirty years old."

"Yes, I know."

"So now I'm asking you what you want to do? Would you like to go to America?"

"What about you? What would you do?"

"Never mind me."

Charlotte put down her fork. "How can you say that, 'never mind me,' just like that? You want me to go away? To leave you? Is that what you want?"

He could see how agitated she was and he tried to calm her down. "No, that's not what I want. What I mean is, I want what's best for you."

Charlotte looked at him suspiciously. "Did you meet someone?" she asked. "Is that why?"

Jakob couldn't help smiling. That was his own first thought about his daughter when Harry first brought up the subject. "No, I didn't meet someone."

"Are you sure?"

"Sure, I'm sure. I promise you. I'd tell you if I did."

"So why do you want me to leave?"

"I didn't say that."

"You said America."

"I just said . . ." He was becoming a little frustrated. This was exactly what he'd feared all along. "Please, don't get upset. It was just an idea, nothing at all. It's just that you talk about Hollywood, it's so glamorous . . . I just wondered if you'd ever thought about it."

"I don't think Doris Day lives in New Jersey."

"No . . ." said Jakob slowly. "No, maybe not."

For some reason, that ended the discussion, and they ate the rest of their meal in an uneasy silence. Jakob felt terrible. He knew he'd hurt her feelings and that was the last thing he'd wanted to do.

It was wrong of him, he knew, to blurt it out like that. He should have given it more thought before he'd said anything and he was angry with himself for not doing so.

Nevertheless, despite her reaction, he still considered the basic concept to be sound. America was the land of the future, and that's what he wanted for her: a future.

She needed room to grow, with enough distance between them that she could cut her ties to him, that she could meet new people, start afresh. He could see that now.

It was all very clear. Harry had been right. She was his daughter, not his wife. She shouldn't be here in Stamford Hill, rushing home to heat up his stew. She deserved so much more than this.

Charlotte was devastated, shaken by the very notion of leaving her father, and just when she'd begun to feel some stability. How could he say such a thing to her? Her mother had sent her away and now her father wanted to do the same. Was it for the same reason, she wondered?

Despite her father's denials, she couldn't help thinking that maybe he had indeed met someone, because there was no other explanation; unless, of course, she'd disappointed him in some way.

Perhaps she wasn't such a good daughter after all. Perhaps she talked too much, laughed too loudly, and that's why both her parents needed to push her out.

In her confusion, she tried to go through all the possibilities, but nothing made any sense. Yet however she felt in private, when she next met Sadie she tried her best to keep her expression the way it had been before, all smiles, all fun, in line with her own pre-determined policy.

Whatever she was feeling on the inside, she wouldn't let it show on the outside. The sun could reflect, even if it couldn't penetrate.

"America?" said Sadie, after Charlotte had explained it. "Did he mean it?"

"I don't know."

It was a fine Wednesday afternoon in the late spring of 1950. After a quick snack at the Lyons Corner House on Shaftesbury Avenue, they'd walked over to catch the new Dior fashions on display along Regent Street.

They were far too expensive for either of them even to contemplate, but they wanted to see and admire them nonetheless.

"Maybe you'll go to Hollywood, like I told you," said Sadie, gazing in at a store window. "You could meet Cary Grant. Maybe you could become Mrs. Grant."

Charlotte smiled, as always, at Sadie's humor, but her mind was still struggling with its own preoccupations. "What do *you* think?" she asked Sadie. "Do you think he meant it?"

"Didn't you ask him?"

"He said he wanted what's best for me."

"What's wrong with that?"

"It's what my mother said."

"So? That's good, isn't it?"

Charlotte nodded, but her hesitancy was obvious, and for one anxious moment, she thought about telling her friend everything: about her mother and Karl, all the things she'd never told anyone; but in the final reckoning, she just couldn't bring herself to do it.

She was too ashamed, not just of her mother's betrayal but of her own disgust and jealousy, multiplied a million-fold by the overwhelming guilt of knowing her mother's fate.

Ultimately, inevitably, she forced herself to maintain the illusion, so she just stood there without answering. In front of her were the world's most stunning styles, yet she saw nothing.

Behind her, cars and taxis and buses rumbled past, a cacophony of engines and horns, but she heard none of it. She was trying to hold back her emotions while keeping a pleasant expression and she didn't know how long she could keep it going.

Sadie must have been aware that something was amiss, because she said, "Charlotte, listen to me. Are you listening?"

Somehow, her voice managed to break through, and again, Charlotte just nodded, a weak, automatic gesture.

"No, you're not," said Sadie, "you're miles away. I want you to listen to me."

With some reluctance, Charlotte turned her head. "I'm listening."

"Good, so what you have to understand is that it's up to you. It's your choice. Nobody can force you to do anything."

"I had no choice with my mother."

"That was different."

That was when something changed in Charlotte and she responded with instant venom. "How do you know? You weren't there." However, the very moment she said it, she regretted it. She turned to hug the short figure of Sadie and held on to her tightly. "I'm sorry, I'm sorry. I didn't mean that. I'm so sorry."

Sadie struggled for breath. "All right, let go, I give up!" Then, when she was released, she added, "You can mother me, just don't smother me."

This made Charlotte giggle and she calmed down, thankful that she had such a friend. She pointed to one of the dresses in the window. "That's like the one you lent me, remember?"

"Except it's about five thousand pounds more expensive. Maybe Cary Grant will buy it for you."

This produced more laughter, and it was enough to let them continue with their afternoon. They had to get to the Odeon, Leicester Square, in time for the matinee, *The Heiress*, with Olivia de Havilland and Montgomery Clift.

The matter of America was forgotten for several months, and Charlotte was able to settle back into her life, unperturbed by the possibility of disruption. Yet the wounds were still there underneath, and on some nights, they just tore her apart. The vision of her mother chasing along the platform as the train left still haunted her dreams, and Charlotte would wake, dry-mouthed and aching.

It was a torment that she alone suffered, because only she knew the full extent of it. The idea of the same thing happening again—to see her father, this time, on a different platform—was just too much for her to bear. It therefore came to her as a surprise when the envelope was pushed through the door one morning in 1951. It looked official, and when Charlotte picked it up, she saw that it was from the US Embassy on Grosvenor Square.

It was addressed to her as *Miss Liselotte Goldhill*, technically incorrect, but an understandable error with so many refugees now changing their names. With unsteady hands, she ripped it open. This was another letter, she was certain, with more bad news. It wasn't difficult to guess that her father had applied for an American visa without telling her. When the words came into focus, the first thing she noticed was that it was a form letter.

It began "Sir/Madam," and went on to say that her name had been placed on the registration list for US immigration, as per the request, but that she was part of an over-subscribed quota, and there was no telling when she might be contacted again.

Her reaction was relief as much as annoyance. Unlike when she and her mother had waited in line at the embassy back in Vienna, she was now very thankful that she was mired in some bureaucratic procedure and that the application would not be progressing any further.

However, she was also immensely upset that her father would do such a thing without asking her and she resolved to let him know how she felt as soon as he returned that evening. Yet it didn't happen that way. He called her in the afternoon to say that he'd been summoned to an urgent client meeting in Ilford, just beyond London's eastern perimeter, and couldn't make it home before nine or ten.

Don't wait for dinner, he told her, and don't worry, because he'd grab a quick sandwich on his own. It was such a thoughtful consideration on his part that she couldn't stay mad at him and, as the day wore down, she found she'd mellowed from her morning's indignation.

When the light faded, she called Sadie at home and told *her*, instead, what had happened.

Sadie's response was typical. After listening to the long monologue, all she said was: "Well . . . I suppose Cary Grant will just have to wait."

This struck Charlotte as so funny that it completely removed whatever edge remained and allowed her to regain her inside-outside balance. Once again, she chose to instruct herself that whatever she might be feeling—hurt, bitterness, regret, guilt—she would present a serene face to the world. Superficial though it may be, she knew this was the only way she'd be able to cope with the silent anguish that just wouldn't go away.

To camouflage her emotions and offer some respite for her deeper anxieties, Charlotte counted herself fortunate that she had several reliable sources of fun in her life. There was Sadie, of course, with her sisters and her friends, always ready to laugh. However, it was also true that the animals which she and her father kept prompted considerable amusement.

The small parrot always made her smile when it chirped out the few words it had learned, and the stray cat would demonstrate its gratitude by bringing back gifts of dead mice and leaving them at Charlotte's feet on the kitchen floor, but it was the dog, Bobby, who was the truly intelligent one. He even managed to take the bus on his own.

Often Jakob would take Bobby along on weekends to see Harry and Leah, who had recently moved back to London and now lived just a couple of miles away. The dog became used to the journey, and one morning, when he managed to slip unnoticed out of the house, he decided that he would go for a jaunt.

According to the bus conductor, the little terrier climbed aboard the big double-decker all by himself, was impeccably behaved while on board and seemed to know exactly where he was going. Either he counted the four stops, or else he recognized certain landmarks through the window but however he accomplished the feat, he alighted from the bus at exactly the right place, and trotted off around the block to show up on Harry's doorstep.

When Harry opened up to collect his newspaper, Bobby licked his hand, wagged his tail, then accompanied him back into the kitchen to enjoy scraps from the breakfast table: a suitable reward for such a brave odyssey.

Another diversion that entered Charlotte's life around this time was the purchase by Harry of a new television set. It was a giant wooden box with a tiny fourteen inch screen and a rabbit-ear aerial, which showed one station in black and white, with limited programming and an often scratchy reception.

Yet, whenever she had the opportunity, Charlotte would take Bobby on his favorite bus ride to go watch whatever they were broadcasting at the time.

She liked the news, of course, and was profoundly moved when they announced that the much-loved king, George VI, had died and was about to be succeeded by his eighteen-year-old heir, Elizabeth. The announcers tried to herald the change as "the birth of a new Elizabethan Age," but Charlotte wasn't even aware of the first one and had to go look it up in the library.

Of far more interest to her was the Winter Olympics, held coincidentally the same month, with the British team in Norway all wearing black armbands. She especially liked the figure skating, recalling how much she enjoyed the sport with her youth club during those Vienna winters.

Her attention focused, like the rest of her adopted country, on Miss Jeannette Altwegg, the reigning British and world champion, who managed to win gold despite rumors of collusion amongst the Soviet Bloc judges.

Charlotte's cousin, Frank, also showed up occasionally to watch the newsreels of the games, and she was able to continue the friendship that she'd allowed to slip. His own favorite sport was ski jumping, which he'd always wanted to try—just like flying, he told her—but he also enjoyed the ice hockey.

It was a lot like soccer, he explained, except played on skates instead of studs. When the Canadian team triumphed, as expected, it gave him the chance to ask her if she'd ever thought about going to Canada.

This startled Charlotte for the moment. She hadn't even realized that Frank knew about her father's failed application on her behalf to the United States, yet here he was, now asking very casually if she'd ever considered its frozen neighbor to the north.

"Did my father ask you to say that?" she asked him, her voice accusatory in tone.

Frank immediately reacted to the change in attitude with a tactical retreat. "Keep your hair on," he replied, "it was just a simple question."

The entire topic of emigration was put to rest for the time being, only to be reawakened, like all things, in the spring. For Charlotte, it appeared to happen innocuously, but she soon understood that it had been set up by her father, this time with the willing collusion of Harry and Frank: an entire family conspiracy to get her away.

It began with a seemingly innocent suggestion by Frank to go for a stroll one Sunday afternoon. His new fiancé was visiting her parents, and Jakob was working that day, so Frank asked Charlotte if she wanted to go feed the pigeons in Trafalgar Square, something he hadn't done since he was a boy. It sounded innocent enough and she thought it might be a pleasant way to spend a warm April afternoon.

"If you like," she answered.

"Just don't bring the dog," he added. "Dogs and pigeons, not a good mix."

These birds had always been as much a feature of Trafalgar Square as Nelson's column and Landseer's lions, which made the place not only a must-see on any visitor's itinerary, but also a place for locals to bring their kids.

In terms of location, it was central to everywhere, so their expedition became something of a sightseeing tour, and Frank took pleasure in pointing out the various sights, just as her father had done when she first arrived.

He showed her the National Gallery along the northern edge of the square; Whitehall with its government ministries leading away from the south; and through Admiralty Arch was the grandeur of The Mall, the ramrod-straight avenue which led all the way to Buckingham Palace.

After strolling for a couple of hours, they wound up their excursion in the square itself, where they bought small packets of bird seed from the vendor. Being a Sunday, there were large crowds out feeding the pigeon population and, predictably, most were families.

It was a joy to see the children's small faces beaming with excitement as the flocks fluttered around them, and without feeling at all self-conscious, Charlotte was more than happy to join them. Next to her, Frank looked on, smiling, as the greedy birds fussed and argued, clambering all over her arms and shoulders, up to half a dozen at a time.

It was all immense fun, but unfortunately, Frank had to go and spoil it. At the end of the afternoon, he suggested that, instead of going directly to Charing Cross to catch the Underground, they stroll up to Piccadilly Circus.

She had no objection, but no sooner had they approached the neo-classical edifice of Canada House, just to the west of Trafalgar Square, she knew he'd been tricked.

"Hey, look where we are," he said, obviously feigning surprise. "Let's go in."

Charlotte glared at him, suspecting the entire day had been nothing but a ruse. "You knew we were coming here, didn't you?" she asked with some vitriol.

"Well . . ."

"Don't lie to me, Frank."

He looked a little embarrassed at being exposed. "Yeah, maybe your dad might have suggested we pop in, you know, while we were here and all."

Charlotte was clearly upset at what appeared to be yet another betrayal. "How could you do that? Why didn't you say something?"

"Your dad's only thinking what's best for you. Come on, what can it hurt? We'll just take a look, pick up some pamphlets." Then he said again, "What can it hurt?"

Before she could prevent him, he took her arm, linked it into his, and held on to it firmly as he eased her across the pavement and into the building. She was still robust and could have resisted more stridently in any manner of ways, either verbally or physically, but this was the center of London, and she didn't want to cause a scene, all too aware of her father's constant warnings not to make any trouble.

That Sunday night, when she arrived home, her father was already there.

"Have a nice time?" he asked her.

In response, she simply dumped the pile of pamphlets on the table. Some were glossy travel brochures showing the Rockies, with people pointing out the grizzly bears from train windows, but others were more directly concerned with prospects for potential immigrants.

In that booming post-war period, the dominion was wide open for naturalized British subjects, and not only were work visas readily available, there were even offers of financial aid if the applicant qualified.

It was quite a change from the situation back in Vienna, and different, too, from the current American policy where the relevant quotas, in this case, British and Austrian, were totally over-subscribed.

"Why?" Charlotte asked her father. "Why Canada? It's not America, it's not glamorous . . ."

"Sit down, *liebste*," said Jakob. "No, first get yourself something to eat, then come sit down."

"Why don't you answer me?"

"I will, I promise. Now, please . . . you need to eat."

Her father had already taken his meal, so Charlotte fried a slice of bread and a couple of sausages in chicken *schmaltz* for herself, then came over to sit by him at the table. She was still livid, and although she was trying to fight the emotion by following her self-imposed rules, it wasn't easy.

"So?" she said.

He'd been reading some kind of business report, glasses perched on his nose, but now he removed them and turned his full attention to his daughter.

"All right, now listen to me carefully, once and for all. It's no good you being here with me. I'm not a husband, I'm your father, and I can look after myself just fine, thank you very much."

As soon as she opened her mouth to interject, he held up his hand to stop her from doing so. "Please . . . pay me the respect of listening. It's time you found a life of your own. Now I know we have nobody in Canada, not like in New Jersey, but there are two cousins from Poland, Stefan and Roman. You haven't met them yet. They survived the war, and they plan to go to Montreal . . . and I want you to go with them."

"But . . ."

"No arguments, not yet. I want you to think about it. Read the papers you brought home and meet the boys. I think you'll like them. Then we'll make a decision. Will you do that? For me?"

Other than blind refusal, there was not much Charlotte could say to this. He was being so reasonable, yet she just couldn't bring herself to embrace the idea. "It's cold there," was all she could think to say.

"Not in the summer."

"They all live in igloos."

"Now you're just being silly. We'll talk about it some more when you're less upset."

"I'm not upset," she insisted but then felt compelled to add, "You tricked me, and Frank tricked me. Do I deserve that? Do I?"

Jakob had to concede the point. "All right, *liebste*, no more tricks, I promise. Just tell me you'll think about it."

Charlotte shrugged and continued with her meal. She had nothing else to say.

They all met at Harry's place one Sunday and Leah deigned to make tea for everybody.

The brothers from Poland were already there when Charlotte and her father arrived. At first glance, they seemed nice enough: two young men from Krakow, sallow and slightly built.

The elder brother was just a year younger than Charlotte, but apart from the age similarity, she found she had little in common with either of them. They were polite enough, to be sure, but their eyes were wary, and it was clear they'd been relying on each other for so long that the rest of the world seemed alien.

At her father's encouragement, Charlotte told them she'd come from Austria on the special train, the *Kindertransport,* and Stefan, the more intellectual of the two, nodded his understanding. Roman, who was the stronger, revealed nothing at all, and neither of them seemed willing to volunteer their own story.

When she made a point of asking them how they'd managed to survive, they replied that it would take too long to explain. It was enough, they said, that they were still alive. The only other question she posed was why they were thinking Canada of all places, but their answer was just as minimal.

"A new life," was Stefan's only reply.

So that's how their conversation ended, with neither Charlotte nor the brothers especially interested in each other. For them, she was outside their tight, two-person fraternity, and for Charlotte, these long-lost cousins were engaged in a venture that she was extremely reticent to join.

On the way back, Charlotte and her father didn't speak until they were on the bus. Bobby, tugging at the leash, had it in his head that he wanted to go upstairs on the double-decker, so Jakob traipsed up after him and Charlotte followed, even though they were only traveling the four stops.

On the top deck, people were smoking which made Charlotte's eyes water, and she found it hard to answer when her father asked her what she thought about her new cousins.

"Are you crying?" he asked her.

"No, just all this smoke. I don't know why the dog wants to come up here anyway."

Jakob laughed. "It's because he once smelled some meat in a woman's shopping bag, so now he thinks that every time he comes up here, he'll have the same smell. Maybe he thinks this is where all meat comes from . . . upstairs on the bus."

Jakob chuckled again but Charlotte didn't find it all that amusing.

"I don't think anything about them," she admitted, responding to his first question.

"You must have some opinion."

"They seem all right."

"But you're not too impressed."

"I didn't say that."

"No, but I can tell."

"You always think you know what I'm thinking, but you don't."

He turned to look at her, not entirely sure what had brought on such harsh words. "What have I done, you talk to me like this?"

For a while, she didn't answer. She just sat there looking out the window with the dog now perched on her lap, until her father dug his elbow into her.

"I'm talking to you."

She turned to him, her expression giving away the simmering resentment that she felt. She urged herself to keep control. She even tried a mental count, but in the end, she just couldn't hold it back. "You know what you've done," she said to him, spitting out the words.

"It's for the . . ." He didn't even manage to finish.

"It's for the best, I know, you told me."

At that, she got up, dumped the dog onto the seat and pushed past him into the narrow aisle. Then, without saying anything more, she made her way along the swaying bus and down the stairs, getting off one stop early just so she could be alone for a while. She needed to breathe, to be away from the smoke and away from her father, too.

It was still light, and she found herself alone outside a newsagent's. There were placards advertising yet another story in the *Evening Standard* about the young Queen Elizabeth.

This time it was which dress she might wear for the coronation, and which couturier might be so honored with the task. Normally, Charlotte would have been intrigued enough to have purchased a copy, something to chat about with Sadie, but not today.

All the pain and confusion she had felt leaving Vienna had returned, swirling around and fogging up her thought processes. She was conscious of the fact that she was not an adolescent any more, that she should be acting her age. She told herself to be mature, to be sensible, yet it was tearing her apart.

Why did her father want to send her away? Hadn't she worked to make him happy? No matter how much she considered it, she couldn't seem to work it out. Nothing made sense to her, and as she tried to figure it out, she just walked; somewhere, anywhere, like she'd once wandered around the Augarten, lonely and totally lost inside her own mind.

Here, at least, there were no Nazis and no curfew, but she was still faced with another parent pushing her out, and this time, she didn't even know the reason. She longed to be able to stop in at Hugo's repair shop but there was no Hugo here. Had he survived the war? Where was he now?

She longed to sit with him and drink tea with him and pour out her troubles to him, and the fact that he wasn't there just added to her sense of sadness.

Finally, she came across a group of boisterous girls, arm-in-arm, laughing loudly with faces flushed as they emerged from a pub. It was closing time, which made Charlotte to realize how late it was getting, so she gradually made her way home.

When she arrived, she found her father still up, waiting for her in his armchair, half-asleep with the cat in his arms.

"Where have you been?" he asked her. "I was worried."

"I'm not a child."

He looked at her from across the room. "No . . . No, you're not," he said quietly. "*Liebste*, come, come sit with me."

She didn't want to sit down, she just wanted to go directly to her room, but she did as her father requested. He obviously had something to say, and once she was seated opposite, she simply waited for him to speak. In the meantime, he was tickling the cat's ears.

It had a thick coat and a throaty purr, and there was no other place it preferred to be. At Jakob's feet was the dog, as usual, which turned his head upward to gaze at him with mournful eyes, as if jealous of the attention he was giving the feline. The parrot was in his cage, already asleep, his beak tucked into his back feathers.

"You say you're not a child," Jakob began, "but now I want you to think back to when you *were* that child. Eleven, twelve years old . . . It doesn't matter what age. Do you remember?"

"I remember everything."

"Good, good. So now I want you to remember how you were, your personality, your character."

"I don't know what you mean."

He smiled and nodded his balding head while he continued to stroke the animal. "*Meineliebe* Liesl . . . You were so strong, so independent, don't you remember? You went hiking in the mountains and you came back even stronger. I was so proud of you."

"You're not proud of me now?"

"I'm always proud of you, *liebste*, always. What I mean is . . . Back then, you had a different spirit. You wanted .

. . I don't know the word. Maybe adventure, maybe fun, I don't know. But these days . . ." He paused as if to gather his thoughts.

"This is hard for me. I don't want you to go halfway around the world, of course I don't, but you need to get back that feeling. That's who you are, that's your character. All this . . ." He waved his hand to indicate the apartment in general. "All this means nothing."

"Nothing?"

"No, no, I didn't mean it like that. Liesl, *liebste*, please don't make this any harder. You know what I'm talking about."

Charlotte was watching the bird sleep but it was just a place she could fix her gaze so she didn't have to look back at her father. She knew that what he was saying was true. That had indeed been her character.

One time, up there in the mountains, she'd felt like she just wanted to go on forever, like Vasco de Gama, or Marco Polo, or any of those other great explorers she'd read about. She breathed a sigh but that was as much as she was prepared to concede.

Very softly, she asked, "Why Canada?"

He shrugged. "I know, I know, America was the first choice, but there's nothing I can do about that. There's no visa."

"I meant my cousins. Why are they going?"

"They have friends there."

"They do?"

"It's not so different from America. A few degrees colder, maybe, but not so different. They live the same way, drive the same cars. It's a rich place, *liebste*, there's lots of opportunity, lots of adventure. Don't you want to go walking in the mountains, all that fresh air?

"Over there, you can keep walking and never get to the end. That's what I want for you, don't you understand? I want you to find your independence again, all that you lost."

Perhaps it was the effect of the parrot, but Charlotte's eyes were drooping, too. She forced herself up from the armchair, then gave her father just one single nod to close off the evening. Once in her room, she closed the door behind her and just fell onto the bed fully dressed. She was more than tired, she was weary, exhausted with the constant questioning and the perennial doubt.

Tomorrow, she thought, as her head settled on the pillow. Tomorrow she'd think about hiking in the mountains, but not tonight.

Here in North America, we generally tend to think that the correct way to behave is to be straightforward and honest in our relationships. For people who don't conform, we have the expression "two-faced," which is used as a derogatory. Yet, this attitude is by no means universal.

Over vast swathes of our planet, it's perfectly acceptable for people to generate great differences inside and out, and what they reveal is often diametrically opposed to what they're really feeling.

For example, I've noticed that in some cultures, politeness and charm are used to camouflage wariness. In others, self-confident or assertive behavior might act as a mask to hide weakness or vulnerability.

In Charlotte's case, as her father rightly pointed out, her natural instinct was to be outgoing, open, generous, and independent in spirit. That was her personality until she was nineteen, but then, when the trauma struck, the disruption wounded her at the deepest level.

It might even have destroyed her, but she chose to develop an external layer as her own method of protection and self-preservation. Mostly, this took the form of cheerfulness or humor, but it could also display a certain cool serenity.

However, it took a while to develop, and that's why she reacted so badly when she thought that her father, too, was pushing her away. It wasn't authentic, so it wasn't yet completely formed.

Later, though, over the years, this mask became an integral part of her character, automatic in its application and completely genuine in its intention, without any trace of superficiality.

Yet always, the primary function was to act as a disguise, to hide the torment and turmoil that caused her very soul to ache. It became so effective that nobody suspected the truth, not even those closest to her, but it was never completely impervious, and that's why, as I occasionally witnessed, the private tears were able to break through.

13

In June of 1953, Charlotte watched on her Uncle Harry's television the spectacular pageantry of Elizabeth's coronation. Then, just three months later, she found herself emigrating to a distant land where, by historical happenstance, that same royal crown still presided.

The vessel on which she traveled was Italian by registry, the Lauro Lines' SS *Sydney* departing from Liverpool—the same port where she'd taken the Isle of Man ferry—with a scheduled arrival in Quebec City five days later. As the ship finally cast off and the tugboats eased it away from the dock, Charlotte leaned on the rail alongside her two cousins and scores of other passengers with her arm raised high, waving down at her father who was standing on the quay, a squat, sad figure trying to look happy.

She was heading off on a brand new adventure, but that's not how she felt. Instead, her mind was filled, yet again, with memories of that last morning in Vienna when she stood on the train and watched her mother vanish into the morning mist.

In some ways, her emotional state was the same, too: a numbing sensation that affected her entire being. It was as if she were dropping off the edge of the world, a voyage of the damned, like the paintings she'd once seen in her mother's art books.

For her father's sake, she attempted to smile and appear willing, a continuation of the ebullient cover-up she'd been trying to perfect, but she couldn't fool her own psyche, and underneath it all, she couldn't have been more miserable. Then it occurred to her that perhaps she wasn't being sent away. Perhaps she was the one who was abandoning her father, just like she'd abandoned her mother. Perhaps she'd just pretended to herself that she was being a good and responsible daughter by obeying her parents' wishes.

Perhaps she secretly wanted to leave them. She felt like screaming at all the recurring images, and even before the ship had cleared the harbor, she ran down to the third class cabin she was sharing with another young woman, a complete stranger, because it was less expensive to travel that way.

Fortunately, her bunking companion was still up on deck, so she had the tiny space all to herself. It meant she could be blissfully alone, to close her eyes and shut everything out, if only for half-an-hour. Yet, still, the thoughts wouldn't leave her—her mother at Theresienstadt, her father at Douglas, both of them behind barbed wire—and beneath it all was her own guilt, eating at her resolve and resilience.

As it turned out, the weather came to her rescue. A major storm served to distract her from this continual self-absorption. The vessel, while relatively new, was designed for the more tranquil waters of the Mediterranean, not hurricane season in the western Atlantic, and for two days it was tossed around like a toy in a bathtub, forcing Charlotte to focus on such basic acts as remaining vertical and keeping her meals down.

At one time, when she arrived in the dining room for breakfast, she found herself on her own. Not even many of the crew were around, and the few who were there tried to reassure her in their macho way that the ship wasn't in danger, that they'd survived far worse than this, but Charlotte wasn't entirely convinced. Not until they reached the estuary of the St. Lawrence did the swell subside, and for the first time on the entire journey, the sun emerged, welcoming her to the new world the way it once did to European explorers dating all the way back to the Vikings.

Charlotte had learned enough to realize that she probably wouldn't have to break new trails or hitch up a dog sled, but nevertheless, she felt like she was venturing into the unknown; and since she wouldn't have her father waiting for her, she wondered who else she might find.

Would there be another friend like Sadie? Could there ever be? It was hard to imagine, but maybe her cousins could introduce her to some people. It would be a start.

For the sake of her father, Charlotte tried her best to be positive and optimistic, but what she really discovered in this strange place was emptiness and loneliness. True, she had her cousins with her, but they hadn't changed. Somehow, she thought that they might become the brothers she never had; that they'd all be sharing this adventure together, three musketeers out to work hard and have fun as they built some kind of life.

Unfortunately for Charlotte, that's not how it turned out. The two brothers had relied on each other for so long that it hardly occurred to them to include this outsider in their plans, even if she was related. Once they'd all cleared immigration in Quebec City and journeyed by rail up to Montreal, their mutual assistance pact just seemed to dissolve.

While the brothers reunited with old friends, Charlotte was left to map out the landscape on her own—and so it was demonstrated to her yet again that people on whom she relied had proved to be undeserving of her trust. She understood that perhaps her expectations were too high, yet she couldn't help but feel betrayed.

So here she was, on a foreign continent far away from anything she'd known. While she maintained her fortitude during the day as she hunted for work, at night, when she was alone at the hostel where she'd found affordable accommodation, she cried herself to sleep.

The city itself was also a disappointment. This was a long way from the supposed glamour of Hollywood, and compared to the great capitals she'd known, Vienna and London, the place seemed like a cultural wasteland, an overgrown pioneer village where each ethnic group had its own enclave. In the east was the majority, the French Catholics, even more devout than those back in Austria. Towards the west were the English-speaking Protestants, mostly Anglicans and Presbyterians. In the north were the Italians and Greeks, and in the southwest, the Irish.

There were also sizeable numbers of Chinese, Ukrainian, Portuguese, Jamaican, and Haitian, as well as a small community of African-Americans, direct descendants of the slaves who'd made that terrifying run north.

Wedged right in the middle of all of them was the Jewish population with its own familiar divisions, the entire spectrum from orthodox to liberal, all huddled around the long boulevard known as The Main, which divided east and west. It was here that Charlotte was instinctively drawn because it meant basic survival: a job, an apartment, and a neighborhood full of equally-minded refugees who might show some empathy; but this was not where she wanted to be.

The area felt too much like Brigittenau or Stamford Hill to be comfortable. She didn't want to live in yet another ghetto, so while she couldn't be too selective in terms of employment—since her only real skill was as a seamstress, she was limited to working at a Jewish-owned garment factory—she decided to hunt elsewhere for a place to live.

It was possible, she thought, that her father wouldn't have approved of her living beyond the safety of the community, but he was the one who'd pushed her out, telling her she needed to become more independent, so that's what she intended to do.

The crisp, colorful weeks of autumn were already giving way to the icy blasts of Charlotte's first Canadian winter, but that didn't stop her determination, and each weekend, she took excursions by streetcar or bus in order to discover unfamiliar areas. She usually had an address in her coat pocket, a scrap of newspaper torn from the classified ads, but she was looking for the right district more than the right apartment. In the meantime, work at the factory was exhausting. Although she and the other machine operators were seated while they worked, it was a strain on the back, and the noise caused many of them to experience chronic headaches.

Days were eight hours long, but that could increase to ten, or even twelve, during a rush period, and such extended shifts were compulsory. There were few breaks, and the pay was barely enough to cover the necessities, but at least the foreman, a rotund man with flabby arms and puffy cheeks, had a sense of humor. He laughed along with his girls until his chin wobbled, and it was only his attitude that made the job tolerable. "How can it be a sweatshop when it's minus twenty outside?" he asked.

It was one of his standard jokes, chuckling to himself each time he repeated it, except, in truth, the place was indeed a sweatshop. Some of the younger, more strident workers talked about joining a union, but that issue never went very far because there were always raw immigrants like Charlotte waiting in line to be hired: far too many willing recruits for the owners ever to worry about a shortage of labor.

These owners knew that on any given day, they could instantly fire everybody, and by the following afternoon, every chair would be once again filled, and every machine would be up and running. So, unlike some of her colleagues, Charlotte kept her mouth shut, sharing the humor but not anxious to get involved with anything that might lead to trouble. It wasn't that she was a coward—she'd proven her courage on the streets of Vienna—but survival was what she knew best. The work might be tough on her body and spirit, yet even in the deepest freeze of winter, this was better than a concentration camp, better than an internment camp, and these images became her constant mental comparisons.

She wrote often to her father, always telling him of her accomplishments, never her problems. She could picture him arriving home at night, tired after a long day, delighted to discover a letter with a Canadian stamp waiting for him on the doormat. He'd sit down in his armchair with the cat on his lap and the dog by his feet to read it, and the last thing he'd want to see would be tales of distress. Was he lonely, too, she wondered? She missed her father, she missed Sadie, she missed Harry and Frank, and she missed her evening walks with Bobby.

She couldn't recall why she'd even agreed to the crazy idea of coming here, except for the duty of being an obedient daughter—and look where that had gotten her. More than once during that initial winter season, she considered the idea of simply getting on a boat to go back, and she might well have done so but for the embarrassing fact that she didn't have the fare, and it would have required asking her father to send over the necessary funds.

Then, one weekend, as patches of green were finally beginning to break through the gray slush, she found an apartment in a pleasant area, and it opened up a fresh chapter. It was only three small rooms, plus a bathroom, but it fit the bill. There wasn't much of a view on the buildings opposite, but it was heated, it had a clean stove, and the water ran clear. It even had a small fridge. What more would she need?

This would be the very first place that she could ever truly call her own and she was determined to put all her effort into making it just the way she wanted. The borough was called Outremont, located in the French-speaking part of town, but she'd learned the rudiments of the language at high school, so she didn't really mind. The area was mostly residential with an equal mix of ownership and rentals, but she liked the conservative, European-style atmosphere which gave it a reassuring sense of permanence.

She was so full of plans, she could hardly wait to move in. She would stitch curtains and tablecloths, shawls and bedspreads. She would spend her evenings listening to the radio, cooking and sewing until she got tired, then she'd read a little before a peaceful night's sleep.

This, she decided, would be her own small version of paradise. If she could rely on no one else, not her parents and not her cousins, then she would rely on herself. She'd finally arrived at the stage where she felt she didn't need people at all. They always ended up disappointing her and she just couldn't take any more of that in her life.

Then, at a time when she was least expecting it, she met Joe.

She first heard about him on a Monday, and it came from the young woman at the factory who worked at the adjacent machine. She knew Charlotte was Jewish, and during lunch hour, she told her that she'd been out with her husband during the weekend, and they'd met this really nice man who'd just arrived.

She was sure he was Jewish—and a bachelor, too—and would Charlotte like to meet him? She also confided that if she weren't already married, she might have gone after him herself.

Of course, Charlotte's first response was to say thank you, but no. In this newly independent phase of hers, a blind date was the last thing she desired. However, a few days later, as she arrived home from work, her landlady came out to meet her in the stairwell.

"There was a call for you," she said in English. "A man with an accent. He left a number to call back."

Charlotte had forgotten all about her colleague's suggestion and thought immediately of her father. Since the number to call was local, a man with an accent must have meant a message. Perhaps something had happened. Perhaps her father was sick. All kinds of worries raced through her mind.

"May I use your phone?" she asked. She didn't yet have a line of her own.

"Now? I'm serving supper."

"It might be an emergency . . . *Uneurgence . . . s'il vous plaît?*" The fact that Charlotte tried to speak the language helped the situation.

"Okay, but not long."

Charlotte followed the woman through the untidy apartment, nodded a greeting to the husband and two teenage children, then dialed the number.

"Hello?" said the voice, with an accent even more pronounced than Charlotte's.

"Charlotte Goldhill . . . You called me?"

"Ah, yes, hello, Charlotte. My name is Josef."

"How's my father? Is he all right?"

"Excuse me?"

"My father?"

"What about your father?"

"Don't you have a message from him?"

There was a nervous laugh. "I'm sorry, I don't know your father. I think maybe you're mixing me with someone else. My name is Josef Urban. I was just calling to ask if you'd like to go out with me."

"Go out with you? Where? Why?"

"Your friend said . . ."

"What friend?"

"Your friend at work."

By this time, Charlotte realized what was happening and felt upset, as if she'd somehow been duped. Her reply was brusque. "I'm sorry, I'm not interested, good-bye." Then she slammed the receiver back into its cradle with enough force that the landlady's family, all sitting around the kitchen table, turned their heads to look at her.

"Wrong number," she told them, then left quickly for her own apartment, her face flushed with a combination of anger and embarrassment.

Charlotte had her own meal to prepare, and by the time she was done cooking, eating, and washing the few dishes, she'd not only calmed down, but felt ashamed of what she'd done: not only to the man himself, but also the display she'd put on in front of her neighbors.

She couldn't even bring herself to go and ask to use the phone again. However, she felt she had to do something, so she put on her coat and went along the street as far as the Van Horne thoroughfare, where she knew there was a small café with a pay phone. It was from there that she called him back.

"Hello? Is that Josef?"

"Yes?"

"I'm sorry, I was rude to you."

"Ah, yes, Charlotte . . . That's all right. You wanted news from your father. I was silly to call you."

"No, no, you're not silly. Where are you from?"

"I was born in Poland."

"Like my father."

"Is that so? But I came here from South America. Not long ago, just a month."

"That sounds like an adventure."

"That's one word for it." He laughed.

It was a pleasant sound and Charlotte spent the next hour talking to him. She didn't even realize the amount of time she'd been on the phone until the Greek café owner pointed to his watch. He was waiting to close up. Once again, Charlotte had to make her apologies to Josef, which was why, despite all the promises she'd made to herself, she agreed to go out with him that Saturday evening.

The next day was Friday, and after work, Charlotte went to buy herself some new shoes. She had a dress of sorts which she'd altered herself, black with a bow at the neckline, but she had no shoes even remotely suitable for an evening out. It was late closing at the stores, so she took her time.

The pair she selected had higher heels than she normally wore and she wasn't used to them. The following evening, when Josef arrived at her building to pick her up, she came down the stairs, tripped, and fell, literally, into his arms. It was just like with Sadie when they first met and it served to ease the tension immediately.

She looked up to see his easy-going face had a ready smile. On his head he wore a trilby hat, not dissimilar to the one her father used to wear back in Vienna, and it gave him a slightly dashing appearance. Charlotte was instantly entranced. From that very first moment, she felt like she'd known him all her life.

The evening he'd planned was dinner, then a movie, but they never made it to the theater. Instead, they just sat after their meal of spaghetti Bolognese, drinking endless cups of coffee and talking. In addition to Polish, Yiddish, and partial English, he spoke fluent German, so communication was no problem at all.

Somehow, using German in Canada didn't seem as negative as in London, and nobody looked at them strangely. There were many immigrants speaking many languages, she told him, some she'd never even heard before, but everyone seemed to get along. It was one of the few positive things about the place.

By the end of the evening, Charlotte had learned much of his life story, and even when compared to her own odyssey, it was quite something.

Apparently, when the Nazis invaded Poland, Joe and several of his friends escaped into the forest. Few chose to do that because it was a brutal existence—the insect-infested summers, the frozen starvation of the winters—yet, somehow, they not only survived, they actually formed a roughshod partisan group, dedicated to the unlikely aim of striking back if at all possible.

In the first instance, they built ramshackle shelters and stole food from local farms to keep themselves going. Then, later, they joined others, both Jewish and non-Jewish, who shared the same intentions, and in this collective state, their resistance became a little more determined.

For six long years, this was how Josef and his group lived: sometimes as predators but, more often, as prey. Many around him had died, but in all that time, he was never shot, never wounded, never seriously sick. For that, he considered himself the luckiest man of the war.

When the hostilities had ceased, he found himself running a transit camp for survivors, paid for by Haganah, the Jewish defense organization, whose principal motive was to transport as many of these homeless, exhausted refugees to the British mandate of Palestine. It was not an easy task since Her Majesty's government had chosen to blockade the route in deference to Arab opinion.

After a couple of years in that role, he'd met a woman who was originally from Brazil, an aid worker at the camp. They'd married and went back to her home country, where Josef set himself up with a small roadside store selling cheap jewelry. Not only was the business less profitable than he'd hoped, but it turned out his new wife was stealing from him, transferring their joint funds to her family behind his back.

When he finally discovered the fraud, he was more upset at the lack of the trust than the missing money, so he just walked away, as simple as that, finally arriving in Montreal through some contacts he'd made in the jewelry trade.

Here, he wasn't running his own business, he was working for a furniture upholsterer, a skill he'd first learned back in Poland, but he was gently philosophical about his job, just as he was about his entire life's experience—and this was the quality that Charlotte most admired about him.

In return for his own lengthy tale, she told him a little about herself, too: about growing up in Vienna, her life under the Nazis, her escape to London on the *Kindertransport,* and how her mother didn't make it, just one of the six million Jews who had perished.

Of course, in all this, she said nothing about what happened with Karl. On this matter, she'd already decided she would never say a word to anybody.

At the end of the evening, he walked her home from the restaurant. By this time, she was already calling him Joe, but they didn't hold hands and they certainly didn't kiss. He was very proper in his manners, very respectful of her modest sensibilities, a characteristic she liked about him; so much so that when she arrived at work on the Monday morning, she was able to announce to her colleague, the girl who'd introduced them, that this was the man she was going to marry.

It wasn't an excited statement while still fresh from a first date but was spoken with quiet assurance and utter confidence. She'd never been more certain of anything in her life.

As was to be expected, Charlotte's father expressed a strong desire to meet this mystery man, this former *partisaner* from the forests with whom his little girl seemed so enamored. She knew well enough that she no longer needed parental approval to do anything, but instead of objecting to the imposition, she decided to keep the peace by reverting to the role of dutiful daughter and was gracious enough to ask him over, an invitation he accepted within a few weeks.

Unlike Charlotte, Jakob traveled by air now that he was a little more prosperous, his first flight since his rapid exit from Prague. It was a long, circuitous route across the Atlantic because the turboprops in service didn't yet have the range: from London's new airport at Heathrow, through Shannon in Ireland, then Gander in Newfoundland, before touching down at Montreal's Dorval.

As he descended the steps of the aircraft and spotted his daughter waving from the terminal, Jakob paused to raise his hat, looking for all the world like some foreign diplomat arriving on a state visit.

Charlotte wasn't sure what her feelings would be when she saw her father again, not even certain whether she still held any resentment. Nothing had really worked out the way he'd suggested.

She wasn't hiking in the mountains, she was working in a factory, and her cousins hadn't exactly looked after her like brothers, either. Despite all of that, she'd met Joe, and for that, she was prepared to forgive a great deal. So, once her father had cleared customs, she accepted his big hug the same way she did all those years ago when she, herself, had arrived at Liverpool Street station.

"You'll stay with me," she informed him.

"No, no, I told you in the letter. A hotel is fine, anything will do. Please. I'm not here to, well, interrupt anything."

"Interrupt anything?"

"Between you."

"What? No, no, don't worry, Joe has his own place."

This was an outright lie. In fact, they'd been living together for a while now but Joe was willing to stay with friends while her father was in town under the guise of old-fashioned decency.

As it happened, Jakob liked Josef immediately. The two were well-suited, spoke a similar range of languages, and were proud to escort Charlotte on a grand sightseeing tour, one on each side of her, taking in all the aspects of the city that none of them had yet seen.

There was nothing spectacular there—no Hofburg Palace and no Westminster Abbey—but there were impressive houses, wide cars, and vast supermarkets with an immense range of foods from every corner of the world.

Jakob had never seen such a bountiful assortment, and he was left shaking his head at how rich and energetic this country seemed compared to Europe, still recovering after the enormous destruction and deprivation.

It wasn't a long vacation because, as usual, Jakob had business commitments, and it felt like it was no time at all before they were sitting in Charlotte's tiny kitchen, sharing a last cup of coffee while waiting for the taxi to take him back to the airport.

"Thank you," he said to her softly.

"You're welcome," she replied.

"No, what I mean is . . . thank you for showing me the respect."

"Respect?"

"*Liebste*, I know I'm getting on a bit, but do you think I turned into an idiot in my old age? You think I don't how it is with you and Joe living here together? No, no, don't answer, don't spoil it. I just wanted to say thank you for showing me the respect . . . nothing else. I'm glad for you. He's a nice fellow. You deserve a chance to be happy, *seitgesund*. You're a good girl, just like you've always been, and for that I'm very grateful."

It was a fine speech, and Charlotte clearly appreciated it, although she knew that things could never be quite the same between them as they'd been before.

He'd once been her protector, someone on whom she could rely even when he wasn't there, but she'd now grown far beyond such childish needs. Besides, she now had Joe.

The happiness for which Charlotte had striven for so long finally arrived. It didn't last long enough, nor was it sufficient to heal a soul that had been ravaged by far too much raw emotion. The wounds were too deep, and the scars too fresh, but for this brief period of time, in the late fifties and early sixties, she came the closest she would ever be to the state of contentment and well-being that many take for granted.

One of the things she just adored about Joe was his love of spontaneity. This was the definition of freedom, he always told her: this possibility of doing anything at a moment's notice, plus the willingness to seize the opportunity.

Sometimes, for example, in the middle of winter at sub-zero temperatures, he would take Charlotte walking up to the top of Mount Royal, a good hour by foot, and they'd drink hot chocolate from the summit overlooking the city. Nobody could ever call it hiking in the mountains but it was the next best thing.

Another favorite adventure, especially during the summer months, was to wake before dawn on the weekend. They would then climb into the car and take the southbound highway, reaching the US border by sunrise and her father's cousins in New Jersey in time for brunch.

"Driving into the morning," Joe called it. On these occasions, Charlotte made a pretense of moaning at being roused from her warm bed for the early start, but she secretly enjoyed this independence of spirit. For her, Joe was a man who knew how to live.

They weren't rich, nor did they have any such prospects, so they lived frugally, paying all their debts immediately and even managing to save a little over the years. Then, one day, Joe announced his surprise. His intention, he told her, was to buy a property, something he'd had his eye on for a while.

He'd already talked to agents, and to the bank, so when Charlotte questioned how they could possibly afford such an endeavor, he was able to show her the arithmetic, as well as the building itself. It wasn't large, just three stories on Davaar, an Outremont side street, but all being well, he figured the rents should cover the mortgage, and even more importantly, they would be building some equity for the future.

Personally, she wasn't at all convinced, but she gladly gave her consent because, in the end, she trusted him totally, and trust was perhaps the one quality she now valued more than any other. Sometimes, she even thought that if she'd known Joe in Poland, she'd have probably followed him directly into the forest.

Once they were installed in their newly purchased building, one of their first acts of kindness was to allow a large family—a husband, wife, and six children—to move in on the ground floor. The man, Monsieur Rénaud, was large and hearty, a popular local police officer, but his problem was the kids.

Five out of the six were boys, enthusiastic and rowdy, so it wasn't easy to find accommodation. Nobody was willing to take them until Josef and Charlotte, now Mr. and Mrs. Urban, agreed to accept them. From that time on, the Rénauds became their most loyal friends, ever willing and ever grateful.

Later, at the larger building they purchased on Van Horne, two of those same children even became the couple's janitors. They first employed Lyne, the only girl, then one of the boys, Alain, each of them using the opportunity of a free apartment in exchange for a few hours of work each week. Once again, it was all about trust.

Life was now as close to idyllic as Charlotte had ever known. It wasn't easy—both she and Joe had manual jobs and worked long hours—but they were together, they were remarkably compatible, and whatever they did turned into a pleasure.

Chores were attacked with joy. Whether doing laundry, tossing the garbage, or washing the winter grime from their windows, there was always a joke, always a lightheartedness that eased the load.

Although she knew the inner torment would always remain, she now felt considerably more at ease with her external trappings of good humor. The sun was reflecting brilliantly from her armor, and it seemed as if, finally, the traumatized refugee had at last found her place.

Eventually, even her father came over to live out his years, the continual traveler at last settling down to spend whatever time remained in close proximity to his only child. So it was that in 1965, the old soldier finally passed away in his sleep, content in his heart that he'd done something good in this world by bringing Charlotte into it; and glad, too, that he'd been at least partially responsible for the sense of peace she seemed to have found.

After helping to raise the six Rénaud kids, the only thing missing for Charlotte and Joe was a child of their own, and when she eventually told him she was pregnant, it was if their lives were complete.

This would have been the high point, the final summit, but sadly, it was not to be. After just eight weeks, there were complications, and while the miscarriage which followed was not entirely unexpected, the bad news was the medical opinion that she might never be able to have children at all.

"Not to worry," said Joe gently. He'd taken her for their usual hot chocolate up at the lookout. It was the middle of the day and there weren't too many people around. "I've been looking into adoption."

Charlotte hadn't even considered that possibility but now her eyes brightened. "Really? You'd do that?"

"Why not?"

"But what if . . ."

"What if what?"

"What if the child turns out, you know, not how we want?"

"Then it will be our fault. The child will be whatever we make him."

"Him?"

"Or her. Whatever you want." He smiled, taking hold of her hand and tapping it softly. "At least with adoption, you get to make the choice."

Charlotte nodded. This, too, was something she hadn't thought about. "A daughter . . . Somehow, I always dreamed of having a daughter."

For a few silent moments, her mind went back to her mother and their love-hate paradox which had haunted her for most of her adult life. Even now, she hadn't told her husband anything of the story and wasn't about to relent on the promise she'd made to herself.

To open up the past would do nobody any good, and she was determined not to let it happen. In her mind, this was the new world, so let it stay new. That was how she saw it and that's how it remained.

Filing the requisite papers for adoption proved to be a long process. Fortunately, their credentials were reasonably sound. They'd already qualified for citizenship, they had title to a good-sized property, and they both had the practical skills to ensure a steady income. There appeared to be nothing that could obstruct their progress—until the day that Joe was diagnosed.

He'd been feeling some restrictions in his movements, but said these were minor, nothing to complain about. He'd seen people with far worse during the war. Still, on Charlotte's insistence, he began a series of tests at the Jewish General which seemed to go on forever.

There was always one more appointment, one more examination. Eventually, the doctor in charge, a senior man with a grave face, delivered the verdict.

"It's a condition we call Amyotrophic Lateral Sclerosis," he told them. "It affects certain aspects of the central nervous system which control voluntary muscle movement . . . and I'm afraid it's progressive," he continued. "It causes the upper and lower motor neurons to weaken through atrophy." Then he looked from one of them to the other, as if he'd explained everything and was waiting for a response.

"What does that mean?" asked Charlotte, not at all shy to display her ignorance; not when she needed to know something about Joe.

"What it means," the doctor replied, "is that it will get steadily worse."

Still, the reality failed to get through.

"How bad will it get?"

The doctor looked at them both for several seconds, at last understanding that his careful answers hadn't yet penetrated. Now he wasn't at all sure how to offer further explanation, so he just came out with it, the words as blunt as hammer blows.

"It's generally fatal."

For a moment there was no reaction. Then Joe just sat back in his chair, as philosophical as he was about everything, just one more piece of information for the partisan fighter to digest.

Charlotte, however, was more demonstrative. She put her hand to her mouth to stifle the exclamation, and almost instantly, the moisture appeared in the corners of her eyes.

It seemed as if everything she'd ever valued had been torn from her grasp at one time or another, and here it was, happening again. She couldn't believe it, didn't want to believe it. Even fate itself was betraying her.

"Are you certain?" she asked, her voice plaintive, longing for at least some minor hope. "Are you absolutely certain?"

"Well, you're always welcome to seek a second opinion, but, yes, in this case, I'm sorry to say that I'm fairly sure."

"How long?"asked Joe quietly. "Before I start to feel it?"

"Like I said, it's progressive. I couldn't say when you'll actually feel anything. It can take a while, but eventually, you'll weaken. Usually, it's the limbs first."

"And then?"

"And then other facets of the body's motor function. It's essentially a disease of the neo-cortex . . . that's a part of the brain . . . along with the spinal cord. This is what controls all your main body movement, and this is what will begin to shut down."

"What causes it?"

"That, we don't know. You've never had any family history of this?"

"Not that I know."

"Then I can't really tell you what causes it."

"How about treatment?"asked Charlotte. "Is there something you can do?"

"We can help to relieve the symptoms . . . reduce the effects of fatigue, cramps, constipation, and so on. There are certain medications in case of depression or sleep disorders, and we can advise on daily regimens for nutrition and mobility therapy. But I must emphasize that none of these are what you'd call treatments. All they can do, at best, is to help ease the discomfort."

"Can he stay at home?"

"Yes . . . if there's someone willing to cope."

"I can do that."

"No," said Joe immediately. "I won't have it."

"That's not your decision," said Charlotte firmly. "It's not for you to say what I can or can't do."

The doctor didn't want to get involved and looked at his watch. He had other work to do. "If there's anything else I can do, please don't hesitate to contact my office." Then he hesitated, realizing how cold he might sound. He turned to Charlotte: "But in my view, the best thing you can do now is just provide lots of care and attention."

Charlotte nodded. This she knew how to do, and even while she was still there in the doctor's office, she came to a decision. She would give up her job at the factory to stay home with Joe. They would live off the income from the building, and if that wasn't enough, well, they'd just have to cut back. What she wasn't prepared to do was leave him alone to manage by himself. She'd made up her mind.

By the end of the decade, Joe was mostly bedridden. He had difficulty doing almost anything for himself, but he was still alert, still read his papers and his books, still laughed and joked with Charlotte as she helped feed him, bathe him, and take him to the bathroom. It was as if all the strength she'd built into her body during those formative years was now being utilized in lifting him up and back several times a day.

In the meantime, the political situation in Quebec was rapidly worsening, and Joe took it upon himself to monitor it closely. Secessionists felt victimized by what they termed the "Canadian occupation," and after years of protests and demonstrations, some in the movement had resorted to violence.

Amongst the instigators was a militant group known as the *Front du Libération du Quebec,* or FLQ, who devised crude letter bombs and sent them to the homes of wealthy English-speakers. Other cells went even further, even as far as kidnapping public officials. The first, a British trade commissioner, was released unharmed in exchange for the group's manifesto being read aloud over the airwaves, but the second, a provincial government Minister, was later found dead in the trunk of a car—and that caused all kinds of reaction.

In Ottawa, the federal Prime Minister, Pierre Trudeau, himself a Quebecker, conceived the notion of passing the emergency War Measures Act, a form of martial law. In reality, this took effect by launching a major military presence onto the streets: five thousand soldiers of the regular armed forces to augment the police, with broad-ranging powers of arrest and detention.

This climactic episode in 1970 became known as the October Crisis, and it brought back fears that were all-too-familiar for immigrants like Charlotte and Joe. It had been twenty-five years since the war ended, but the memories were seared into their consciousness like it had all happened yesterday.

One chilly evening, the crisis came home. They'd finished dinner, and Charlotte was settling Joe for the night when they began to hear a commotion outside their second floor windows overlooking Van Horne. Charlotte immediately went over to see what was happening.

"There's police everywhere," she called back. "Cars, flashing lights . . ."

"Come away, Liesl," Joe called over to her. He'd taken to calling her Liesl, partly as an endearment, but partly because it just came more naturally to his tongue.

However, Charlotte was too wrapped up in what she was seeing. "They're getting out . . . and they're coming here! Joe, they're coming here, into our building!"

"Come away, please, Liesl, and close the curtains."

She did as she was asked, but she was clearly alarmed.

"Do you think we should call Monsieur Rénaud?" she asked, referring to their friend, the local beat cop to whom they'd once rented an apartment.

"Let's stay calm," replied Joe. "See what happens."

"Maybe he knows someone, maybe he can help us."

"Liesl, please, relax. It's not Vienna, and it's not the SA. Nobody's going to hurt us. Don't give yourself a heart attack."

Charlotte tried but she couldn't prevent the recurrence of her deepest traumatic excesses. For a while, her relationship to Joe had been like a soothing relief, but his long decline into debilitating illness, coupled with the increasing insecurities of the world around her, brought the inner torments back towards the surface, threatening to break through as they had so often in the past.

As the panic began to set in, recollections of *Kristallnacht* played in her mind: those heavy boots on the stairs while she and her mother were huddled in the closet. Even the smell came back to her, that nauseous aroma of damp and disinfectant. Instinctively, she turned off the lights before coming over to sit on Joe's bed, squeezing his hand tightly as she listened, once again, to men entering the building and rushing up the stairs, past their front door, all the way to the top floor.

This time, the voices were not German, but French. There was some scuffling and they could hear loud arguing, but it was all soon over. By the time Charlotte decided to risk a peek into the street, she saw little except for car doors being slammed shut.

"They're leaving, they're driving away."

"Good," said Joe simply. "Did they take anyone?"

"I don't know, I couldn't see."

The following morning, they woke to a sky of sullen gray, but the street was clear of police, and everything was eerily normal. It was as if it had never happened and there was nothing about any local raid in the early bulletins.

Charlotte made breakfast, then waited until eight before calling the janitor, only to learn that one of their own tenants, a nice enough man, had apparently been an active member of an FLQ cell living right there on the fourth floor.

What happened to him, they never found out, but the shock of the discovery was also a lesson. From that time forward, they never rented an apartment to anyone off the street, accepting only referrals.

The law's heavy hand served to quell the violence and the fears generated by Quebec's October Crisis passed into the annals of local history.

Yet for Charlotte, the crisis continued each and every day as her husband became ever more paralyzed. These long days were often followed by exhausting nights as she watched him fade before her eyes. Soon, he could hardly hold the newspaper. Then he found it difficult to move all but a few muscles. With Charlotte's constant care, he somehow held on for eight more years until his strength was totally depleted, and on a bitter January night, his body just gave up the struggle.

He had no last words because, by that time, his throat was constricted and he couldn't speak, so Charlotte just sat there next to him, with his thin hand in hers, feeling helpless as the life drained out of her wonderful Joe. For over a decade, Charlotte had fed him, changed him, and medicated him, getting little rest herself because she also had to take care of the building: its upkeep, its tenants, and the financial management.

By the end, the result of her long toil had manifested itself in her hips, which had taken the brunt of the heavy lifting and were in dire need of surgery. Worse, however, was the toll it took on her mental state. Being with Joe had been the happiest period of her life, but now it was over. The gods of destiny had snatched it away just like everything else.

She'd lost her mother, her romance, her school, her home in Austria, her life in England and her best friend, Sadie; then her cousins when they left her to fend for herself, her father when he passed away, and even the unborn child whose life ended while still inside her.

All that she'd ever loved had been taken from her as if by malicious intent—and now Joe was gone, too. The only way she knew to handle it all was to resort to her tried and trusted persona, the duality she'd adopted all those years before, and so back came the charade. On the outside, she was once again Charlotte the Cheerful, but inside, she was devastated.

Only by wearing the mask of good humor could she continue, and she threw herself into charity work, donating time and effort to all manner of causes. She helped out generously at the creative center attached to a local synagogue, then became an organizing member of the local chapter of ORT, a Jewish-run retraining service for immigrants. All the while, she still managed the business she and Joe bought together, the thirteen-apartment structure on Van Horne.

In the true spirit of survival that had brought her through all those other critical moments, she refurbished herself with dignity and with grace—and it was at that stage of her life, two years after her husband died, that she and I first met.

The behavior of Charlotte's cousins, Stefan and Roman, was especially difficult for me to comprehend and remained a mystery until much later. In general, they were polite enough to Charlotte, and no doubt in their minds, there was nothing untoward about this kind of relationship with a cousin.

They kept in touch and invited her over on family occasions like Passover, but Charlotte always had the vague feeling that, under the circumstances, they could have been so much closer. Only when she discovered the facts of their own astounding story did she begin to realize why they acted as they did.

The startling truth was that they were members of a unique group known as Schindlerjüden, the name given to the hundreds of men, women, and children who were saved from the camps by the Nazi businessman, Oskar Schindler, and since made famous by the Steven Spielberg movie, Schindler's List.

It was in 1942 that their entire family was transported from Krakow to a nearby ghetto, the two brothers together with their parents and their little sister.

After they'd arrived, the first to be removed from them was their mother. Then, their father managed to escape, but he was soon recaptured, and they found out that he'd been subsequently tortured by the Gestapo.

At the end of that year, the brothers were sent to a labor camp, leaving behind their eight-year-old sister. They never saw her again, nor did they learn what happened to her. The following year, they were again transferred, this time to Plaszow, where the kommandant was the same ruthless sadist as the character played in the movie by Ralph Fiennes. He shot prisoners for sport and kept a pair of vicious hounds, trained to attack and kill on command.

Somehow, despite the threats and the beatings and the fourteen-hour workdays with little food and no hygiene, the brothers managed to stay alive, relying only on each other.

Finally, it was in 1944 that they first learned they would be sent to work under Schindler, a sociable profiteer and paid-up member of the Nazi party.

At first, he only wanted the Jews as unpaid labor, but then over time, he gradually began to recognize them as human beings, and it was under his protection that they survived the rest of the war. Eventually, they were liberated by the Russians.

Nobody who knew Stefan and Roman had ever been aware of their history, not even their wives and children, and certainly not Charlotte. Then the movie was released, and for Stefan in particular, the experience of seeing it all right there on the screen was so poignant that he felt he just had to talk about what happened.

It was a total change of heart, from completely silent to conspicuously vocal, and from that time on, he spoke to any audience that would invite him, whether it was in a school auditorium or a church basement.

On one of these occasions, I accompanied Charlotte to hear him talk and found his hour-long presentation to be both moving and absorbing. When he asked for questions, the first was inevitably about the movie. "How accurate was it?"

At this, he smiled, replying that Liam Neeson, the Irish actor who played the title role, was taller and more handsome than the real Oskar Schindler; also that the Russians who appeared at the end hadn't arrived on horseback, they had come in a truck.

Apart from those minor details, he said, the entire portrayal was uncannily close to what had occurred, and he congratulated Mr. Spielberg on having done such a fine job.

14

Charlotte and I were first introduced at the urging of her best friend, my Cockney cousin, Sadie. From the start, Charlotte told me so much about the fun they'd had back in wartime London and what a source of strength Sadie had been, that when we heard she was coming over on vacation, I fully expected it to be a joyous, spontaneous reunion.

Sadie was accompanied on her transatlantic visit by her younger sister, Ruthie, with whom she still shared an apartment. Neither had married, and I was glad to see that they'd hardly changed since I had known them in England.

While Ruth was as mature and dependable as ever, Sadie was still the bright spark, full of her Cockney confidence and that quick, ready humor. She even repeated her silly Viennese joke just for the sake of old times, with that same deadpan delivery. "You do know that the Blue Danube isn't blue, don't you?"

The sisters stayed for several days, but although Charlotte tried her best to be the genial hostess, their relationship was nothing like before, when she and Sadie smiled at their hardships and laughed their way through the Blitz. Charlotte still attempted to wear the same mask of cheerfulness that she'd first perfected back in London, but somehow, it didn't work its magic quite as well, and all I could think was that perhaps Joe's passing was just too recent for it to be otherwise.

The visit, however, did serve as a kind of catalyst for Charlotte to begin divulging her life story, not to Sadie but to me. At that time, she still hadn't told me very much, but afterwards, she was not only ready to talk more about what she'd been through, she was actually anxious to do so. It was as if she'd been waiting all this time to confide in someone and that's when I started to become more than just a casual acquaintance.

Gradually, and without even realizing it, I turned into her confidant. It seemed as if I'd arrived at the right moment in her life, and because I was ready to listen, she dropped the masquerade like a burden that had become too heavy to carry any longer, and she began to open up. However, that was only with me. As she often told me, I was the sole person in whom she'd chosen to confide. When others came to the apartment, whether friends or tenants, she transformed instantly, from her soul-searching introspection to the welcoming mother-figure, ever generous with coffee, cake and cookies, no matter who it was. There was always a bowl of nuts or candies on the table and always a smile.

The strange thing was that it didn't appear false. Both sides of her personality were genuine. That outer sense of lightness came from an earlier, more innocent stage of her life, and it was more a case of restoration than invention. Did these people she greeted so warmly ever suspect what lay underneath? It's possible, but I don't think so, and I wasn't about to tell them. The last thing Charlotte needed at that stage of her life was another betrayal. She'd never have forgiven me, and in all honesty, I'd never have forgiven myself.

Only once did I ever ask her to speak in public, and even then, it was only in a historical context. Every year in November, the Holocaust Memorial Center has a ceremony to commemorate the anniversary of *Kristallnacht,* and on each occasion, they invite a living witness to provide a personal account as testimony. At first, when I suggested that she might wish to volunteer, she declined, telling me that she'd never before spoken in public and that she would be too embarrassed to do so.

However, when I reminded her of the reality, that she might well be one of the last of the generation who could make such a valuable contribution, she agreed, albeit with some reluctance. To add some measure of reassurance, I told her that I would write her speech myself, and that she would be surrounded by friends and supporters.

As expected, the event was solemn and respectful, presented in a darkened room with just a solitary spotlight on the various presenters and speakers. When it was Charlotte's turn, she carefully mounted the rostrum, slowly unfolded the notes I'd prepared for her, and then read in her own accented way the story of that terrifying night, when she and her mother had held on to each other in the broom closet listening to the rampaging boots on the stairs.

In front of her, the hushed crowd was suitably moved and responded at the conclusion with enthusiastic applause. In the front row was the Israeli ambassador, who congratulated her on helping to remind the world of what had happened, as well as the Austrian consul, who was especially pleased that Charlotte had chosen to mention the non-Jewish janitor, Frau Graebner, as instrumental in having saved them.

After being formally thanked for her words, Charlotte was helped down and introduced to members of the audience. One was a woman her own age whom she'd never met before but who leaned over and gave her a big hug. To Charlotte's astonishment, the woman told her that she, too, had lived in that very same building on Staudingergasse during exactly that period.

Although they didn't know each other back then, the coincidence that this woman would be present at this particular memorial event was uncanny—or perhaps, as Charlotte told me, it was destiny—and the two of them went on to become friends.

At no time during the evening, however, did Charlotte ever hint at her own personal story. Once again, she'd managed to display her most eloquent persona, and it was only when we were back together in the privacy of her apartment the following week that the reaction set in. The memories had all been reawakened, and the entire spectrum of emotions just poured out of her: from courage to fear; from remorse to guilt.

Seeing her like that, I felt responsible, thinking I might have talked her into something she really didn't want to do, but when I was finally able to ask how she had felt about giving the speech, she just shrugged.

"It was necessary," she said simply.

All those years, I didn't just visit Charlotte to listen to her stories, or to eat lunch. There were practicalities, too, and the trust she was developing sometimes added to my sense of responsibility towards her. Although she remained fiercely independent, she often asked my opinion about some issue that bothered her: some offer she'd received in the mail, or some discrepancy in her finances; in which case we'd scrutinize her ledgers, all those neatly penciled entries, until we found the error.

On a couple of occasions, she even asked me to go with her to present her case to the rental board, a provincial government administration that adjudicates disputes between owners and their tenants.

However, by far the greatest such challenge was in helping Charlotte to sell her building. For thirty years after Joe died, she'd resisted all advice, all offers, due in large part to the fact that his memory was so tied to the place.

This was the property they'd purchased together. This was where they'd lived their most joyful years and this was the place, too, where his life had slowly ebbed away, and out of respect for his memory, she was never going to leave.

It was only when her hip joints worsened to the extent that she could hardly walk that she began to consider the notion, and even then, she was reluctant. That's when I mentioned to her that selling didn't necessary mean leaving.

"What do you mean?" she asked me. "Where will I live?"

"Why not just stay here?"

"Stay here how? If I'm selling . . ."

"All you have to do is put a condition in the sales contract that you can keep this apartment for as long as you like."

It was evident that this straightforward option simply hadn't occurred to her. "I can do that?" Her voice was incredulous.

"Sure you can do that. All it means is that you'll be a tenant instead of the landlady. You'll live here without having to manage the place."

"But what about the rent? Won't I have to pay rent?"

"We can negotiate that, too. And anyway, you'll have the capital in the bank. It'll be more than enough to cover it." However, as obvious as this solution sounds, I didn't want to try to sell her on the concept. As with everything else, it had to be her decision, or it just wouldn't have worked.

"I don't know," she said. "Let me think about it."

"No hurry. Whenever you're ready, we'll talk about it some more, all right?"

As it happened, it took several more months of hesitation, but eventually, her movements became so difficult that she had no choice. Managing the place had just become too much for her, and she was weary of the effort. Then, one day, she simply made up her mind.

"All right, I'm ready to sell," she said, almost as soon as I walked in the door. "Let's get on with it. What's the first step?"

In some ways, we were lucky during the process; in others, far less so. Although I was a novice in dealing with this kind of multiple-unit real estate, my brother-in-law happened to be in this exact business.

He wasn't an agent, but he was a professional manager, and he knew his stuff. His first recommendation, before we did anything else, was to obtain an evaluation from an independent source. It would cost a few hundred dollars, but as I explained to Charlotte, it would give us a benchmark, a place to start, and she agreed. He also gave us crucial information about how valuations were calculated based on rental income, depreciation, taxation, and all the other factors; also what potential purchasers would be expecting.

Such advice, however, was where our good fortune ended, because by the time we received the analysis and were preparing to start the sales process, we'd already entered the severe recession that began in 2008.

All over the US and across most of Europe, the real estate market was a disaster zone. Although the crash was never as catastrophic in Canada as elsewhere, nobody at the time knew how it would turn out, and here, too, prices began to ease.

I was concerned and suggested we might consider waiting, but for Charlotte, the economic environment didn't matter. She'd made up her mind that she was ready to sell, and she wanted to go ahead, no matter what the result.

"So the price is reduced," she said. "So what? If that's how it is, that's how it is."

Yet in addition to falling values, there was also another factor to consider. Charlotte had been a landlady for so long that being a tenant in the same apartment was hard for her to accept, and she had a great deal of insecurity about any potential arrangement.

For example, would the new owner manage the building to her own high standards? Would it be kept clean and tidy? Would it remain a quiet and courteous place to live? Would this owner be as sensitive to tenant needs as she, herself, had been? After all, some of them had been there for decades.

Would they even be allowed to stay, or would they be forced out as the entire edifice was converted into condominiums?

All of these questions would have to be answered, and the only way I could see to do it was to forsake the open market in favor of finding purchasers through personal contacts and then conducting an interview process. Ostensibly, this would be to uncover their intentions, but in reality, it was to see whether Charlotte actually trusted them.

As I'd already guessed, it would be up to me to arrange all of this. I suppose that, in theory, I could have refused my assigned role as chief advisor—and perhaps I should have done so—but my heart wouldn't let me. I'd listened over the years to her entire life story, so I couldn't bring myself to let her down by simply opting out.

She would have undoubtedly felt abandoned all over again and I just couldn't bring myself to do that to her. She didn't deserve it, and it wouldn't have been right. I therefore began my duties by canvassing around and then, one-by-one, we sat down at her dining room table to meet the various prospects I brought in: all the partnerships and consortia and private interests which might conceivably be willing to buy in this harsh economy under the stringent conditions that we set.

It was a difficult process, yet there was an unexpected side benefit. As we sat together during those long and sometimes tense negotiations, the bond between us was sealed. Charlotte knew she could depend on me, so she stayed calm and thoughtful throughout with none of the emotional turmoil that might have been expected.

In the end, none of the potential purchasers quite fit the bill, and we'd just about run out of options when my brother-in-law introduced us to an agent, a young man called Pierre, in whom he had total confidence. Pierre was of half-Russian, half-Lebanese descent and had obviously been raised in a good family with strong integrity. Most importantly, Charlotte liked him.

What surprised us was that, instead of placing the building on the open market, Pierre himself saw the opportunity and decided to make us an offer. He would gladly figure out an excellent deal for Charlotte, he told us, in which she'd be able to remain in her apartment as long as she wished by full contractual agreement.

As for the rest, he would maintain the building to its current standards, and eventually, it would become his nest-egg, as he called it. The place would one day be for him exactly what it had been for Charlotte and Joe: an investment that could act as a source of income during retirement. This not only made logical sense, it was also a motive that Charlotte was prepared to believe.

It had taken eighteen months, but we'd finally accomplished our goal, and we were both very much relieved. Just as significantly, the trust between us was now total—and that's when it happened.

At last, Charlotte felt secure enough that she could reveal the most intimate details of her life story. Something as bland and boring as a real estate transaction had served as a catalyst, encouraging her to relate to me that most profound of secrets: the ultimate trauma between herself and her mother.

A more pragmatic benefit of the building sale was that she now had sufficient funds to obtain the health care she needed. She would have the finest medical treatment, a nurse visiting her home on a regular basis, plus bi-weekly appointments at a brand new facility specializing in geriatric disabilities, where she had access to the highest standards of physiotherapy and counseling. It helped but not a great deal. Despite all the treatment and attention, there was still no way to prevent the continued degradation of her mobility, and she soon found that she was no longer able to stand at all, even with the support of her metal-framed walker.

For Charlotte, the situation was intolerable. As she told me repeatedly, if she couldn't get around and do things for herself, she didn't want to live. She'd lost her independence, and suddenly, the physical had taken over from the emotional as her main source of anxiety. She'd already had one hip replacement not long after Joe died, and now, according to the opinion at her clinic, the most valid option was for admission to St. Mary's for tests and consultations to see if further surgery was possible.

Although she didn't care for hospitals, she'd become desperate and had no choice but to agree. She just couldn't take the prospect of being wheeled around like an invalid for the remainder of her life, so she went in, fixed her mask of good humor firmly into place and allowed them to conduct their probes. While there, she received many visitors: old friends and tenants, as well as all her cousins from both Montreal and New Jersey. As for me, I went to see her at the end of each day, late in the evening, so I could be the last one there. By that hour, she'd finished entertaining the nurses and orderlies with her jokes, and she was ready for some plain talk.

Often, she wondered what her parents would have thought to see her like that, thin and pale and incapable of looking after herself. Of course, such notions were nonsense but I couldn't change her attitude. She just refused to accept what she perceived to be the loss of pride, of self-respect, and although she was as charming as ever to all who came to her bedside, she confessed to me in private that she'd had enough.

The longer she was there, the clearer the choice seemed to be, and one time she actually quoted to me the motto of the state of New Hampshire, as inscribed on every car's license plate.

It was something that Joe had noted, she told me, because it was exactly how he had felt when he escaped into the forest to avoid the Nazis. "Live free or die." She repeated the slogan several times, and I knew that it had now become her own guidance, too, her way of talking herself into what would be a highly dangerous operation.

In the meantime, the medical staff were still discussing how to proceed. Some were in favor of the operation, some against. It was a fine balance and there was no unanimous opinion because it wasn't just a matter of technical ability. They also had to consider her general constitution, whether she would have the stamina to survive such a procedure.

Due to her advanced age of ninety-one, the risks involved were exceptionally high, but the longer she remained in that ward, the more resolved she became. She stated categorically to anyone who would listen that she wouldn't, couldn't, spend her remaining time in a wheelchair. It wasn't entirely her decision, of course, because the doctors could have simply refused to operate, but the louder she insisted, the more they considered it a sign of her strength and willpower. In the end, they agreed.

Surgery would be scheduled for the following week.

It was the end of July 2010 and unusually warm. The evenings were alive with families strolling, dogs panting, and in the trees, cicadas humming their massed harmonies. As usual, I arrived at the hospital at around nine, so we could talk and summarize the day's events: all the news, both medical and in the world at large.

She also spoke about her affairs: which bill needed to be settled, which person was waiting for a call. Yet, the subject she wanted to talk about more than any other was, once again, her mother. She returned often to the same refrain.

"I think she loved me, don't you?"

It was just another echo of her lifelong struggle to understand her mother's real motives but how could I respond when she was in that condition? The easy way would have been to offer a positive answer, something soothing, but that would have been patronizing, and she would have seen right through it. Even as she lay there at her physical worst, I knew she expected more from me than that.

"We all need to believe that our mothers loved us," I told her. "But they're human, they make mistakes. Sometimes they love us but they still screw things up."

It was just my own two-cent psychology, but she nodded, and for a long time afterwards, we sat there in silence. As gently as I could, I reached out to hold her hand, which had become so veined and frail that she couldn't even wrap her fingers around mine, the way she'd once done with Joe. The mood had become somber, and I was well aware that, despite her bold courage, she was fearful of going into that sterile room, fearful of placing herself so completely in someone else's hands.

Her eyes were still bright, still defiant, but her face had lost all color. When a young nurse came in to check on her, Charlotte did her best to cheer up, but this time, the masquerade wasn't enough to be convincing. An hour went by.

Outside, dusk had descended into night, and I could see the lights of the city, all the way across the plateau as far as the north end, but I could tell that Charlotte was somewhere else: perhaps in Vienna, or perhaps in London, I'm not sure.

Perhaps she was reliving her entire life, reviewing that extraordinary raft of memories to see if there was some clue she might have overlooked, some detail that might have explained things a little better.

At one point, she seemed to return because she looked at me and saw how tired I was. "Go," she encouraged me.

"Will you sleep?"

"What difference? I sleep, I stay awake, it's all the same."

"You want me to call the nurse, get you a pill or something?"

"Pills . . ." Her tone was dismissive. "I feel like I'm starting to rattle, I've had so many pills."

"So, anything else you want? A drink?"

"I'll have a gin and tonic."

That was obviously not what I meant at all, but I was glad to see that her humor had returned—and that's when she gave voice to the thoughts that had been weighing so heavily on both of us. In true Charlotte fashion, she just came right out and said it, enlivened by a broad smirk. "Listen, stop worrying so much. If I make it, I make it . . . and if not, what can I say? It's been nice knowing you."

It was so unpredictable, so much like one of Sadie's old quips, that I just broke up laughing, and so did she. That's how I'd like to remember that evening, because it was the last time we spoke.

She was in the operating room some seven hours, and reportedly, the surgery itself went very well, but her ailing physique just couldn't take the invasive stress. Towards the final stages, she suffered a heart attack, causing her to lose vast quantities of blood.

They tried to replenish it as fast as they could, but her body found it hard to tolerate this new infusion, and one by one, her internal organs began to shut down.

After that, it was just a matter of time, and although she made it to the recovery ward, she never awoke. By chance, I wasn't there for her last breath.

During the afternoon, her blood pressure seemed to have stabilized, and since I'd had nothing in my stomach all day, I accompanied one of her cousins for a quick cup of coffee downstairs in the cafeteria.

I doubt we were gone longer than fifteen minutes, but by the time we had returned, it was too late. The lines on all the screens were flat and the nurses were already completing their notes.

Was it possible that, even unconscious, she'd waited until we'd gone in order to preserve her last shred of dignity, to don the mask one last time?

As I stood by her bed, I must confess the thought occurred to me, and whether or not such things happen, I can definitely say that it would have been characteristic of her to do so.

She fought many battles during her long life, but they always seemed to be from the inside out. The hardships, the abandonments, the fears . . . these were difficult to endure, but they were always secondary to the vulnerable emotions that ruled her personality.

What happened when she was nineteen had affected her for the rest of her existence.

It was a profound trauma which she could never fully suppress, and in order to cope, she was obliged to create her own game of charades that she played out for the world.

This was how she was able to continue, both mentally and spiritually, and the proof of her survival was that she managed to maintain her spark of humor right to the very end.

My great friend, Charlotte Urban, née Liselotte Goldberger, was buried according to custom in her own selected plot at the Baron de Hirsch cemetery, right next to her beloved husband, Josef.

Dozens gathered to pay their respects. The tributes were sincere, and the tears flowed freely for the Charlotte they knew—the gracious survivor with the Viennese accent, the old-world values, and always, that twinkle in her eye—but personally, I focused more on the private Charlotte, the secret Charlotte, the enigmatic Charlotte with her inner torment.

That she allowed me a glimpse of her true self was the highest possible compliment she could have given. Today, I regard those weekly conversations we shared for over a quarter century as an inspiration, not only for her lifelong resilience in coping with extreme circumstances, but also for the courage it must have taken to overcome her internal vulnerabilities and just continue each day.

Even now, whenever I happen to drive past that familiar building on Van Horne, my vision becomes blurred. For me, Friday is no longer the same without my lunch with Charlotte. Sometimes, it seems, all I have to do is push the button for her to buzz me in. As always, the TV will be broadcasting the world's news, Ricky the budgie will be chirping happily, and the dining table will be spread with herring in brine, poppy-seed bagels, sour cucumbers, and hard-boiled eggs.

For dessert, there'll be deep-dish apple cake and a large pot of Viennese coffee, and that's when we'll start to talk . . . and no doubt our conversation will begin with a little geo-politics, then move on to neighborhood gossip, before finally ending up, inevitably, on the topic of her mother: the pret-ty, auburn-haired Franzi, who by her own confession never loved her husband, Jakob, but whose relationship with her only child, Charlotte, still remains open to question.

Maybe if we keep searching long enough, we'll find the answer.

Afterword

This book was something I just had to do.

I must admit that my passion for writing is generally more predisposed towards fiction but after such an unusual friendship spanning a quarter century, I felt I not only had to set it all down but that I had to do so accurately. Every word had to reflect the spirit, the experience and the extraordinary life of Charlotte herself.

Yet, I also know that this is not the memoir she'd have written for herself. She'd have offered the facts but I'm convinced she'd never have confided the traumatic depths that she poured out to me when we met each week over lunch. She'd have been too proud to make such a conscious public confession and that's why the story is told not from her perspective but from mine.

Every aspect is just as she related it to me, yet it wasn't an easy project. As I've indicated, she told me her anecdotes haphazardly, a piece here, a fragment there, sometimes repeating herself, sometimes going back to correct herself.

That's why I asked one of the curators at the Montreal Holocaust Center, Julie Guinard, to check the first draft to see if it all made sense, and it was her feedback that encouraged me to finish it up.

There were many others, too, whose contribution was invaluable and I would be remiss not to take this opportunity to offer my sincere thanks.

First, my daughter, Janine, who not only knew Charlotte well but as a professor of English was able to bring a critical eye to the manuscript; also my good friend, Howard Krosnick, recently retired from the Montreal Jewish Federation, who also reviewed a draft.

For the segment on Schindler, I'm indebted to Charlotte's cousin, Steve Lesniak; and for tales of the London Blitz, I'm grateful to my own cousin and Charlotte's good friend, Sadie Blay, now sadly deceased.

In addition, I'd like to thank Grey Gecko Press publisher Jason Aydelotte for his remarkable enthusiasm, as well as his mother who recommended he accept the book. I've also been impressed by his talented and efficient team.

Mostly though, my appreciation goes to Charlotte herself, who honored me with her trust. I still mourn her passing.

✦ Publisher's Note ✦

Lunch with Charlotte first came to me through blind luck. I was searching for something new to publish, and I chanced to come upon the title and synopsis of the book you now hold, and I immediately felt a shiver.

It was then that I knew I had to publish this book, even before I read a single word. Her story was too powerful, too *important* to let languish any longer. I had no idea how long it had been waiting, but that didn't matter.

Charlotte's story needed to be told.

Upon reading the full manuscript, I was profoundly moved, more so than with any other Holocaust-era tale I'd ever read. I wish I'd had the honor of knowing Charlotte, of listening to her story and hearing her laugh.

I founded Grey Gecko Press to publish stories just like Charlotte's, by authors just like Leon. Stories that might otherwise never have been shared. *Lunch with Charlotte* is, in a very real sense, at the core of why we do what we do, and I could not be prouder of or more enthusiastic about this book.

Thank you for helping to share her story.

Jason Aydelotte
Executive Director
Grey Gecko Press

About the Author

Leon Berger

For me, writing is a passion. I wake early in the morning, usually around 4am, and if I can put in 3 hours before breakfast, I'm happy the rest of the day.

I first began writing when I returned from overseas 15 years ago and I now have 6 novels published, plus my recent work of non-fiction.

In my day job, I'm a consultant specializing in the field of marketing, branding and communications, having worked and traveled extensively across 5 continents. At various times I've been based in London, New York, Singapore and Beijing, but these days I prefer to spend as much time as possible back in Canada.

My home is in Montreal where I got to know Charlotte, the venerable subject of my book *Lunch with Charlotte*. I'm also fortunate to have a country property where I spend my weekends, and it was here that I met the unique animal which inspired my novel *Horse*.

Connect with Leon

Email
lberger@videotron.ca

mation can be obtained at www.ICGtesting.com
USA
4080712

V00001B/14/P

CPSIA info
Printed in the
LVOW05082
289152L